AUDACIOUS

SOMETIMES I JUST TALK CRAZY

—A MEMOIR—

2016 - 2020
FIVE YEARS OF A
SPECIAL KIND OF STUPID

NIKKI HANNA

Published by Patina Publishing
Tulsa, Oklahoma 74120

neqhanna@sbcglobal.net
www.nikkihanna.com

IBSN: 978-0-9978141-5-6

Manufactured in the United States of America

Photography: Michael McRuiz, Tulsa, Oklahoma
Steven Michaels, Tulsa, Oklahoma

Cover Design: Jaycee DeLorenzo, Sweet 'N Spicy Designs

Artwork: Nan McDowell

C O N T E N T S

Contents

SECTION V
RESILIENCE - 277

APPENDIX

PREFACE

While creating this book, I worried it was tremendously egotistical of me to write so much about myself and, even more so, politics—about which I do not profess to be an expert. I began writing primarily to heal myself and considered not sharing the result. Then, as I wrote I learned the most significant lesson of the past five years: Complacency is complicity. With that awareness, I considered, "What if I don't share?"

This book is important because it is about the cost of complicity. If we don't pay attention, we will lose our democracy as extremists and a vengeful, opportunistic leader ravage our country. Parts of this book are hard. When the nicest, kindest man I know couldn't get through those parts, I understood. It was also a hard book to write because it chronicles a disastrous time in our county's history and lays bare the impact on its citizens. I personalized those influences through my experiences to bring the topics down to the individual level—that of a mother, a grandmother, and a tormented, traumatized soul. Still, plenty of uplifting, amusing, and hopeful messages are shared.

Regardless of which side of the political spectrum a person embraces, the topics incorporated herein are going to grate on the reader's sensitivity. Also, many people are ready to move on and put the traumas of the past five years behind them. I understand and appreciate that need. I wish I could say that authoring this book helped me do that, which was my original intent in writing it. But I could find no peace in ignoring threats from the current climate of conflict and extremism in our country. So I persevered the best way I knew how, through writing about them.

I don't judge anyone who finds parts of this book dark and tedious. I get it. My suggestion is for readers to digest the narratives and, if need be, gloss over the bulleted items. They can be overwhelming. I include them to illustrate the breadth and depth of the threats of the last five years and how they might influence the future. A glancing view of them will accomplish that.

A valuable, redeemable quality of this composition is education, especially on the topics of mental illness, stealth mind control, and cults. That information explains our country's evolving extremist society. Everyone would do well to develop a deeper awareness of these influences to protect themselves and loved ones. For this reason, I recommend reading and sharing Chapters 9 on personality disorders and 10 on cults, which are enlightening and worthwhile. Just as important, I believe readers will be enriched by the tones of hope and encouragement, of which there are many in this book. It's not all hard.

INTRODUCTION

While in my sixties, I wrote a textbook for a university's lifelong learning program. People over fifty-five were the audience. In the Introduction, I disclosed I had a sense of what being fifty and sixty was like, but I didn't have experience with being seventy or older. In my late seventies now, I have that. The experience has been rich with surprises—some not good, and they hit hard. Bam! Bam! Bam! The naiveté of my sixties self, when I expected to be vigorous until I died, became clear as reality pummeled me like a marauding wildebeest. The good news, of course, is I'm still here.

I was recently asked, "What surprised you most about aging?" My answer was: The necessity of continuous, day-by-day coping. A good surprise was that time became gentle as it transformed from an enemy I strained against in younger years in to a friend I embraced in older ones. Also, perspectives realigned and gratefulness flourished as every day was viewed as a gift. Wisdom introduced simpler interpretations of events and reset priorities. Frustrating life intrusions faded into obscurity—the *don't matter* zone. I redefined what was important and carved out mental and physical clutter.

In spite of the positives into which I have nestled comfortably, I can't say I've found my lane in the aging arena. It seems as though every positive thought must be qualified with a negative reality. The upsides of the third trimester of life are rich, the lows intimidating. They shaped me in to an audacious and unapologetic scribe. I've taken license here to be both a prickly old woman and a hopeful champion of living a purposeful life, one that enhances the lives of others and creates an inspiring legacy.

This book will, no doubt, be my last in a series of nine, so I'm putting it all out there. Audacious influences surface. The subjects are disjointed, and the mood swings range from ethereal bliss to bitterness and fear. Occasional tirades intrude as I vent and mend. I may stumble a bit in my interpretations, but I plan to stick the landing by being candid and bold, even when the content is risky or does not paint a pretty picture.

The scope of this book runs from the five-year period of 2016 through 2020. I can't interpret the past five years without exposing traumas that have colored them with fright, disappointment, loss, and anguish. It is tempting to avoid such unpleasantness, but my story would be less than truthful if I left out those reactions and the reasons for them. And so, to be authentic, I rant, rave, and speak my mind with the dual objectives of healing myself and informing others.

When teaching writing, I recommend authors write from the perspectives of themselves and of their audience. If they don't write for themselves, their "voice"—probably the most important quality of good writing—will falter. If they don't write for an audience, they won't have one. When I started this book, the plan was to write an essay solely for myself in an effort to heal. As it evolved, I realized I had messages to share, especially for a target audience of like-minded individuals, who might also need healing.

The political environment has dominated my life in the last few years, so I dedicated a good part of this book to that topic. Opinions are expressed without inhibition along with the facts that support them. My intention is not to change minds. I have no grand illusions that fervent right-wing followers will respond to rational information. In the first draft, my position was that those people needed to stay away from me. Since then, I've studied books written by experts and conducted considerable research on cult-like behavior and have softened my position. The message from these studies can be summed up in one sentence: *Hate the cult, hate the cult leader, but love the cult followers.* You can argue about whether most of those who follow Trump are in a cult, but every cult expert I've studied says they are. They behave in a cult-like manner, supporting their leader without assessment or judgment. The lack of rational thought has caused them to be exploited and influenced to act against their own best interests. I don't apologize for my harsh opinions about that and their role in the political madness of the past five years, but I have compassion for their reasons and uneasy situations.

I've included herein information on an odd combination of topics—love, aging, pandemic, mental illness, cults, and politics. All have profoundly affected me and contemplating them is a step toward healing. I doubt I will ever completely mend. Shattered trust from betrayal is tough to overcome.

Venting through writing has healed me before. So far, it hasn't worked this time. I don't recall hating anyone my entire life, but I struggle not to fall into the abyss of hate about what Trump and his greedy, rabid family; crime syndicate cronies; white supremacist enablers; and fake Christian leaders do. I especially try not to have animosity toward his followers who lost their moral compass and betrayed our country through either complicity or outright support of a brutal madman. It's easy to get pulled into a cult, and hard to get out of one because people in a cult don't know they are in a cult. Most will hold their positions regardless of facts. Crushing disappointment in them during the years of Trump's fiasco caused me to drunk-cut my bangs on two occasions. Now, like Melania Trump—a woman cocooned in wealth whose coping mechanism is "I really don't care"—I'm done.

Let me be clear, this is not a self-help book or an inspirational one. I don't pretend to be a role model of any sort. What I am is an audacious old lady writer who is royally pissed and not discreetly so. There you have it. Read on, dear readers—or not. I've lost faith in humanity and, to cope, I aspire to the malaise of "I really don't care." This doesn't mean I've given up. There is fight in the old gal yet.

SECTION I

THAT WASN'T ON MY BUCKET LIST

**If You Live Long Enough,
You Get to Be Cute Again.**

She wears black and glows in contrast to its darkness. She is intuitive and strong, soft but powerful. She speaks her mind with candor and style. She leaves her mark and touches the soul of the troubled. She is both a savage warrior and a tender lover of peace of mind. She is also a wise old woman who is hugely and not discreetly pissed.

Chapter 1

WHERE DID LONELY GO?

*Though devastated occasionally by betrayal
or some other form of emotional trauma,
being alone has never been an issue.*

Except for short, rare occasions, loneliness was never on my radar. Flowing fluidly from a large childhood family into marriage and children, I was never alone. After getting divorced, not having a life partner delivered emancipation. Life became uncomplicated and devoid of intruding distractions, and I quickly adopted the posture of fierce independence. For many years after that, children and a purposeful career fed my soul. Then grandchildren happened, murdering any prospect of loneliness ever. And, at all times in my life, I've had compadres, both male and female, surrounding and supporting me.

I never married again after a divorce more than forty years ago, primarily because of an extreme fear of being controlled, abused, and losing my identity again. So when loneliness should have hit, it didn't, even in my seventies when a health crisis, the political climate, and a pandemic drove significant withdrawal from social interactions. Although those situations did isolate me, they had little influence on my outlook. Loneliness still didn't surface. I relished a break from the intrusions of social activity, folded into myself, and withdrew comfortably into the cocoon of aloneness. I used the seclusion to heal from trauma and to revel in my blessings.

Past good fortunes included three children who grew into caring, rational-thinking, principled, and independent people. I unabashedly take full credit for that. Also, a successful career in which I made a difference gave me purpose and enriched my life. A second career as a writer birthed my magnum opus, *Listen Up, Writer—How Not to Write Like an Amateur*. I reaped the rewards of being a teacher throughout my life, no matter what other role I had assumed. Daunting challenges intruded, but I persevered, lived with bravado, left my mark, and made things better.

My work here is done. Any hint of ambition has faded away like a dissipating fog. Expectations for achievement are low, and anything I do now is frosting. So, this egocentric, grumpy old woman's diatribe can be a piece of crap and it won't matter. I'm writing less for an audience and more for myself at this point.

In the past, I was always preoccupied with purpose and passions. My mother, an Iowa farm woman, once asked me, "Why do you have such a fire in your belly?" A life review while writing my memoirs answered that question. Childhood events instilled in me an unrelenting drive. I had something to prove, and prove it I did.

My father commented one day, when I took a turn inconsistent with the traditional role of women, "You should have been a boy." I was a woman on fire—an ambitious, determined woman with something to prove. Once that was done, I settled into my seventies as a matriarch focused on legacy and determined to make a difference still—or not. Loneliness? It was never there.

Chapter 2

THE HALCYON DAYS

Life is not a straight line. It's more like being drunk and driving down both sides of the road at the same time.

A counselor asked a little boy whose parents were getting divorced, "Tucker, are you overwhelmed with all that's going on?" The boy hesitated for a moment, squinted his eyes, pursed his lips, and then responded excitedly, "Yes! Yes! I have too many whelms!" My life has been filled with too many whelms. In my younger years that was the result of decisions and ambitions. In the past five years, it was the result of aging, a pandemic, and a devastating, unsettling political environment. Never in my life had I been barraged with so many disturbing incidents for such a long period of time.

Over the span of my entire life, though, there have been notable peaks and valleys interspersed with plenty of level ground that felt like sitting on a cloud. Now, I've survived a rough five-year span, from 2016 through 2020, a time flush with ominous storm clouds that foreshadowed foreboding calamities and trepidation so intense it was reminiscent of Dante's Inferno—a climate I could have never predicted.

THEN AND NOW

Sometimes I feel like a puzzle piece you can't tell whether or not it's an end piece. At other times, I feel like the last piece snuggling in.

In the past, I could dance down any cowboy in Tulsa dance halls, easily line dance for an hour a day, and work out six days a week with yoga, weight training, and cardio. Now, at seventy-six, I ride a three-wheel bike fifteen minutes a day.

Single for over forty years, I used to prowl for men with my girlfriends. In Oklahoma this meant fraternizing with men who say such things as "what in tarnation?" and "suffering succotash" and who consider "horsefly" a term of endearment. Enduring Jerry Jeff Walker fans, these men prefer their women a little on the trashy side, and they don't wipe off the counters when they do dishes. Actually, they don't do dishes. They have hound dogs and horses that love them more than I ever could. And when I crawled cat-like into bed in a sexy teddy, one of them asked, "Can we lose the jump suit?" Their needs are simple. They just want their women to bring beer and get naked.

Back then, seeing an appealing man created emotions in me similar to those of observing lightning cracks in the sky. Now, when I see a handsome guy, I assume he's an asshole. If a man asks me out, I must protect him from himself because I refuse to make another unfortunate fellow feel inadequate, which is apparently one of my strong suits.

Fervent ambition drove the acquisition of credentials designed to achieve career and personal goals. Continuous learning, teaching, and mentoring were priorities. Now, I'm in stay-home mode due to a pandemic and a harsh political environment. I'm also distracted by continuous health issues like fat ankles and worrying whether a pharmacist gave me the wrong pills, possibly hormones that would cause me to grow a mustache.

A thirty-some-year career in corporate America exceeded any expectations I had starting out, introducing a world of sophistication and professionalism this Iowa farm girl could not have envisioned as a young woman. At work, I learned to never, ever underestimate the male ego; that men aspire to seize power rather than achieve influence; and that, as a woman, it is lonely at the top.

After retirement, a second career in writing produced nine published books and textbooks and a rewarding teaching occupation. Now, professional goals are non-existent. My focus is on acquiring brain-enhancing herbs of which I take only half doses because I don't want to remember everything.

As a single mother, my success is measured by three exceptional, responsible, and compassionate children I raised, including one I inherited because he had lost his mother. Now, as GoGo, I am grandmother to Thing 1 (my sidekick) and Thing 2 (my girlfriend), and two lovely girls I call *The Sparkles*. This entitles me to unacceptable excesses I would have never allowed my children. These darlings are a reason to create a positive legacy that will inspire the youngsters and their parents.

NOSTALGIA

If you don't look back at your life and conclude you were an idiot, you are not learning and growing.

Looking back, I realize my memories often focused on things I did that were unfortunate. As a result, I concluded I was a foolish teenager, wife, and mother. My style back then could best be described as tacky in a Herculon upholstery kind of way. Then I realized that if I didn't feel I was stupid in younger years, I wasn't learning and growing. That thought gives me comfort, and I now focus more on recognizing progress rather than assessing past behavior.

An exercise I occasionally do in lieu of lamenting past experiences is to contemplate moments in my life I'd like to live over again because they were so special. This introduces a positive reflection on the past. It is so enticing and entertaining that I frequently suggest it as a roundtable discussion at gatherings. Such remembrances produce captivating and meaningful conversations.

PERHAPS I'M NO LONGER A NICE PERSON

I'm not.

My mother once called me "hard-hearted Hanna." That's something you never forget—your own mother calling you that. I don't claim to be a sweet, warm, cup of love, but that was harsh. At the time, she was an Iowa farm woman and I a corporate executive running the production operation of one of the largest companies in a complex and highly-regulated industry. The nuances of the business world were not on her radar.

She scolded the president of my company, telling him he should make the men do the traveling so I wouldn't have to. After many hard-won battles to climb the corporate ladder, Mom's directive to my boss produced intense anxiety. I was relieved when the president looked at me and winked. Raised in rural Oklahoma by a mom like mine, he got it.

Frankly, I don't believe "hard-hearted" was a proper label for me back then. I was a champion of customers, employees, women, and progress. However, the label is apropos now. I'm hardened to a degree I could not have imagined a few years back.

As I get older, my tolerance for foolishness, abuse, prejudices, and political nonsense has dissipated. And the trend toward corporate greed that has gotten out of hand since I left the business arena disgusts me. No executive deserves a $60 million annual bonus—ever and under no circumstances. There is something morally wrong with the huge salaries and bonuses of many corporate executives today. That money could solve numerous national problems if shared with employees.

Also, politics has gone wacko. In 2018 I reached a breaking point and succumbed to hate, which was a shock similar to someone throwing a brick through a window. I dealt with this originally by cutting those I called *toxic people* out of my life, and I did so swiftly and without regret. Then, I studied cult-like behavior and came to realize that many of them—not all—were good people who had been innocently subjected to manipulation and exploitation by evil shysters and despicable teams of entitled cohorts who bend reality. They are so corrupt I don't have the verbal dexterity to describe them. These self-serving predators rob people of their dignity and put democracy on the critical list.

Because of their nefarious role in society and politics today, I no longer extend the concept of tolerance to all. Instead, I'm a tough old bird who now harbors her own prejudices—who loves intensely but hates with a vengeance. I tell myself, "Nik, you are better than that." But I'm not. I have become hard-hearted Hanna. And I'm not sorry. If you read on, you'll understand why.

Love was like getting lost in the depth and complexity of quantum physics. I can no longer fathom it. The inevitable rhythm of new love and dying love seems reason enough to dress a man in camouflage, walk him into the woods, and leave him there forever.

Chapter 3

BROKEN—BUT ON MY GAME

Love is fragile. When it evaporates, which it often does, brace for a tsunami of pain followed by a slow, steady burn. Love hurts.

One Saturday morning my horoscope said, *Romance is intense, and the full moon in your sign can set your love life on fire. Venus and Jupiter make a romantic interaction impossible to ignore.* Excuse me while I put down my coffee dosed with fiber and take off this damned back brace so I can blow coffee out my nose while I laugh.

The pickings are slim when you are in your seventies. Age-appropriate men are chasing younger women, divorced men are broke and often have a young, psycho ex and child support till they die, and the rest just want to do my hair. The last seventy-something old fellow who showed an interest in me thought Ariana Grande was a font, knocked a tooth loose doing the gator, thought a Randy Newman song was appropriate for a wedding, and requested the song "I Shot the Sheriff" from a Reggae band.

Problematic experiences with men stretch back to my marriage as a teenager. After the birth of our second child, my husband and I were driving home from deer hunting in southeastern Oklahoma. He spotted a cabin nestled into trees high on a hill. He said, "If I didn't have you and the kids, I could live in a place like that and hunt and fish every day." Tears welled up in my eyes as I peered into the back seat to observe two sweet babies sleeping peacefully. Not long after, he announced he didn't love me anymore, but he would stay with me because of the kids. Seven years later, I asked for a divorce and set him free to hunt and fish.

As I moved past that time, feelings eventually became neutralized. Over the years, two loving men healed me, and thoughts of past loves no longer trigger negative emotions. I believe this neutral state is as close to being healed as I'm going to get in the romance arena. At this point, I'm grateful for past loves and don't attach deep significance to any bad behavior of others or myself. People are flawed. I've accepted that and moved on.

LESSONS ON LOSING

I'm no longer a woman who will wear
leather so I smell like a new truck.

When people couple up, they develop expectations about the relationship. Often these don't materialize, and severe disappointment reigns. Hope and the attachment factor keep people holding on and going back again and again before making an enduring break. Couples torture themselves with repeated attempts at breaking up. Rarely does a couple make a clean break the first try.

Nina Simone said, "You have to learn to get up from the table when love is no longer being served." This is easier said than done, of course, but it is important. When it's over, it's over. Nothing is any deader than a dead love. Facing that reality is what makes giving up so hard. Healing from a relationship typically takes a year or two, an investment that, at my age, I'm not willing to make.

Romance is often like a truck that runs like a sewing machine. It's frustrating. Taking a bat to your ex's truck or putting a laxative in his chili are not good plans. Truth is, there is no good plan. This is why I haven't had a date in twelve years. In the third trimester of life, I'm determined not to spend another year pining away over lost love. I'd rather be alone. So love is off the agenda. However, during forty-some years of being single, I experienced two long-term relationships and many short ones from which I've accumulated a wealth of wisdom on romance. Plenty of good came out of the experiences, but even so, the reality is that it was a quagmire out there.

The most valuable lesson I learned about love was that it is all about how each partner makes the other one feel. Nothing else matters as much as that. It explains why people are attracted to each other and why some relationships endure and others don't.

After my divorce in 1975, I soon concluded no white knight worth having was going to rescue me. I was on my own. This conclusion fostered fierce independence. I became career focused and determined to take care of myself and my children on my own. If I wanted something, I resolved to get it myself. And I did. Nobody ever gave me anything. I've never wavered from this position. I went on a quest for credentials, built a resume, and worked hard. That drive for independence and my youthful, unfortunate marriage experience are why I never remarried.

Never underestimate the vulnerability of the male ego. Most men eventually feel inadequate in the presence of an ambitious, self-reliant, and accomplished woman. Men are hard-wired to rescue. It is emasculating for a woman to do so. It doesn't make them feel good. I've had a tendency to encounter men who had experienced bad luck and was compelled to save them. I've done so several times. Doing so was great fun, and I left a few as better men. But in the long haul, it didn't end well for me. Rescuing is the man's job. Eventually, they reclaim their masculinity by finding desperate women to rescue. And who can blame them for that?

I also learned that when you date younger men, they send you music online you have no idea how to open. When they take you out to dinner, you'll be eating jalapeño poppers at Sonic followed by great sex on a futon. When you date an older man, you wake up in an AARP t-shirt. When dating a cowboy, odds are you'll wake up in an NRA t-shirt and celebrate special events at a Bass Pro Shop.

When a younger man leaned up against the wall in my office, looking better than any man had a right to, I knew I was in trouble. He chased me hard until I finally acquiesced. After seventeen years, he left me for another woman fifteen years my junior. This lesson didn't take, and I repeated the process. The next pup left me for a woman thirty years my junior. The lesson took this time.

I like to think that as I aged, I become more interesting. However, experience suggests interesting doesn't count, and I don't pair up well with any category of men. So I give up. Love is no longer on the agenda. Pursuing men makes me feel like a dog barking at cars.

When a man asks me out, I must protect him from himself. I respond with, "Men don't like me." They often argue the point with, "I like you. I really do." I respond with, "Well, you would get over that."

Actually, if a man were a sensitive lyricist who delivered poetry in a magical, rhythmic cadence, perfectly nuanced, and at just the right moment, I might. . .Oh, hell. No.

Chapter 4

THE DEBRIS OF LOVE

Grief is love with no place to go.
It is the price you pay for love.

Love is a powerful mistress not to be trusted. Although romantic loss is a shared human condition, it is also uniquely individual. I've been the object of bad behavior that produced pain and grief with no place to go. It has caused me to ask several times, *What do I do with my shattered heart?* I never got an answer.

I stayed when I should have left. The signs were there that love had run its course. I hung in out of commitment or stupidity. I'm not sure which. So rejection and heartbreak hit hard, and they own me still. Hardened like cement as a result of romantic betrayals, my capacity for forgiveness is now nonexistent. I don't understand the concept. I don't ask for it, and I don't give it. Any feelings are neutral—and even irrelevant—at this point. Strangely, this is a comfort.

Although any initial bitterness has subsided, the skittishness remains. This perspective is common among older women. I won't get into all the reasons, and I won't write a book on the top ten dates I wish I'd never had. Let it suffice to say disappointment abounds in the romance arena, and I've had my fill of it.

Sometimes it's not the loss of love, but how it happened that lingers. Interestingly, when love was true, the breakups were not as painful and recovery was swift because we both wanted the best for each other. The troubled relationships—characterized by infatuation rather than love, or those where love had run its course and betrayal ensued—were the ones that hurt the most and were the hardest from which to recover. This was because of disloyalty and severe disappointment from expectations not met, each piling on an extra layer of hurt.

I dated a variety of men. One otherwise wonderful man's idea of enjoying the outdoors was being drunk in a gazebo. He went to the liquor store for breakfast, and was so snockered when I broke up with him I had to do it again the next day. That was a lesson learned.

Occasionally, I encountered a verbally abusive fellow. Narcissists are charming initially, but they are usually void of cultural content and once you peel back the charm and veneer, the meanness becomes obvious. These relationships were short lived. With the first red flag—in lieu of tasing—I ghosted these guys.

There are good men out there, and love is a gift, but I no longer trust that it will last. I won't subject a man to my emotional baggage, and I cannot endure the prospect of spending any of my few remaining years pining away over love gone wrong.

I used to journal. I didn't do so when life was good. I wrote out of desperation and floundering—when times were harsh, when festering hurt overwhelmed, or when I needed to hold on to the will to survive. While reading these journals now, as a seasoned woman with a hardened heart, fresh interpretations about what happened surface. I am embarrassed by my foolishness in younger years although regrets are few and many memories sweet.

NO LONGER
THE ASSHOLE WHISPERER

Now, instead of concluding "It's not you, it's me," I have determined, "It's not me, it's you, goddamnit."

I'm no longer the woman who sucks in her stomach and stands up straighter when I see an attractive man. Instead, I assume he's an asshole. And I stopped being the asshole whisperer years ago.

In younger years, I was eager to accept personal accountability and was therefore quick to make excuses for others—to justify their bad behaviors. As a result, frayed edges become ragged wounds. Now, red flags wave ferociously. No one can measure up. And I am alone.

I've been told that to heal you must honor your experiences. I've been blessed with a couple of great loves with fabulous men. And I've dated my share of good men. It was the betrayals from men leaving me for younger women that left the most recent and deepest scars.

As a result, I am not soft. Experience has made me hard. No man wants a hard woman. Although bitterness and disappointment have burned out, hurt and heartbreak own me still. I am broken—a damaged woman. The upside of that is that I am also wise and unencumbered by the potent distractions of romantic interests.

All that being said, I still relish the fellows as long as I can keep them in the friend zone. Hugs are harvested, which comfort but don't complete. Serious relationships are murdered lest something inside me breaks again. Though yearning persists, I don't have another breakup in me.

Being alone in old age wasn't on my bucket list, but it's okay. The void it provokes is cured with grandchildren. Being with them is where the light hugs me.

SECTION II

THE THIRD TRIMESTER OF LIFE

Aging—Where the Light
and the Dark Collide

Geeks don't say it outright, but when they walk into my house I get the feeling they are there to make me feel stupid. Perhaps that is because the only contraptions I can successfully master are a stapler, a pencil sharpener, and a seat belt—sometimes.

Chapter 5

AGING—WHERE THE LIGHT AND THE DARK COLLIDE

Initially, aging stalked me. Then it crept up and grabbed me by the soul like a lion downing its prey.

I prefer not to write about aging. Doing so suggests it is the most important thing about me. Perhaps it is. At seventy, the aging bitch slapped me—hard. And age became profoundly relevant. Growing old is not a choice, but happiness is, which involves such things as a sleeping baby settling on my chest; being attacked by a litter of puppies; napping anytime I want; and curling up on a cold, windy day encased womb-like in a quilt so thick crisp air cannot penetrate it. And it involves gratefulness.

THE IMPERTINENCE OF AGING

Nature makes no promises, but at its core, it is the result of natural laws and is consistent—except when it's not.

Aging issues hover like angry poltergeists. Not ready, I feel as though growing old is happening to someone else, and I am just a voyeur. Although reality is a formidable and angry truth not to be denied, this time can be encore years —better than the original show. Embracing that prospect, I am resigned and resilient, and I press on.

Part of redefining yourself as an old person is deciding what kind of patriarch or matriarch you want to be. A person can never *not* lead, and how a person acts in the sunset years counts. The challenge of the aging experience is to remain positive in the face of troubling obstacles.

An old person sometimes feels like an outdoor dog looking in the patio window at folks eating steak. To be relevant, that person must challenge dismissiveness. As family, neighbors, caretakers, the medical profession, and others interfere and control, an older person remains relevant by focusing on sharing his or her greatest asset—wisdom.

We old folks must not ignore the pressing issue of doing aging—and even dying—in a way that makes it easy on those we care about most. This requires sacrifice and a determined stance against negativity. I call this "aging *beyond* well," which is aging in a way that is a gift to others—a way that does not cause them to fear their own futures. Delivering a positive aging experience and, ultimately, a good goodbye, are opportunities with the potential to enhance the lives of loved ones—or do the opposite. Because the end of life will be fresh in survivors' minds, managing this time well may be one of the most important things a person does in their lifetime.

Without a doubt, I am in the final stage of my life. I'm not afraid of death. I recall when my daughter and I were dancing with cowboys in a Dallas dancehall, and I felt as though I was exceeding my cardio capacity. As I sat down to recuperate, another man asked me to dance. I did, assuring my daughter, "If I die two-stepping on a Dallas dance floor, know that I died happy." I just don't want to die vacuuming or scraping concrete out of a casserole dish.

I realize I'm a ticking time bomb on the path to an end I prefer to ignore. Statistically, I should be dead by now. However, I am an off-the-charts realist and pragmatist, so I face the inevitable head on. I may be more afraid of aging than dying. Ghost-like, aging torments with the terror of something grave. Dreams of losses nudge me awake at night. As coffee soothes, a gnawing anxiety remains. There will be no more sleep this night for I fear I cannot save myself.

Reality is harsh these days. When I run into old friends I haven't seen in a while, my reaction is shock: *Oh, they're still alive.* And aging raises curious questions, such as:

- Can I do this? Can I survive it? The answer is "no."

- How soon after getting up in the morning is it okay to take a nap? Whenever.

- If I don't acknowledge aging, will it go away? Of course not.

- Does putting raisins in my coffee instead of on my oatmeal mean I have Alzheimers? Perhaps, but probably not.

- As a writer, can I go against the trend and develop a successful new genre: *Old Adult Fantasy*? Nah. There is no market.

- What can I do when expensive new front teeth that make me whistle when I talk? Whistle.

- When needing to make a medical appointment, should I work on my living will instead? No.

- If Sam Elliott's character dies in a movie, can I handle it? Ah, hell no.

PIVOTAL DEFINING MOMENTS

*There were times when I made a turn
down crazy street, and I didn't signal.*

Although thoughts often roll around like marbles in my head, defining moments stop me dead in my tracks. They leave tattoos on the brain—searing marks that change everything. Cutting deep, some incidents cause wounds that leave scabs and scars that shape a person.

One of those instances was when I retired and learned that at sixty you begin to disappear. On break at a writers' conference, I stood in a circle of young, enthusiastic women scribes. As we chatted, I realized I was being cut off and my comments ignored. The realization that to the young I was irrelevant stormed into me.

Defining moments apply to both mental and physical issues. Before my personal experience with aging, my only intimate exposure to it was through my mother. I was dutiful and devoted to her as she aged to eighty-eight but didn't understand what she was going through until I began living those experiences myself. The lack of "lift" in Mom's legs required she roll off the sofa onto the floor, crawl to a chair, and pull herself up. This produced giggles from her and me. When it happened to me, I realized you laugh so you don't cry.

At this stage of life, hard situations intensify. Friends announce they are dying, and when people ask you how you are, you say, "I woke up." I occasionally have some kind of spell in the night. I feel sick and weak, like I'm fading away. My doctor had no clue what this was, and her eyes glazed over when I described it. Because of that as well as spiking blood pressure, a persistent ache around my left shoulder, and an alarming family history, I spent two days in a heart hospital for tests. This involved sitting in a wheelchair in a hallway in a long line of big bellied old men while being shuffled in and out of testing rooms.

Nothing was found. The cardiologist suggested I go back to my primary care doctor. "She will probably adjust your blood pressure meds," he said. This was not reassuring, and the change in medication resulted in fat ankles, which was unacceptable. The next drug produced a constant cough, which made me unpopular with friends and family. So I resigned myself to nighttime spells, which have not killed me yet.

I've learned over the years that any condition that persists but does not intensify is unlikely to kill. I live with many such conditions, so I've stopped worrying about them. I relax into nighttime spells and eventually go back to sleep —if I don't throw up. When I wake up, I'm surprised. *I'm still here.* Gratefulness abounds, and I revel in the glory of living a long life. Not everyone gets to do that.

The aging process vacillates between being soft, like fine dust settling on patio furniture, and being fierce, like Santa Ana winds whipping up a fire. The roller-coaster effect of these swings is disorienting, but a person can nestle into acceptance and refuse to be held hostage to the inevitable consequences of living so long.

NEFARIOUS VULNERABILITIES

I stare at the naked waffle woman in the mirror and fantasize that I look better from the back. But I don't.

The complicated manifestations of aging pop up and dart about like sparks from a bonfire. On a sidewalk, a vaguely familiar reflection appears in a window, and I wonder, "Who is that old woman?" Then, reality storms in. It is me. In the shower, I discover on my face the reading glasses I searched for all morning. I find another pair on my head. I get on the scales and wish I weighed what I weighed when I first thought I was fat. Getting up from the sofa, I list to the right. To maintain balance, by feet follow my upper body, I make a full circle, and end up on the sofa where I started. The people hiding in my attic steal the remote, my slippers, and my last PayDay candy bar. And I don't know the difference between HD and analogue.

Old people have a lot to contend with, and it's a good idea to avoid pissing them off. We may appear fragile and vulnerable, but our temperament is inconsistent and our spirit underestimated. Coping is a tough gig. Sometimes someone else is going to pay for issues with which we deal.

It's hard to be pleasant when you're in pain, bombarded with threats, and constantly intimidated by fear. You might leave the house feeling foxy and intending to be an upbeat, charming gift to the world—your goal: to make everyone's day. The plan is to smile, compliment the grocery store checker, banter with a postoffice employee, and tease your pharmacist that regardless of what everyone else says, you like him anyway. But something can set you off and you move instantly into *don't fuck with me, buddy* mode.

Many of the downsides of aging are relatively minor, but they are constant, cumulating, persistent, unpredictable, and mean-spirited. Mental decline teaches that the best you can hope for is that your body does not outlive your mind.

- The progression of short-term memory loss becomes glaringly clear when you decide not to flush the toilet so the water will not affect your shower temperature, and then you flush the toilet.

- During excursions in the car, every block or so you remind yourself where you are going.

- Technology delivers frustrations on the level of untangling outdoor Christmas lights.

- While helping a grandchild with homework, you discover you cannot do third grade math.

I forced myself to attend a party when I wasn't feeling well because the hosts were good friends. A girlfriend and I visited there. I complained about back pain, the fact that I couldn't wear eye makeup because of an eye condition, and an allergic reaction to a lip balm that had me looking like a sock monkey doll. She said, "You sure do have a lot going on." A few days later she drove me to the eye doctor while I whined and sobbed from the pain of a torn cornea from dry eyes. She said, "I'm so sorry you're in such pain." My response, "And I have an ingrown toenail." Such distressing, complex situations are not unusual:

- Compadres no longer speak of sex. They talk about estate plans and colonoscopies.

- There used to be so many men and so little time. Now it's. . .never mind.

- Noises that used to be made during sex are now made when getting out of bed.

- The perfume industry discontinued the production of Jungle Gardenia.

- When a help-desk child asked if my cookies were activated, I called him a rascal. And I didn't know what a browser was.

What bothers me most about being old is not the health crises, mental issues, or the inability to adjust to the world of technology. It is being unreliable—letting people down. I used to be so dependable. Now, I'm afraid to commit to anything. I mess up my calendar or get sidetracked by unfortunate incidents. I often feel as though I'm dumb and dumber simultaneously.

THE STRUGGLE TO MAINTAIN

When there is no progress, you run sideways,
knowing soon you will be backing up.

Aging amplifies emotions. Upsides and downsides are exaggerated as compared to earlier years. I vacillate between being frisky one minute and fragile the next. A body flaw interpreted as a lovely tarnish one day promotes anguish the next. I might admire the dignified face staring back at me from a mirror one minute and recoil from it later. As a result, I worry I'm bipolar.

The steadiness of earlier years is a loss. Unrelenting challenges introduce instability through a constant series of small events punctuated occasionally with large ones. To cope, I brush off the constant barrage of minor, everyday incidents with an indifferent "Oh, well," after which I ignore the event or start cleaning up the mess.

Bigger issues, like mental failings or an acute health incident, create tension that must be managed. Such destabilizing harassments are emotional triggers that cause me to shake like a baby rabbit in a human hand.

I accept that I must be in a constant state of adjustment these days. Coping is the new normal. Fortunately, the writing profession fits well into this intermittent world of good and bad times, and it helps me maintain a joyful disposition. It is work from which I don't need a vacation. And, although technology tortures me continuously, it also affords vital connections and a robust writing career.

And then, there is the blessing of grandchildren— the future sparkling brightly. They taught me that building couch-cushion forts and sitting in a large box with a flashlight do not mean you look foolish. Need I say more?

THE "WHY BOTHER" SYNDROME

You are only as strong as your weakest part.

In my sixties, I worked at staying fit. In my seventies, the "why bother" syndrome kicked in. That was not where I wanted to be. It was where I was. In 2016, I took a medication that attacked tendons and ligaments in my body. In addition, it affected my brain, limiting my ability to write creatively. These were significant losses that dramatically changed my life. This happened shortly after a diabetes diagnosis, the evolution of heart issues, and frightening eye problems. My ability to manage all that in a positive manner melted away. Overwhelmed, my mental state shifted into severe coping territory.

I hunkered down and healed, but like so many ailments, the conditions never completely went away. Instead, they coalesced into a cumulated mess. Overcome, I retreated into a "why bother" mentality.

Before all this, I worked out, ate healthy, used makeup, got manicures and pedicures, went to the hair salon regularly, wore nice clothes, and raised my computer stand to improve my posture. After that crisis, I could no longer go all out. I melted into feebleness. My zest for life waned, and I was no longer *put together* and *finished off*. "Why bother?"

These limitations introduced new freedoms, though. Without the distractions of "bothering," time was available for mental activities. Inner strength was tested, and it prevailed. Life became simpler, consumerism faded, and mental and physical clutter was eliminated. Focus switched from *things* to *people* and from *image* to *substance*. The light collided with the dark. I found my moorings and became vintage with game—sort of.

As an old person, if you think things are going well, you obviously have no clue what is going on.

Chapter 6

VINTAGE WITH GAME—OR NOT

Please, Lord, don't let me die on the toilet like Elvis.

I am a woman laced with contradictions. I resolve that I am vintage with game. Yeah, that's it. I've still got game. Nah, I don't. Not really. Yes, I do. I do. I really do. No, I don't. Yes. No. Yes. These contradictions are the result of having the good fortune of surviving. There are downsides—many of them. But wrinkles don't hurt, and just being here is a win. Aging is replete with pros and cons.

At sixty, you begin to disappear. At seventy those around you know not to ask how you feel because you will tell them. In your eighties, statistically, you are going to die, and people begin to talk about you as though you are not in the room. At ninety, well, at ninety you are probably dead or soon to be so.

I peaked in my fifties and was still vital and robust in my sixties, although aging had clandestinely stalked me for years. When I hit seventy, health issues crept up, tackled me hard, and beat me up. Bam! Bam! Bam! These hits influenced all aspects of my life.

Now, I dress like a French cafe slouch and feel somewhat like a wounded dog hit by a car. Writing contributes to the style shift. Writers tend to be a slovenly, introverted bunch. Amazingly, I don't care. I've learned that no one cares what I look like but me. And how I feel is my burden alone. Still, my earlier perspective on appearance is at war with my aging identity, and I am a woman laced with contradictions.

REALITY SQUARED

Aging—a cruel master—is life happening. And there are upsides, like naps and, well, naps.

I define myself as an old lady rocking leggings like a bloated, sloppy, badass bitch. Doing so is a defensive action. In the battle between nurture and nature, nurture may have its influences, but in the long run, nature will have its way. Belly fat ain't going away, no matter how much weight is lost, and the ultimate outcome is mortality.

Old age teaches us we cannot always manifest our destiny. I may very well die vacuuming. Drowning in a sea of discontent, I'm irritated with those who are so upbeat they shit rainbows and fart glitter. When one such rainbow woman said to me, "You don't look a day older than fabulous," I wanted to respond, "Yeah, well then, can you explain why looking in a mirror is equivalent to spotting a tapeworm in the toilet?" It took intense discipline not to say that. This doesn't mean I don't celebrate the magnificent being reflected in a mirror and see the resilience etched in that deeply inhabited face. But reality is two-sided, and let's face it, I look like a Russian scrub woman.

I have a sense of humor when my body is so wonky it's as though it came from Ikea and was put together without instructions. My arms resemble swim floaties, body parts move around—down mostly—and when I experience a raging urinary tract infection I tell a doctor, "I have a UTI. My twat is on fire—and not in a good way."

With a chin numb from dental work, a noodle from lunch stuck to it, causing a workman at my house to stare at me peculiarly. I worried he wanted me. After he left, a mirror eliminated that concern and introduced disappointment.

Doctors tell old people the most important thing they can do to stay healthy is not to fall down. Well, good luck with that. I often feel like my mother these days—especially when I fall. Those incidents were the only times she swore until her last few years when she swore while playing cards. My swearing, after falling and when playing Solitaire (manually, with cards), resurrects memories of her.

Retirement has delivered many blessings. The stresses of working have faded. Time was my enemy then, and I fought it hard. Now, time is gentle. It is my friend. Increments of time are gifts from the universe. Every day is a new start—a gift. I relish mornings when I sit in my warm, cozy flat drinking coffee while observing out the window people going to work in rain and snow. And all those years of hard work have allowed me to be financially generous to others. This is a joy I didn't expect because I never thought to aspire to it. Another surprise was the joy of learning.

THE FOREVER GIFT OF LEARNING

Gandhi said, "Learn as though you will live forever."

Learning creates *legacy squared*. It is a magnificent way to invest in oneself. Sharing what is learned, invests in others. When a person learns something new, the brain builds new connections. Anything new at my age is a good thing. What is learned is enduring and can be held forever. No one can take it away. (This is a useful fact to teach children and grandchildren.) Although easily befuddled these days, I continue to learn. Each decade of my life has fostered a prolific abundance of enlightenment and awareness through learning. Here are some examples:

What I learned in my fifties:
- Once an asshole, always an asshole.
- A man cannot put a flower in his butthole and call it a vase, but he will try—hypothetically speaking.
- A man must earn me, and it would be a hard sell.
- Dreams don't always come at you screaming.

What I learned in my sixties:
- When with grandchildren, wear cheery colors.
- Don't let losses eat up your smiles.
- It's time to be reasonably self-indulgent.
- People are savages on the Internet.

What I learned in my seventies:
- No one cares what I look like but me.
- Coping rescues and gratefulness blossoms.
- Overwriting is literary masturbation.
- There is a special kind of stupid in politics.

What I expect to learn in my eighties:
- If you live long enough, you become cute again.
- Each day is a rare gift from the universe.
- You matter by being all about the others.
- It's lonely to be the last man standing.

THE EBB AND FLOW

Minor inconveniences come in waves.
Major ones crash in like tsunamis.

One day you're feeling *extra*; the next day, *inadequate* —one day *bad ass;* the next *a failure.* You can be upbeat and hopeful and then, suddenly, a desperate, whiny bitch.

You may ask yourself, *How did I get here?* The answer would be that you survived. You beat the odds. You may question whether the disorienting ebb and flow is a good thing, but it is life happening—playing itself out.

An old journal of mine reflects the embarrassing immaturity of younger years. Lessons and achievements show progress and the price of that growth. Wisdom sometimes makes one intolerant of the young. It's tough to suffer fools when you are so well-seasoned. However, a person's own youthful history demonstrates that everyone starts out naive and finds their own path to awareness.

A person's disposition is influenced by what is personally defined as happiness, which is different for everyone. For me, expressions through writing are worthwhile and often healing. Sharing them preserves lessons for posterity. As I chronicle experiences, I think about my grandchildren and subsequent descendants reading them someday, which makes me feel productive and purposeful—attributes that are hard to come by in the latter stage of life. I'm hoping my successors will appreciate the heritage and perhaps even conclude that grandma was way cooler than they thought.

The final stage of life introduces fresh challenges. Historically, you might have caught a college roommate wearing your clothes. Today, you spot a lady sitting in your spot in the assisted living lunchroom. Great sex is traded for a senior sixty-nine, which involves rubbing each others feet at the same time. The best you can hope for is that your body gives out before your mind. There are up-sides: taking naps, eating whatever you want, and doing things you shouldn't. Writing is the universe showing off, and memoir means you won't die with your story still in you. And you are less likely to be abducted. Such positive thoughts are followed with "brace yourself," and negative ones with "I'm still here." Thus the magic of the ebb and flow.

When turning sixty, you might have at least one-third of your life ahead of you. That's a lot of time to waste by coasting.

Chapter 7

PASSION AND PURPOSE

To leave the world better, fighting for relevance and creating legacy are primary themes for the third-trimester of life.

It is likely I only have ten to fifteen years left—if that. My response to "How are you?" is often that I am only "mostly okay," or I lie and say, "fine" because I don't want to be a downer. Sometimes I even ask myself, *Am I okay?* And the answer is *no*.

Self-talk often includes the phrase: *This, too, shall pass*. And it does, or at least it has so far—mostly. The third trimester of life is not primarily about these things, though. It's about giving back. I've had my run. It's time to focus on legacy—leaving things better for others.

JUST TRYING TO MATTER

You can't give away what you don't have.

When asked what she was up to one day, June Carter Cash responded, "I'm just trying to matter." Not a bad plan.

Everyone matters, of course, but consciously focusing on mattering promotes a purposeful life.

I tell young people who are unsure of themselves and suffering self-esteem issues: "Just by *being*, you are *enough*." Everyone is born worthy. An important accomplishments of my career was an anti-suicide presentation I introduced to seventh graders in Junior Achievement. I didn't call it that, of course, but it was designed to help them survive youthful hard times. I drew a line across classroom boards to symbolize a lifetime. Then I erased a two-inch space shortly after the beginning to represent the junior high and high school years. I explained that many upsetting incidents they think are so devastating during that time will seem insignificant in the whole scheme of life once they are older and looking back. This put a fresh perspective on the traumatic teenage years.

Then I pointed out the long line ahead of that empty space when they will be in control of their lives. There is hope in their future. Good decisions are key, and they can make them. I also told them they will make mistakes and gave advice on how to forgive themselves and to recover from them: *When things are bad, remember: It will get better. The universe gives us the gift of units of time. Every day you get to start over.*

It is common for people to encourage the young by telling them: *You can do anything you want to do.* Someone said that to me once, and it did inspire me. But I've observed too many people struggle to do things that are inconsistent with their innate talents. I encourage people to take that inspiration a step further: *Find what you were born to do and do that.* This idea came to me when I observed terrible singers on American Idol. Some of them lacked the innate talent to ever realize singing goals and were struggling against inevitable odds. I also noticed at work how many employees were mismatched to their jobs and didn't realize it. Everyone has unique and natural abilities just waiting to be tapped. The key is to discover them. They are the path to realizing potential as well as to finding happiness.

One of my messages to grandchildren, and even myself, is a wise and wonderful confidence-builder—a quote from Christopher Robin in *Winnie the Pooh*:

> You are braver than you believe,
> stronger than you seem, and
> smarter than you think.

This is so inspiring that I've purchased gifts for children with this quote engraved on them. This thought even keeps me going. Whatever circumstance crosses my path, I try to leave it better. Sometimes frailty and weakness get the better of me, and I fail at this. When that happens, I remind myself that if I'm not dead yet, I'm not done yet, and I carry on. Tomorrow is a new day. I can re-start. Everything I do still counts. I matter.

MATTERING—LEAVE IT BETTER

You become much more interesting when your focus is on making a difference for others.

I was seventy-two when diagnosed with diabetes. Despair festered, and I was mad. Then, I rationalized that if I had not lived to be that old, I wouldn't have gotten diabetes. With that perspective, gratefulness blossomed. I'm generally upbeat but not immune to feeling down. Each decade delivers some form of physical degradation or emotional crisis that threatens my good nature.

At seventy, I thought I had moved past all that nonsense, leaned into threats to my sanity, and learned to roll with the flow. I had accepted the philosophy that endurance is key when trouble surfaces. So why do I occasionally feel like an ungrateful, brooding child hankering for a tantrum? Because the challenges are relentless. This is why coping skills are vital. I apply mantras: *Oh, well; Bummer; This, too, shall pass; Don't affect me none; Stay the course;* and my favorite, *Work the problem, Nik, work the problem.* Then I move on.

The past sometimes haunts me and inhibits my enjoyment of the present. I have to remind myself that thoughts are made-up stories, some of which are significantly distorted and laced with regret. People tend to judge themselves more harshly than others do. I suspect most people who contemplate their early years are embarrassed by the naivety of immaturity. That's okay. As I've taught my children, if you don't look back on earlier years and feel you were an idiot, you are not evolving. I remind myself of that when old lady nonsense surfaces.

BEING BOLD

Sometimes I do things I shouldn't.

I've gotten more brash and audacious in my old age. My children are accustomed to the fact that their mother sometimes does things she shouldn't. They appear to not judge, and they cope well with the consequences. We old folks don't have a lot to lose. When someone is upset with something I've said or done, I accept responsibility and tell them right off, "I'm not a nice person." *Nice* is boring and *refined* tedious, and it's hard for others to argue with an old lady who doesn't defend her position.

Unfortunately, because of politics in recent years, I am a woman hugely frustrated. The older I get, the less I am willing to suffer fools. I require they stay away from me. Not being a nice person, I have nothing to say to them. The meanness and foolishness endorsed by some people, of all ages, has cost our country and innocent people so much that I no longer know how to be lovely. It takes intense discipline to *not* tell a sweet granddaughter being bullied by a mean girl to "Punch her in the mouth."

I'm disillusioned with humanity and shocked by what people are capable of. The selfishness and the lack of common sense and discipline during a pandemic have damaged my attitude toward others. I'm now afraid of people, supposedly normal people who act selfishly and irresponsibly. And I'm appalled at their lack of discipline.

I boldly attack political issues in this document because, for me to matter, I'm compelled to stand up to evil. So I diligently study and share my take on the threats to democracy and humanity.

I've mellowed in recent years in some respects and have become fired up by others. I respect boundaries, except when I don't. When I go after something, I do so with the enthusiasm of a panther after prey and sometimes with a vengeance that is intimidating. For such actions, I'm *not sorry*. I am politically radicalized, and for good reason.

Our country has lost its moral compass. Because of that, the rest of this book takes on a different tone. It flows from intimate topics of love and aging to an impolite political environment that has colored the last five years and a pandemic, which I call *The Trump Virus*. I know. This is name calling, but Trump set the bar on that so low I'd have to dig a hole to get under it. He likes attaching his name to things, so I'm happy to deliver. Also, an extremist movement has gained momentum with a more sophisticated playbook. Is this okay? Aw, hell no! As an audacious, resolute old woman determined to *leave it better,* I'm calling it like I see it.

At all cost, avoid a victim mentality, and never lose your sense of humor. If you fall down and a cohort calls you "Safe!"—laugh. If you do something inappropriate, say "I didn't mean that weird-like." And if you are striving to survive or to protect others, fight with a vengeance.

Chapter 8

A BRAZEN, DIABOLICAL PANDEMIC

Unleashed on a selfish, undisciplined public, the pandemic crisis showed who we really were. And that was heartbreaking and ugly.

A friend said to me, "If my dad could land on Normandy Beach in World War II and survive, walk from there to Berlin while being shot at all the way, I can stay in my lovely home during a pandemic." I wish more people had found a reason to do so. Americans have proven themselves to be undisciplined and selfish beyond belief and, in the case of many Trump followers, easily manipulated to the point of ruthlessness.

At times of crisis, the world doesn't need selfish, undisciplined, numb, cult disciples. It needs the brave, the bold, and a shitload of rational thinking, common sense folks willing to sacrifice for the good of all. Unfortunately, this nation didn't get that, and its citizens didn't have a leader who could give it to them. They had just the opposite.

After seeing something about the pandemic on the news, my grandson, with tears in his eyes, said to his mother, "I don't want my GoGo to die." That set the tone for my sequester strategy. I don't want those I love to worry about me. They have enough to worry about. Also, I don't want them to have to live with killing me if they, or I, are careless and one of them infects me. What an unfortunate thing for them to have to live with. I'm not inclined to want to kill anyone either. So I'm careful, and I make severe sacrifices. I do so as much for others as for myself.

Sequestering diligently was an extraordinary sacrifice that I made for well over a year. When pandemic fatigue set in, I resisted it and stayed home. I didn't refill my car gas tank for over a year. I abandoned beauty processes, let my hair go gray, clipped my nails to the quick, and taped my broken eyeglasses together. No one sees me, anyway. I was determined not to be lying in an intensive care bed with manicured nails, painted toenails, and beautiful hair.

I had no visitors and amassed supplies in my garage, cupboards, freezer, and under my bed. The only place I went for fourteen months, other than a couple of mandated medical exceptions, was to a twenty-four-hour grocery store once a month at five o'clock in the morning—masked and gloved. When I got home, I closed the garage door immediately after putting the car in park to avoid conversations with neighbors. I unloaded the car and put perishable groceries on the stairs to carry upstairs to my flat. Non-perishables were quarantined in the garage for a week to allow germs to die. I stripped out of my clothes and left them on the garage floor, being careful not to shake germs into the air before applying another dose of Purell to my hands and inside of my nose. (I'm not obsessive.) Since this is done only once a month, my nose endured the assault.

The first time I got home from grocery shopping during the pandemic, out of habit I hit the automatic garage door button to close it, forgetting it was already closed. The door started going up as I stood there—buck naked. This created terror on the level of discovering a tarantula in the bathtub. In a panic to reverse the upward motion, I accidentally hit the button that opened the other garage door. At this point, the door closest to me was halfway up. I immediately hit both door openers—hard—stopping the upward motion. Another hit sent both back down, sparing my neighbors a sight which might have scarred them for life. It would not have been pretty.

Regrouping, I gathered up grocery sacks and climbed the stairs, removing my outdoor shoes at the top landing before entering my flat. I carried the groceries into the kitchen where I prepared a portion of the counter with a considerable dose of disinfectant. Once the groceries were wiped down and put away or set aside for germs to die, I showered and washed my hair. Okay. Okay. I am obsessive. But one reason I do all this is so my children don't have to worry about me. However, when I tell them my routine, they worry about me.

ISOLATION EXTREMES

*I've worked over thirty jigsaw puzzles
in twelve months—some of them twice.*

I'm seventy-six years old, which statistically means I will die of something within the next five to ten years. But I'm determined it's not going to be from this virus, primarily because it would mean someone killed me. No one needs to live with that. And I still have purpose. I might put my car keys in the refrigerator and my toothbrush in the cookie jar, but I still have purpose. I'm able to convey wisdom and lessons learned, even though, admittedly, I am not always a good role model.

After five months of isolation, I had exhausted every avenue of entertainment and projects. So I decided it was time to create solace through music. I ask the Echo lady, Alexa, to play Joe Cocker, Michael Bublé, and Queen. And I created *My Favorites* list which included these songs:

Jason Aldean asked me to take a ride on his "Big Green Tractor." This produced a pleasant country buzz that had me two-stepping around the living room.

Don Henley and Glenn Frey's "The Last Resort," one of my all-time Eagles' favorites, spoke to my ecological leanings.

"Love Hurts" and "I Want to Know What Love Is" stirred emotions related to love gone wrong, although I really didn't need to hear that crap.

Journey's "Can't Fight This Feeling Anymore," reminded me of a boyfriend, sitting shirtless on my bed playing it on a guitar. The lyrics were effective at the time—now, not so much.

"The Story of Love" and "The Glory of Love" further tormented my sentimental mind, after which Train's "Soul Sister" had a rallying effect.

Then, Garth Brooks swept me away with "To Make You Feel My Love," a song from one of my favorite movies, "Hope Floats."

Several Keith Urban love songs soothed my soul.

"What a Wonderful World" by Louis Armstrong reminded me of grandchildren whom I had not seen in over a year. So I cried—hard.

My all-time favorites, Prince's "Purple Rain," and Nate Ruess and Pink's duet, "Just Give Me a Reason" always raise my spirits.

A new track, which I call my pandemic song, "I'm Not Going Anywhere," gave me goosebumps.

Contemplating other songs to request from Alexa, I wondered: What ever happened to that raspy bitch, Kim Carnes, and will I ever get over the loss of Prince?

After depleting my favorites song list, I requested Alexa play seventies music. That decade included several defining moments in my life reflected in music of the era. If Alexa played songs I didn't like, I asked her to skip them and move on to the next one. When "Highway to Hell" came on, reminding me of an old boyfriend who installed surround sound in my house, I yelled "SKIP!"

I also skipped brooding music. That included The Eagles' "Hotel California," which never did do anything for me. I preferred "Take It Easy" with Winslow, Arizona, in it. I recuperated from the flu in a motel there on a road trip from California to Oklahoma. My grandkids gave me the flu, which makes the event special. Any form of camaraderie with them is a positive experience.

Bob Seger's "The Fire Down Below" was not well received. Since my estrogen level was .001, I didn't need to hear that. "SKIP!" Waylon sang about "getting back to the basics of life," which I did in 2016. I appreciated the reminder and the reinforcement of my decision.

THE "I DON'T CARE" COPING TACTIC

*When I tell myself I don't care, it's because
I care so much I fear I will go mad.*

There is no understating the impact of the pandemic on the mental state of most people I know. That influence is reflected in my thoughts and emotions as I document them here. Admittedly, I am for the first time in my life out of control and unrestrained in my attack on the corruption and incompetence that fed this viral attack on humanity. And I do not apologize for my angry responses. Not sorry.

Aging issues were exaggerated by fear and isolation fostered by the pandemic. I lost both my mental and physical equilibrium. I was out of shape physically—and I didn't care. My hair turned gray and thin—and I didn't care. When I got off the couch and waddled around the house, slouching and bouncing off of furniture—I didn't care. Because of the political climate, I had written off some friends and even a few loved ones—and I didn't care.

My morning coffee routine changed. I avoided most televised news. And attention-seeking famous folks eager to capitalize on notoriety by supposedly helping people through the pandemic crisis with online posts irritated me:

Elizabeth Hurley (whoever she is) or January Jones (whoever she is) in bikini pics didn't do anything for me, nor did Kylie Jenner revealing stretch marks on her butt. Vera Wang's toned abs and skinny legs were plainly repulsive. And Brie Bierman (whoever she is) baring her butt on "pool day" did not make isolation more tolerable.

I didn't need to know about twenty-five foods I should never buy from China. Nor did I need Shake Shack's recipe for cheese sauce.

The fact that John Goodman drove a certain kind of car was irrelevant. So was seven bikini styles that will be everywhere this summer. Can we get over the bikini crap already, please?

I couldn't care less that Will and Jada Smith cheated on each other. Geez. Nor was I interested in why *The Rifleman* went off the air.

I didn't need to know Lucille Ball's granddaughter looked just like her. She didn't.

And why would I care what the black diamond on a measuring tape is for?

What did work for me? Sam Elliot in his underwear in *The Ranch* on Netflix. And I liked the lady from the CDC who wore tablecloths around her neck while reporting on the pandemic. She should get an award for the stank face she made when Trump suggested drinking or injecting bleach and disinfectant.

When the Internet was introduced to the general public, my boyfriend used it to hook up with an old girlfriend—a common occurrence today but a novelty in 2003. Within six weeks he left me. I decided the Internet made people stupid. Twenty-some years later, I still think that, although for different reasons. I appreciate its redeeming qualities, though, even when they make me feel stupid.

SEQUESTER—A TIME TO NEST

The Bible tells us there is a time for everything. I'm not a religious person, but I can relate to that wise premise.

With sequester, I melted comfortably into solitude. I got into cooking, which is conducive to listening to music. Pink Floyd's rich, full music, Phish's quirky tunes, and anything by Aretha Franklin or Tina Turner are favorites perfect for food preparation. Cooking tasks took on a new, slower pace as I discovered patience I didn't know I had. I sorted carrots out of mixed vegetables, cut onions into tiny minced pieces instead of large chunks, diligently broke pecan pieces into even smaller ones, and adopted a new habit of washing dishes and cleaning up as I cooked.

I ignored my diabetic diet and ate anything I wanted. I saved bacon grease to pour into almost everything that required heat. I was generous with spices and flavorings, doubling the vanilla in recipes and coffee and adding liberal doses of almond extract to desserts.

I dug out old Iowa recipes from when I used to cook and prepared many of my favorites. Dishes were divided into single-service portions and put in freezable packets for the future. I would have preferred to share my dishes with neighbors rather than hoard them for myself, but with the pandemic, giving away food made me feel like a terrorist.

I gained twenty pounds the first nine months, after which I redeemed myself by introducing an intermittent fasting plan championed by Dr. Oz. I lost thirty pounds in five months. This was not done to look good. I was way over that. It was a health thing, and I felt much better without the excess weight. I still ate pretty much whatever I wanted, but giving up evening snacks and breakfast, I consumed only two meals a day. Amazingly, I was rarely hungry.

I ordered a three-wheel bike from Amazon. My son assembled it for me, and I rode it every day the weather allowed. A notorious gray-haired old lady in pajamas peddling away on an oversized tricycle and honking a clown horn, I became a neighborhood novelty. I stocked the basket with a substantial umbrella in case of a dog attack and two twenty-dollar bills in case of a human one.

At three o'clock every afternoon I put on my outdoor shoes and got the mail. I took along an anti-bacterial wipe to open the mailbox and to wipe down any mail not tossed in the garage trash. I sequestered mail in the garage to de-germ for three days before bringing it into the house. I wiped down the garage door opener, light switch, and anything else I had touched, took off my outdoor shoes, entered my flat with mail from three days ago, washed my hands and applied hand sanitizer for good measure.

I distracted myself by sitting on my balcony, sometimes during a polite rain, watching neighbors walk dogs and birds feed in the grass. I hovered in my comfortable home and felt extreme gratefulness every morning when I woke up just to have another day.

I was off Facebook, but monitored my children and friends through telephone calls, email postings, and FaceTime. Occasionally, I zoomed with organizations I belonged to, which was always a blatant assault on my self-esteem since my face looked like a reflection in a spoon and my hair like a tangle of fishing lures. When I ran out of projects and my house and garage were organized and polished to a shine, I began writing an essay out of desperation for something to do. I got carried away, and it transitioned into this book.

A level of fear pervaded everything I did. It hung in the air like hostile apparitions. It's disturbing that older folks have to live their final years in such fear. It took seven months for the virus to reach me personally when three friends died in one week. I hurt so deep for the losses, our nation, and innocent people that I lost myself mentally in the fiasco. So much of what happened was unnecessary. While undisciplined, selfish no-maskers and deniers called the virus a *hoax*, there was no national strategy and few personal sacrifices. There were just lies, denial, and chaos.

I will never be the same as I was before the pandemic. My faith in humanity has been murdered. Resigned to more losses, I became numb, except for a new emotion—hate. For the first time in my life—at the ripe old age of seventy-three—I succumbed to hate. Who would have predicted that would happen?

SECTION III

HOW EVIL OWNS PEOPLE

**The Solution: Rational Thought,
Critical Thinking, and Awareness**

Never underestimate the power of an alternative reality created by a greedy, entitled cult leader. And never, ever fail to appreciate the malleability of the human brain.

Chapter 9

MENTAL ILLNESS—
PERSONALITY DISORDERS

Nothing will make you crazier than
trying to figure out a crazy person.

From a journalistic perspective, it is unusual to write a book so disjointed it hops from love and aging to politics and a deranged bully. I do so for four reasons: (1) I'm so traumatized that I no longer care about journalistic craft. (2) All these topics influenced the last five years of my life so much that ignoring any of them would be lying by omission. (3) I needed healing; writing heals me. (4) Bizarre material, though disturbing, promotes lessons worth sharing. Everyone needs to be aware of menacing mental illness disorders and the nuances of cults in order to protect themselves and those they love as well as to answer these questions:

How is it people can be manipulated to the extent they lose their ability to reason—that they act against their own best interest? How can nice people give up their humanity? How can they sacrifice compassion in support of a greedy, vile madman? How can seemingly sane people ignore facts and be indifferent to the raping of our country and the abuse of the most vulnerable among us? How can lies be turned into truths?

The answer to these questions is a lack of awareness on the part of followers about the power of cults, the vulnerability of the human brain, and the ability of power mongers to destroy rational thought in followers by defining an *alternative reality* for them. Consumed with power, Trump focused more on lying, seeking attention, manipulating, and disrupting through conflict and chaos than on running the country.

Many psychiatrists, including those in The World Mental Health Coalition, have publicly suggested Trump's mental illness includes *narcissism* so extreme it could be labeled *malignant narcissism*. This, combined with a *histrionic* personality disorder—a condition wherein a person requires constant attention—creates a person addicted to rallies and manic tweeting that enticed a disturbing number of loyalists to follow him like sheep. Many—groomed by Fox News, talk radio, and religious leaders for years to accept any lie propagated—have traded critical thinking for blind acceptance of any ridiculous lie, idea, or antic Trump dished out. They subjugated their thinking to his *alternative realities* even to the point of acting against their own best interests. Acquiescing to his self-serving nature and that of his cronies (who have been accused of crimes in unprecedented numbers), followers ignored, accepted, or endorsed The Trump Crime Syndicate. The degree to which followers responded to manipulation by such leaders is illustrated by their willingness to overlook behaviors and, yes, even atrocities.

Historically, one lie could discredit a politician. *The Washington Post* reported 30,534 lies and misstatements Trump told over the four years of his presidency. He acted in ways contrary to the public good in over 10,000 situations, some of which are listed herein. Any one of them alone should have taken him out of the running for someone to admire and follow. None did. Why not?

An obsession with power and a lack of empathy makes a narcissist dangerous. A counselor once warned me as I was leaving a relationship with one that narcissists are vindictive and controlling; therefore, it is almost impossible to leave them. And they are dangerous when you do. I did leave and suffered three years of aggressive attacks, constant harassment, and even assault, which left me emotionally scarred. I was fortunate to have survived it. Since then, I've studied this disorder and collected a library of books on the subject. The behavior of a narcissist is blatant. Red flags wave furiously all around them. Now, I can spot one within a minute or two of meeting them. I knew a guest in my home was an extreme narcissist before we took the stairs from the entry up to my flat. I wish for everyone that level of awareness.

That people continue to support Trump and his aberrant behavior is astounding. Followers are either like him and are okay with it or they have succumbed to an artificial reality. Constantly manipulated and exploited by this cunning con man and his support system, they enable him. One can argue whether Trump's followers are in a cult, but experts tell us they are. At any rate, they are cult-like in their behavior. And one thing we do know about cults is: *Those in a cult don't know they are in a cult.*

The *Handbook of Diagnosis and Treatment of the DSM-IV Personality Disorders* is used here to describe behavior consistent with personality disorders. Published by the American Psychiatric Association, this diagnostic manual is used by mental health professionals to diagnose mental disorders and to define treatment.

I'm not a psychiatrist, and I'm not diagnosing anyone, but I'll take the word of many psychiatrists in this country who have publicly stated they believe Trump has mental disorders based on his behaviors. According to historians and Trump's niece, Mary Trump, Ph.D., his childhood background tracks closely with that typical of a malignant narcissist. And his father's behavior showed signs he was one as well. It is likely both nature and nurture played a role in the extreme extent of Trump's conditions. Take a look at the criteria for *narcissistic* and *histrionic* personality disorders and draw your own conclusions.

NARCISSISTIC PERSONALITY DISORDER

Before getting into narcissistic behavior as a mental disorder, it's important to understand that narcissism is a matter of degree. Everyone has some such qualities. Otherwise, they would be taken advantage of and unable to engage in self care. When diagnosing a person with a personality disorder, psychiatrists consider the degree of observable behaviors on a spectrum. Following are traits of a person whose behavior is so high on the spectrum that, per experts and sociologist Stephen Kent, a University of Alberta professor, they would be classified as having a narcissistic personality disorder to the degree of *malignant narcissism*:

- Lack of empathy

- Dominant, self-centered, conceited, boastful, pompous, snobbish, and exhibitionistic

- Arrogant, indulgent, and having an exaggerated sense of self-importance

- Aspires to grandiose goals of power, wealth, and ability

- Impatient, hypersensitive, easily offended and subject to fits of rage and rants

- Dominates conversations and seeks admiration

- A sense of entitlement and expectations of favorable treatment

- Externalized blame

- Lying, exaggeration, taking liberties with facts, distortion of facts, and self-deception

- Inflexible, disdainful, irresponsible

- Extreme self-confidence. When confidence is shaken, the response is criticism and rage

- Perceptions of others vacillate between adulation and devaluation

- Manipulative and often charismatic

- Preoccupied with feelings of envy

- Exploitive and controlling

Anyone you know?

Narcissists have an exaggerated sense of self-importance and operate under the illusion of specialness coupled with grandiose and often unrealistic goals of power, wealth, and brilliance. With an intense need for admiration, they are thin-skinned and extremely vulnerable to criticism or being ignored, to which they respond with contempt and rage. They lie with abandon and believe their own lies. When stressed, they can be irresponsible and exhibit risky behavior. They are disdainful of those who don't support their exulted beliefs. Other people are considered inferior, weak, and exploitable.

Narcissistic behavior includes *projection*, which means they are transparent and telegraph what they are thinking or planning while accusing others of doing that same act. So an accusation from a narcissist is often a confession of what they are thinking. Their intentions are blatant red flags. A man I know handed his girlfriend a glass of ice water on a hot day. She accused him of trying to poison her. They were not getting along. Understanding the concept of projection, he was smart and left before she poisoned him.

Probably the most prominent and encompassing narcissistic behavior is a *lack of empathy.* This hallmark of narcissism leads to superficial relationships with minimal emotional ties or commitments. If someone is puzzled by you doing something kind for someone in need with no expectation of anything in return, you are likely dealing with a narcissist on the high end of the spectrum.

A common trait of strong narcissists is lying and deceit as well as self-deception. Emily Fox wrote in *Born Trump* that one of Trump's longtime friends said, "He believes his own lies and creates his own realities."

Narcissists often see their children as an extension of themselves and seek for them the same favors they expect. Other than favored descendants, they are loyal to no one.

Professionals suggest that severe narcissism is derived from both nature and nurture. This means the condition is likely inherited. From a nurturing perspective, the root of these tendencies are parental indulgence, role modeling of narcissistic behaviors, and overvaluation of the child. Biographical information suggests Trump had a cold and absent mother and learned exploitive, manipulative behaviors from his authoritarian, narcissistic father. It is likely there were a plethora of negative influences—both inherited and environmental—that shaped him.

For four years, people in this country were buffeted about by radical social and political uncertainties, a world-wide epidemic of fundamentalism, and a pandemic. And, as we lost our moorings, we were subjected to absolute dogma by Trump, a radical, greedy, off-the-charts opportunistic leader who conned and exploited citizens with self-serving solutions far removed from what we needed at that critical time.

HISTRIONIC PERSONALITY DISORDER

Combined with the *narcissistic* personality disorder, the *histrionic* disorder can be particularly destructive. The posting of over one-hundred tweets in a day and a constant barrage of rallies suggests Trump is in some sort of manic state and in desperate need of attention. The most obvious sign of a histrionic person is a constant and intense craving for praise and attention. Behaviors include:

- Manipulative, flirtatious, and attention seeking
- Uncomfortable in situations where they cannot be the center of attention
- Charming, capricious, and superficial
- Infantile behavior
- Entitled to special care or gratification
- Impulsive exaggerated emotions and inability to delay gratification
- Constantly demanding approval and praise
- Inappropriately sexually seductive
- Overly concerned with physical attractiveness
- Displays rapidly shifting and shallow emotions
- Unfocused and diffused thinking style

- Excessively impressionistic speech lacks detail and is highly subjective as opposed to objective

- Relies heavily on hunches and intuition

- Easily impressed and influenced by others

- Easily becomes side-tracked

- Embraces drama and exaggerates emotions

- Considers relationships more intimate than they are

- Externalizes blame

- Shows self-dramatization and theatricality

- Exhibits hyper-responsive behavioral patterns

Anyone you know?

Like most mental disorders, histrionic behaviors occur along a spectrum. Anyone on the high end of the scale will demonstrate many, if not all, of these behaviors. Trump's obsession with tweets, rallies, and "performing" suggests extreme self-dramatization and theatrics.

Trump craves attention and worship. His desire for a military parade, over ten parties in the White House after his election defeat, and a grand ceremonial send off when leaving the White House for the last time reflect these cravings. At over 500 rallies, which distracted significantly from presidential functions, he performed like a stand-up comedian while instilling fear and hate. Although he puffed and bullied, he portrayed himself as a victim. These events were pity parties wherein he complained about being misunderstood and maligned. He continued holding them even after being elected. It is reasonable to predict he will carry on his attention-grabbing ways when out of office.

Trump's constant quest for praise and recognition explains why he makes up awards. Claiming a nonexistent

Nobel Peace Prize, lobbying to have his face on Mount Rushmore, and posting his picture on phony magazine covers at Trump properties reflect histrionic obsessions.

Because of his obsession with attention and the inability to delay gratification, Trump broadcasts his grandiose plans. Braggadocios comments throughout his term as president signal his authoritarian ambitions. He is easily impressed and influenced by corrupt facist leaders and dictators, a typical narcissistic tendency.

A dichotomous thinking style that is global and unfocused is common to this personality disorder. Overgeneralization, emotional reasoning, and an aversion to detail impedes competence, inhibits personal growth, and encourages infantile behavior.

Histrionic men often indulge in macho behavior, called *Don Juanism*, to reassure themselves they are "real men." In spite of his repulsiveness, indications are that Trump fancies himself some kind of ladies' man.

Narcissists who are also histrionic are skilled manipulators who use crafty methods to "stir things up." They perpetuate a constant state of conflict and chaos. Seeing themselves as victims, they blame others for their troubles while demonstrating little self-awareness. In marital counseling, this is the guy who tells the psychiatrist, "You need to straighten her out."

I'm not a psychiatrist, so I'll leave any official diagnosis related to Trump to the professionals. As a layman, though, I consider him a nut job.

Do this. After finishing this book, read this chapter and the next one on cults again. And, if you are to read one book to understand what has happened to our country and its people, I recommend *The Cult of Trump*, by Steven Hassan. Awareness, the essence of enlightenment, offers protection from victimization.

Political views are not facts. Opinions are not facts. Thoughts are not facts. Facts are facts. Anyone not getting that has been sold an alternative reality. Never underestimate the power of mind control and the human brain's susceptibility to it.

If you think you are not in a cult and you are not wearing a mask for political reasons during a deadly pandemic, you are in a cult. No rational thinking person would do that. No one capable of critical thinking would do that. No genuine Christian would do that. Only those untethered to reality would do that.

If you believe not taking protective measures during a pandemic is about personal freedom, you are responding to an alternative reality—a lie. It's not about personal freedom. It's about common sense, rational thought, critical thinking and protecting and caring for others. It is about not killing someone.

Chapter 10

SUSCEPTIBILITY TO CULT INFLUENCES

Cult members have no idea they are in a cult.

If you question whether Trump supporters are in a cult, know that top experts in that field are convinced they are. People who felt spurned by the political establishment were lured into a cult by clever, sophisticated tricksters. Trump is not clever and is far from sophisticated. He is more of an uncouth bungling thug, hell-bent on achieving self-gratification. But he's cunning and supported by a network of manipulative people who are brilliant cult builders.

In the 1990s, Newt Gingrich, Fox News, Rush Limbaugh, talk radio, and evangelical leaders politicized religion by building a religious cult. Trump inherited it in 2015. Through dissemination of distorted information and strategic thought manipulation, the Gingrich playbook allowed Trump to quickly amass power. Extreme right-wing broadcasters teamed up with Trump and his advisors Steve Bannon, Stephen Miller, evangelistic religious leaders, and radical right-wing Republican leadership to strategically dish out classic mind control to gullible, vulnerable masses of unsuspecting souls. Dr. Phil's counseling of those being *catfished* (taken advantage of through the Internet) illustrates peoples' shocking capacity for gullibility. Something similar has happened to many vulnerable

Americans who have been *catfished* to the point where they enable and endorse abhorrent behavior of a man determined to destroy democracy while taking advantage of them.

What causes seemingly normal people to trade respect for facts and truth for propaganda—to accept any *alternative facts* manipulators suggest? What human vulnerabilities cause people, at the persuasion of another, to act against their own best interests and core values? What blinds them to those who exploit? Why do they subjugate themselves to greedy, self-serving leaders? How can a once loving person accept dishonesty, cruelty, and abuse? The answers reside in the study of cults.

Most people are unaware of the powerful forces of exploitive, hidden agendas behind hype and the formidable mind control techniques that trap cult followers. Folks dissatisfied with their lives are vulnerable to false promises and bogus ideologies. In cult-like situations, they are courted early on and exploited later. They have no idea where they are headed until they are hooked. Then, they are so compromised they don't realize they are being used.

One requirement of a cult is a charismatic leader. When coming across one, a person would do well to put up their guard. Leaders can be good or bad, depending on their motives and actions. The ones with empathetic natures who are concerned with the good of others and who act in an ethical manner are good leaders. Those lacking empathy, who demonstrate self-serving motives, seek power, and aspire to enrich themselves at the expense of others, should be avoided. They take advantage with impunity because they believe themselves entitled and perhaps even "chosen" by a supreme being—their excuse for being rich and powerful.

Cult leaders depend on sustained deception to cultivate followers and to estrange them from mainstream society. They create fanatical fear of external forces and then offer protection from them. These forces include family, the government, or any person or organization outside the cult.

Anyone can be swept into a cult without realizing it. It's unfair to conclude that those who have been are inadequate in some way. No one "joins" a cult. But the most intelligent and accomplished among us can be conned into one. Deceptive recruiting practices and proven thought-reform techniques do not discriminate. Once a person is hooked, rational thought fades, critical thinking is compromised, and the person is at the mercy of the leader and his henchmen. Disenfranchised people sliding from middle class into poverty are particularly susceptible to cult influences, so much so that in the hands of a cult leader, they are like turkeys voting for Thanksgiving.

Those outside a cult who love a cult member are victims, too. They become collateral damage as the cultist becomes alienated from them. For me, as an outsider, the shock of Trump's reign caused less angst than did the willingness with which ordinary people embraced his evilness. I've always known there were evil people in the world. The surprise was that empathetic, loving, and compassionate people could turn into cult-like fawners, devoid of reason and divorced from facts and reality. As indifferent as cattle, they endorsed cruelty and the absurd. This was devastating. Relationships with them turned toxic, and connections were severed to save myself.

In an effort to heal, I've devoted myself to an intense study of personality disorders as well as cults and their persuasion processes. I've done deep research and collected a library of books on these topics. Before that effort, I hated Trump's followers as much as I hated his ways and his cohorts. My views softened once I learned people were unaware of his mental illness and the potent effectiveness of techniques used to attack their psyche and alter how they think.

So, when my future and that of my country and loved ones hung in the balance under Trump's influence, I understood his mental issues that predicted *where* he was headed, as well as the *why* of his motivations, and the *how* of his strategy. Trump is an aspiring fascist leader seeking to overturn our government. Many people ignored his behavior and were—and still are—unaware of his madness. They followed him blindly in the face of his lying, exploitation, corruption, and bullying like a junkyard dog.

Trump requires constant adoration. According to Factbase, his Twitter rants reached a peak of over 100 maniacal posts on one day on May 8, 2020, and over 56,600 during his presidency. After years of this, I ignored the 2020 primaries. I no longer cared who ran against Trump. I just wanted a president not obsessed with tweeting.

As the extent of Trump's madness became clear, I eased reluctantly into hate—a new emotion directed at his regime and his supporters initially. I shut them out. Now, with a deeper understanding of how cults operate and of the human vulnerabilities in that regard, I'm more sympathetic toward followers. I will not be reaching out to them, though. I don't wish most of them goodwill or bad will. I'm neutral in that regard, except for the most radical among them who are violent. But my compassion remains compromised. For that, I'm not sorry. I resent that four of my final years had to be lived in an environment of hate, fear, and lunacy—that I was subjected to so much intense and appalling nonsense and chaos that devastated so many people, almost destroyed our country, and left me fearful of the future.

My future is short, though, and it is not for me that I'm most angry. I'm mad—beyond mad—because of what has been done to my children and grandchildren. Also, Trump and his followers hurt and killed people, some I knew and loved. For that, I harbor a deep and enduring grudge.

Some suggest reconciliation with Trump supporters now that he is out of office. They recommend anti-Trumpers *hate the cult, but love the cult members.* I haven't been able to do that. The betrayal of humanity is incompatible with forgiveness to me. Also, I understand cults and certain mental disorders. Trump is not going away and neither are his followers. They are just beginning. He said so himself.

UNDERSTANDING A CULT

Because you think something in your head doesn't make it true. It is a thought, perhaps one pounded into you by someone else.

To grasp what has happened to our country, it helps to understand cults. I recommend these books and sources:

Cults Inside Out by Rick Alan Ross

Cults In Our Midst by Margaret Singer

Losing Reality by Robert J. Lipton

The Cult of Trump by Steven Hassan

The Family, by Jeff Sharlet, also on Netflix

The Brainwashing of My Dad by Jen Senko
on Amazon Prime, iTunes, and *youtube.com*

Information about cults on the Internet include TED Talks on YouTube where ex-cult members speak. Ross' website *rickross.com* and his online library site *Cult Education Institute* are impressive sources.

Criteria for a political cult includes: (1) a self-serving, charismatic leader and a power structure to support him, (2) use of mind-altering practices, and (3) exploitation of group members. Ross further defines a destructive cult as:

An organizational structure led by a charismatic and authoritarian leader who creates a significant power imbalance that hurts or exploits people. The leader becomes a dominant force in the person's life. The objective is to destabilize a person and introduce mind persuasion techniques to control him and cause him to subjugate his needs to that of the leader.

People often get sucked into cults because they are searching for love, acceptance, and community—a place to belong. Or they are seekers, exploring deep, meaningful psychological understanding. Or they may be looking for wealth, opportunities for self-improvement, the solution to a problem, or some other life enhancement. Some need to be unburdened. All are influenced by the ancient primal need —originally vital for survival—to be part of a tribe and to follow a strong leader. Cult members rarely consciously join a cult. They are groomed and lured into one without realizing it. This is why they don't know they are in a cult.

Cult leaders brilliantly identify a person's *ruin*— something that tortures them: a regret, a loss, or some other unfortunate experience that haunts them. The cult offers a solution for that ruin and a cultist is born. This is powerful persuasion. *Otherwise reasonable people will believe anything if someone provides a fix for their ruin.*

Cult builders target people when they are most vulnerable and unanchored. Once they've reeled the person in and created *heightened suggestibility*, they build on that with potent manipulative tools. The leader sells himself as the *only* person who can resolve their issues. Trump often claims he is the *only* person who can do something.

Total loyalty is required of cult members, but their leader is not loyal to them. He uses and discards them at will. Evil cult leaders are manipulative, controlling, self-serving, grifters, and often even perverts, who put power and wealth above all else while followers put loyalty to the cult above all else.

Ross says, "...the human mind is far more fragile, persuadable, and malleable than we would like to think. This is especially true when people are distressed, experiencing hardships, or passing through major transitions that destabilize their lives." Many Trump supporters were in that state when he entered politics. Soldiers were there when a raging Rush Limbaugh and the radical right-wing noise machine was added to military broadcasting channels, subjecting vulnerable soldiers to mind control. The Oath Keepers extremist group, made up mostly of military veterans, reflects the unfortunate outcome of this action.

When being bombarded with *mind persuasion* techniques, people are sucked into the cult-like thinking of *willful ignorance*, which means they only accept information that supports what their leader has persuaded them to believe. All other information, even factual evidence, is rejected. For example, Trump followers believe he is a Christian, contrary to all evidence otherwise. If you ignore what he says and consider what he does, it's clear he is irreligious and amoral. He exploits, hurts and uses people, is mean and selfish, and rarely goes to church. Still, according to Steven Hassan, Trump's right-wing supporters—including the New Apostolic Reformation (NAR), the Catholic Opus Dei, Ayn Rand Libertarians, mega churches of Rick Warren and Pat Robertson, and most right-wing evangelicals—view Trump as ordained by God to establish a Christian nation.

Cults typically have a dual set of ethics—one for cult members and another for non-members. It is acceptable to deceive and take advantage of outsiders. This explains why so called "religious" people are okay with children taken from parents at the border and other hateful atrocities.

Bombarded by inherently deceptive tactics, the judgment of cult members becomes clouded, and they depend on their leader to make value judgments for them and to define the parameters of reality. *Cognitive dissonance* sets in—a mental state of distorted thoughts, beliefs, and attitudes. The person is so compromised he loses the capacity for rational thought and evidence evaluation.

Without reasoning skills, people are easily controlled and primed to act against their own best interests. This is why, when the pandemic hit, Trump followers took up the mantle of denial and rage. Masks were politicized. Those who refused to wear them hurt others. This is cult-like behavior. It also explains why Trump was able to extort nearly $300 million from followers while contesting the 2020 election with a lie. A looser cult, the NRA, has a hold on many—not all—of its members and has politicized guns. Cults are desecrating our country.

AWARENESS OF
BRAIN-ALTERING TECHNIQUES

The best way to keep loved ones out
of a cult is to teach them about cults.

Fortunately, mind altering programs do not change people forever, nor are they one-hundred percent effective. However, the extent to which people are influenced by cult practices is startling. This is because *people in a cult don't know they are in a cult.* It's difficult to convince a person they are in a cult, let alone get them out of it.

The key to avoiding cults is awareness. Most people have no knowledge of grooming strategies cult leaders use, nor a sense of their effectiveness. So they don't see the red flags early on. Thought reform is corrupt, subtle, and insidious. It is amazingly powerful. Education is key to saving people from the evil clutches of abusers. It and critical thinking should be standard curriculum in middle and high schools.

A cult can be composed of only two people—an abusive leader and a single, submissive follower. The determining factor is behavior. Educating teens on the nuances of cults is advisable before they start dating or go off to college.

In the early stages of a relationship, both individual and group cult leaders are devoted and charming. They groom victims, moving them along a path of gradual change, one that eventually ends in the leader taking advantage. Controlling behavior might be interpreted by a victim as being treated "special" initially, during the courting phase. The first signs of a problem are often jealousy and isolation. Controlling people don't share their partners. These behaviors are early indicators of escalating control and abuse to come.

To understand cults, it's helpful to be familiar with the thought processes cult leaders try to destroy:

Rational thought: involves clear, rational, open-minded thinking—informed by evidence.

Critical thinking: involves the process of thinking—how a person evaluates information.

The difference between *rational thought* and *critical thinking* is subtle, and they are often used interchangeably. Both are cognitive functions. Following are mind-altering processes used to neutralize these thinking functions and to achieve *cognitive dissonance*—the inability to apply rational thought:

Coercive persuasion: This is a process designed to control a person through mind-altering techniques that persuade victims to accept a certain allegiance or doctrine against their desire, will, or even knowledge. It can be accomplished through psychological torture or through stealth. The goal is to destroy loyalties to others and exact total allegiance and obedience.

Compromising followers' thinking patterns and persuading them to respond to emotions rather than truth makes them *fact resistant*. This is done through: (1) isolation; (2) single or limited sources of information; (3) repetition and continuous messaging, (4) inducing emotions, (5) strong in-group social pressure; (4) rewards for cooperation or punishment for non-cooperation (can be physical or psychological). Any attempts at applying independent judgement are thwarted. Over time, such actions covertly change people. Depending on the type of cult and the messaging, followers become unpleasant and enraged, even militant, or numb and dazed-like.

Ross says *psychological persuasion* happens in groups of people by fostering a fellowship sub-culture wherein emotions and feelings become a substitute for cognitive processes. A state of *engineered enlightenment* results, the power of which is frighteningly demonstrated in its most radical form by mass suicides in religious groups.

Joseph Goebbels, said, "If you repeat a lie often enough, it becomes the truth." The concept of *perception is reality* reflects this principle. Tony Schwartz, co-writer of Trump's *The Art of the Deal,* articulated this premise: ". . . in the primitive simplicity of their minds they [the broad masses of a nation] more readily fall victims to the big lie than the small lie, since they themselves often tell small lies in little matters but would be ashamed to resort to large-scale falsehoods. It would never come into their heads to fabricate colossal untruths, and they would not believe that others could have the impudence to distort the truth so infamously."

Coercive persuasion through stealth, whether individual or group applied, typically involves subtle but intense influences that incite rage. Over time this subverts people's sense of integrity and promotes a new set of values. For those who watch Fox News all day every day as their single source of information, thought processes and values are significantly influenced through distorted information and the repetitive use of mind-altering tactics. Big lies, little lies, and misstatements—continuously applied—manipulate followers. Disturbing messages enrage. Viewers lose the ability to assess communications and become addicted to reacting to information with powerful emotional responses.

Gaslighting: When manipulators covertly plant seeds of doubt in an individual or a group, they are *gaslighting*. This causes people to question their memory, perceptions, and judgment. By using misinformation, denial, misdirection, and other disorienting tactics, the gaslighter destabilizes victims and delegitimizes their beliefs. Targets might initially feel as though they are losing their minds.

Once this is done, the gaslighter reshapes his targets' realities and thinking processes on his terms, thus controlling them. This induces *cognitive dissonance*—the inability to apply rational thought or to evaluate evidence. Gaslighting also lowers self-esteem, rendering victims dependent on the gaslighter for emotional support and validation.

The goal of gaslighting is to undermine victims' ability to distinguish truth from falsehood, right from wrong, and reality from delusion, thereby rendering them pathologically dependent on the gaslighter for thinking, opinions, and feelings. The target then becomes susceptible to believing lies and conspiracy theories.

Isolation: Separating people from those outside the cult makes other cult tactics effective. Followers are taught that outsiders are evil, and the cult will protect them from "the others." Isolation is key to holding on to cult members. It requires convincing followers that people who believe differently from them are the enemy. A polarizing *us vs them* mindset is fostered. Thus, *perceived persecution* of cult members induces a victim mentality that encourages them to dismiss any critique of their leader or the cult coming from outside the organization.

Propaganda: This is information of a biased or misleading nature used to promote a cause or point of view. It influences opinions, emotions, attitudes, and behavior. *Propaganda appeals to emotions, not intellect.* Distorted information is widely and deliberately spread to harm a person, a movement, an institution, or a nation. This includes: rumors, doctrines, principles, and conspiracy theories. Authoritative sources of information are often made up. Credence is given to a divine source, group-endorsed opinion, or vague sources, such as "everyone says," "people are talking," "some people think," or "an extremely credible source." On the Internet in 2016 (and still today) it was clandestine Russian communications.

Information control: Cult leaders drive followers to a single source or limited sources of information where messages are controlled. Cult members accessing only those sources are easily manipulated through biased information repeated over and over. This is why Trump, most Republican politicians, and evangelicals have championed Fox News as a *single source* that keeps viewers in an idealogical silo. Other sources have recently emerged under Trump because his policies encourage fringe groups.

Convincing followers that objective fact-checkers, such as Snopes, Politifact, and Factcheck, are unreliable is an example of cult information control. Some cults even prohibit members from accessing the Internet except for sites focused on cult messaging.

Through a single source of information, viewers are hammered with propaganda and taught how to respond to counter information. Back when I used to talk to Trump followers, I could easily tell if they watched only Fox News. If I made a good point on any topic, they changed the subject to Benghazi. They all had the same Fox News script full of mis-information ready to deliver.

Trump's disenchantment with Fox after it called the presidential race for Biden, has caused other sources to gain ground. After Trump's administration approved its merger, Sinclair Broadcast Group acquired over 290 local television stations across the country (Channel 8 in Tulsa). Sinclair's hidden agenda is radical right-wing messaging. It requires these local stations to broadcast documentaries and news scripts disguised as objective news. An unaware public assumes the news is local and reliable, as it was in the past. It's not. Sinclair stations can be identified by Googling *Sinclair*.

(National news broadcasts on Sinclair channels are not controlled by them.)

Wrapping a fact in lies: An effective tactic used by cult leaders and biased communication channels is taking a truth —a fact—and wrapping exaggerations and falsehoods around it. Followers who've lost the capacity for critical thinking buy the whole thing—even the lies—because there is a highly publicized fact in there somewhere. Fox uses this technique to neutralize facts that are contrary to its goals.

Loaded language: This powerful tactic uses rhetoric to influence through easily memorized and expressive words and phrases with strong connotations. Short, snappy, one-liner soundbites, slogans, and mantras are designed to exploit stereotypes and invoke emotional responses.

Speaker of the House, Newt Gingrich, used this mind-altering tool to attack Democrats in the 1990s. He collaborated with his political action committee to publish a list of negative words for the Republican news machine (Fox News, talk radio, the Internet, religious leaders, and politicians) to use when referring to Democratic legislation or actions of the Clinton administration. For example, proposed legislation was labeled *a scheme*. The term was repeated over and over by right-wing broadcasters. Other examples of words include: *corruption, traitors, sick, radical, shameful*, and *pathetic*. This tactic was so successful that loaded language has become a political *go to* activity. Today, the Internet makes this technique even more effective.

Trump uses loaded language when he refers to *the deep state*, a phrase that insinuates the FBI, intelligence services, and other governing institutions are evil organizations with sinister motives. Other examples are: *fake news, witch hunt, stop the steal, lock her up*, and *drain the swamp*. Fox uses *fair and balanced,* and *no spin*. If someone claims *no spin*, look for the spin. If they claims *no bias*, look for the slant. Reliable news sources don't market objectivity. It's a given.

Insider language: The leader is the bearer of "the word." Members are expected to accept it without question. Cults use it to create a subculture reinforced by made-up and redefined words that spread and reinforce an organization's dogma. Such jargon implies a leader's brilliance and insight, adding to his mystique and increasing his ability to influence.

Sacred science: A black and white, closed system of logic, this interferes with rational thought by neutralizing critical thinking and heightening susceptibility. It creates an aura around creed or dogma that encourages followers not to question basic assumptions but, instead, to accept them on "faith"—without evidence, analysis, judgment, or criticism. Sacred science is an easy sell in an established, no-evidence based environment in which blind faith is a common expectancy. This is why those who interpret religious dogma literally are especially susceptible to political cults.

Substituting emotional responses for logic: This involves persuading followers their beliefs and feelings are more important than facts. Thus they abandon critical thinking and substitute emotions for cognitive reasoning. The result is *anti-intellectualism*. Politicians use a popular emotional issue to persuade voters to vote or act only on a single emotional issue and to ignore other points. Trump did that quite successfully with the pandemic by making mask-wearing about personal freedom. Persuading followers that Democrats want to get rid of Christmas is another example of this. Abortion is an effective emotional, single-voting issue tapped by both political parties.

Social proof: Also referred to as *groupthink*, this technique operates under the assumption that what is true is *what other people think*. What is right is *what other people do*. What is real is validated by a large group of "others." This introduces peer pressure—an incredibly potent force. The Tea Party exploited this tactic in the 1990s by providing people a group to belong to, which tightened the Republican cult's grip on followers. A generous supply of groupthink and peer pressure resulted. Later, Trump's rallies encouraged groupthink by offering a cohesive group to followers.

Some experts equate social proof to "herd mentality" wherein a herd of cattle follows a leader off of a cliff, even if the individual cows have pastured around it and know it is there. Riots and group suicides demonstrate the potent power of this concept. History is rich with examples of groupthink gone wrong. Once people rage as a group, it's hard to turn the frenzy around. No amount of logic will do it.

Fox News, talk radio, and radical right-wing evangelicals successfully altered the minds of unaware viewers in the 1990s and delivered to Gingrich a bevy of followers in the Tea Party ready and willing to put the movement's objectives before the country. The adding of right wing messaging to the Armed Services Network expanded this influence to vulnerable service men whose lives were in a state of flux. Soldiers were particularly susceptible to cult influences and still are.

Those watching only Fox News and listening to talk radio were pummeled with false or distorted information, which fostered an *alternative reality*—far removed from facts. A continuous barrage of brain-altering techniques and misinformation was blasted all day, every day to an unknowing public. The goal was to make people angry and keep them that way so they rage as cult crusaders. And rage they did. The *social proof* from tight-knit groups raging together produced followers eagerly and enthusiastically accepting information without logical evaluation or evidence.

The Republican media machine nurtured and delivered to Trump a cult rich with members incapable of rational thought, addicted to rage, and primed for exploitation. Trump lied to them and disseminated distorted information all day every day culminating in The Big Lie that the 2020 election was rigged and he was elected in a landslide.

Followers, suffering from heightened susceptibility, believed that nefarious lie, in spite of all evidence to the contrary.

Is there hope Trump supporters will ever leave the cult? Robert Lifton says there is, but interventions may be necessary. Rick Ross has performed over 100 professional interventions, about 75% of which were successful. He maintains that education about cult leader behavior is more effective than mental therapeutic techniques or challenging cult beliefs. (When Dr. Phil saves someone who is being catfished, he doesn't deal with beliefs or the psychological issues of the victim or the scammer. Instead, he focuses on educating with facts about the catfisher's exploitive behavior.)

Once a person is in a cult-like relationship, it's hard to get out. Why? A follower accepting that they were fooled and renouncing their beliefs is tantamount to disavowing one's identity. Also, it's humiliating and mentally traumatic for a cult member to admit they were wrong and used. And the loyalty and emotional equity a person invests in a group makes it difficult to abandon those relationships and disclaim common beliefs. Reliable people don't easily renege on commitments. Exit costs, which include intimidation, emotional badgering, financial penalties, relationship losses, and shunning, also discourage followers from leaving.

A COVERT POLITICAL/RELIGIOUS CULT

The intersection of religion and political power.

In addition to inheriting a national bevy of cult followers, Trump also benefited from *The Family*, a well-established, powerful, and clandestine fundamentalist organization of religious leaders. It is composed of tightly-bonded politicians at the centers of power in Washington, D. C. In addition to influencing politics and supporting each other, they recruit and groom religious political leaders in this country and around the world. Their central mission is to establish a ruling class of Christian-committed men in the United States and around the world. According to Steven Hassan, Trump's cabinet included no less than nine devoted evangelicals, including: Jeff Sessions, William Barr, Rick Perry, Sonny Perdue, Ryan Zinke, Tom Price, Ben Carson, Elaine Chao, and Betsy DeVos

This group wields considerable political power at the upper levels of the government through its immense influence on Christian congressmen. It is covert. They believe the more invisible you make an organization, the more influence it has. Oklahoma legislators have been heavily involved in this underground movement for years, and few citizens are aware of it.

Jeff Sharlet exposed this powerful, low-profile organization in his book, *The Family*, now a documentary on Netflix. Every American should watch it. According to him, this is why Senator Jim Inhofe misses so many Senate sessions. He spends considerable time, sometimes on taxpayers' dollars, traveling to Africa and around the world recruiting powerful kings and dictators of developing countries to Christianity.

The Family calls these leaders "Wolf Kings." They are recruited without regard for ethics or corruption. The criterion is power. *The Family* admires history's strong men: Hitler, Stalin, and Mao. Leaders who kill homosexuals and drug users or whatever else, are prospects for membership. They label them *imperfect leaders* who, because of their power, are "chosen." *The Family* is not focused on recruiting followers—whom they call sheep—whose place in the party hierarchy is with Trump, the evangelistic masses, extremist groups, and as voters.

The Family and other evangelistic Christian legislative leaders teamed up with Newt Gingrich, Speaker of the House, in the 1990s, to introduce a toxic political environment that exploited government safeguards. A master of partisan, scorched-earth warfare, Newt's rabid political style weaponized ethics rules, unleashed mind-altering techniques on a naive public, and played the media like a fine guitar. He swallowed the Republican party and shaped a dysfunctional political environment that infects Congress to this day.

Julian Zelizer's book, *Burning Down the House*, describes Newt as a ruthless, diabolical cutthroat. An expert at provocation and spin, he knew politics was more about perception than substance. He persuaded Republicans to vote as a block on all issues, a scorched-earth approach that destroyed compromise and bi-partisan politics. The primary goal was to reverse the election of Bill Clinton. Later, Mitch McConnell, Senate Majority Leader, took up the mantle with the goal of hamstringing Barack Obama. These men cared not about legislation or the people's business.

In 2015, the Republican political/media and religious coalition handed Trump, in the form of *The Family* and the Tea Party, a slew of zealous, indoctrinated supporters and spiritual warriors—untethered to reality—who never deviated from party lines and were primed to support an aspiring fascist president. Make no mistake, *The Family's* legislators put their loyalty to religious associations above that of country. Their support of Trump's ridiculous lie that he won the 2020 election in a landslide and their opposing his impeachment reveal where their loyalties lie.

The radical Christian right is highly cohesive and organized, both at the level of the masses and at that of its elitist leaders. Coordinated efforts convinced 74 million Americans Trump was "the chosen one." In reality, these followers were fooled. They ignored that the wealthy realized millions of dollars in tax cuts while they were hard-put to realize noticeable benefits from tax reform. In spite of Trump's hype, he threw them crumbs, and they ate them.

Trump's team was further empowered by the influences of Steve Bannon (a destabilizing, norm-bashing cult-master whose stated political goal is disruption and deconstruction of the *administrative state* in order to replace it with an authoritarian government) and Stephen Miller (an extremist, white-nationalist, facist enthusiast who said, ". . . the powers of the president to protect our country are very substantial and will not be questioned.").

Cult expert Robert Lifton dedicated a chapter in his book *Losing Reality* to Trump, whom he calls "the most bizarre and persistent would-be owner of reality whose ideas readily change and reverse themselves." Lifton notes extreme grandiosity in Trump's claim to be a *very stable genius* when, in fact, his mind is unorganized and undisciplined, and his thoughts remarkably fluid. Incapable of strategic planning, Trump reacts to external stimuli intuitively in the moment. *His plan is that there is no plan.* Everything is off the cuff. Although he has no conviction or discipline, he does have a narrative: He is the *only one* who can fix America.

In addition to *The Family* cult, the less covert New Apostolic Reformation (NAR)—a Pentecostal and charismatic movement that uses the cult playbook—has grown by millions. At a D. C. Trump Hotel luncheon in 2018, worshipers held hands in the air during a prayer: "In Jesus name, we declare the deep state will not prevail." Some spoke in tongues. The group laid hands on Trump. They declared that governmental leaders throughout his administration were giving their all for God's dream for the nation.

A scattered and flaky Trump tapped into shrewd and powerful co-conspirators who, through cults, enabled him to mislead followers. Why does he do it? To get attention and to exploit. Why do leaders support him? To get re-elected or they fear him. Why do followers buy it? Because they are in a cult and they don't know it.

SECTION IV

A POLITICAL TRAGEDY

The Trump Effect

The country has become more violet, extremists are emboldened, and gun violence is epidemic. Citizens are so traumatized that they are tired, numb, and disengaged. Those who retreat into the pleasures of privilege because these things have not directly effected them yet should brace for the time when they do.

Complacency is what got us into this mess. Complacency is not a solution. It is complicity. The past five years have taught us that democracy is fragile. The path to peace of mind is doing more than just voting. It's participation and activism. Do something. Say something. Support those who take a stand. Make a difference. Influence. Matter. Do all this and leave the world a better place.

Chapter 11

THE FLEECING OF AMERICA

*Politics is all about power and money.
Rare is the politician who puts country
and what is best for the masses first.*

Sometimes unpleasant situations can be made gentle by words, but there is no softening this truth: Most politicians go into office with modest wealth and come out multi-millionaires. And some seek power, influence, and brotherhood through a Washington religious/political cult, *The Family*. This combination is deadly to democracy.

How that happens is a complicated question beyond the scope of this book, but no doubt, greed, exploitation, power mongering, flaws in the system, and citizen complacency are at the heart of this problem. Many politicians do barely enough to appease constituents while filling their pockets. Some use the fuel of evangelistic enthusiasm to hold on to and to game followers.

The country's founding fathers anticipated many threats to democracy, but they missed one. No doubt, they had no intention of creating a government wherein grifters could fleece taxpayers and the Federal Treasury for years with no mechanisms in the Constitution to prevent it. They were admirable men, not self-indulgent power mongers and; therefore, they did not contemplate that threat. Term limits for Congress could have minimized this problem by creating a legislature less attractive to greedy opportunists. Once a politician gets a taste of the power, financial incentives, and perks inherent in our current governing system, he's not about to vote for term limits. Rare is a legislator today qualified for *Profiles in Courage.*

President Trump has taken political malfeasance and personal corruption—hallmarks of his Administration— to a new high. His loud and proud arrogance, temper, vindictiveness, impulsiveness, disturbing ignorance, and extreme incompetence reflects the abject failure of the Republican party. Although corruption is common in politics, Trump's rampant greed and exploitation in the political arena have brought the country to a new level— the brink of fascism. He used politics to enrich himself and his family and as a path to absolute power. It's a challenge to find anything good in him or his policies.

Many citizens voted for him because of perceived business acumen, which was actually a series of failures. A master manipulator of the media, he created an artificial image through the smoke and mirrors of *The Apprentice* and books he *didn't* write. His media savvy netted him millions in free publicity. And over 10,000 pounding Trump tweets during the 2020 election were mostly lies, boasting, bullying, infantile whining, self-promotion, or petty obsessions of some sort. But, as Press Secretary, Sean Spicer, said, "Trump's tweets are official statements." And his followers took them that way. People bought the fantasy. It's impossible to overstate the role Trump's use of social media had on influencing his base through false information.

Tweets were primarily victim status reactions dished out through threatening or vindictive insults. A *Politico* article by Dr. James Kimmel, Jr. at Yale University School of Medicine, revealed what he calls *grievance addiction.*

Imaging can now show brain activity. Scientists have noted that the brain image of someone who is compulsively vindictive looks similar to the brain of someone hooked on drugs. This suggests Trump's constant vindictiveness is an addiction. He cannot control his urges to seek pity and lash out at perceived enemies. Playing the victim card, he uses his attacks to fire up voters and to generate donations.

How effectively the victim persona worked for him is illustrated by this comment from an elderly Trump supporter, "I feel so sorry for him. They are mean to him and blame him for everything." Although a victim, Trump is a savage attacker on the Internet as well as an ogre and a petulant, self-absorbed, insecure child. Name-calling, bullying, and vitriol prevail and reflect weakness. Yet his followers worship him and consider him strong.

Trump has no sense of humor. He said, "I don't kid." At rallies, he acts as though he thinks he's cute and behaves more like a child or a clownish stand-up comedian than a politician. This riles up the crowd but has no measure of intelligence or sophistication, and it doesn't make them laugh. Trump is not funny. And he lacks dignity. Through his messaging, he promotes fear and encourages followers to be sexist, racist, selfish, hateful bullies. He praises them accordingly. This man, who bragged he was rich and promised to pay for campaigning out of his pocket, asks them for money.

As a Republican turned Democrat, I've been accused of being a socialist, vegetarian, atheist, communist, lesbian— none of which are a bad thing in my mind, except communist. I am not a loyal liberal. I'm a moderate Democrat. I've supported many Republicans over the years. To this day, I admire and would support others; however, when the right-wing news machine teamed up with Newt Gingrich in the 1990s to use mind-altering techniques to influence voters, I was offended by the political radicalization. I also realized that moderate Republicans could no longer vote issue by issue. If they didn't consistently vote with the extreme right-wing block, the party ran more radical candidates against them in the next primary to oust them. As the Newt model rolled out to local governments, Republican politicians everywhere were forced to always vote the extreme party line. Moderates were, and still are, neutered. Also, Newt required Republican legislators to spend a good portion of their time fundraising for the party rather than legislating or interacting with constituents. So I stopped supporting them.

Mickey Edwards, a respected, influential Oklahoma Republican in the House, a champion of bi-partisanship, fell victim to Newt's intimidation. Ousted by his fellow Republicans in a primary, he wrote a book, *The Parties vs the People,* detailing his political demise. In it he describes the political shift that ended bi-partisanship and compromise in Congress and negatively influenced state and local politics as well. Nothing has been the same since. Then came Trump.

He, his family, and cohorts focused on bilking the government rather than running it, beginning with a corrupt inauguration on through to the refusal to concede defeat in the 2020 election, which almost brought democracy to its knees. This is not just conjecture. His own words and lack of respect for boundaries repeatedly conveyed his facist intentions. He ignored real crises and invented fake ones. Under his leadership, politics—if you can even call it that—descended even deeper into a level of mischief that ultimately led to citizens and the country being exploited by a corrupt administration with a self-serving leader who, in the role of Commander of Tweets, poisoned America.

These are damning words, but I stand by them. Anne Lamott said, "If people had wanted you to write more warmly about them, they should have behaved better." Take a look at the following and draw your own conclusions.

CONFLICTS OF INTEREST

After the shock of Trump's election, many people, myself included, tried to comfort those who were troubled and fearful. I told them Trump wanted to be liked, so he wouldn't be so bad. Others said he was a billionaire business man so he couldn't be stupid. Boy, were we wrong.

It's a sad, sorry situation when the people who are supposed to be our nation's protectors are greedy, self-serving predators who suck the life out of the Federal Treasury and the country's citizens, especially when their victims are the middle class—the backbone of this country—and the vulnerable. It's even sadder, and immensely frightening, that people being taken advantage of rally around such a leader in a cult-like manner, worshiping him and abandoning all semblance of critical thinking, integrity, and loyalty to country. Maybe what J. R. said in *Dallas* is true, "Once you lose your integrity, the rest is easy."

It's unlikely we will ever completely recover from the consequences of the Trump fiasco. Charlatans have gained too much ground to abandon fleecing the government and their constituents. Radical fringe groups have been emboldened. And for some reason, which I shall never understand, many people are okay with all that. Are they so manipulated they've lost all sense of reality? Apparently so.

Trump and his appointees, many of them his family and cronies, have demonstrated a blatant disregard for propriety, mores, traditions, boundaries, ethics, and legal and governmental requirements. Among many other infractions, they have repeatedly and blatantly violated The Emoluments Clause in the Constitution.

> This Clause forbids government officials from accepting "any present, Emolument, Office, or Title, of any kind whatever, from any King, Prince, or foreign State"

Emolument defined: payment, fee, charge, consideration; salary, pay, wage(s), earnings, allowance, stipend, honorarium; income, revenue, return, profit, gain, proceeds; reward, compensation, premium, recompense; informal perks, pickings; perquisites.

As Trump, his family, and cohorts foraged for opportunities to enrich themselves by absconding with as much wealth as possible, they trampled on this and other requirements. Who knows the extent to which Russian comrades have financed them.

Evidence suggests one reason Trump didn't concede the 2020 election was that he used that time for a last-ditch effort to exploit his base and stuff his coffers. Through solicitations during that two-and-a-half months, post-election timeframe, he amassed around $300 million in donations from followers by projecting a victim mentality and selling lies.

Trump, his family, and cronies have shown themselves to be greedy, corrupt scoundrels. (I won't apologize for the name-calling. Trump set the bar.) The incidents listed below clearly establish that they were grifters who recognized no limits when it came to bleeding money from American citizens and swindling the government. Power and money were all they cared about and exploitation was the name of the game. With a blatant disregard for ethics and the tasks of the presidency, Trump and his family cozied up to like-minded, affluent con men with similar values to focus primarily on manipulating and plundering our country as well as its naive and less-fortunate citizens.

––––––––––––––

– **May 5, 2016** – For Cinco de Mayo, Trump—a self-promotion aficionado—posted "The best taco bowls are made in Trump Tower Grill. I love Hispanics!" All indications are that he does not love Hispanics.

– **November 13, 2016** – In a *60 Minutes* interview, Ivanka Trump promoted a $10,800 bracelet in her line.

– **November 18, 2016** – After Trump's election, 100 foreign diplomats gathered at Washington, D. C.'s Trump International Hotel. Trump did not divest himself of this business, although he promised to do so.

– **January 11, 2017** – Trump's lawyer, Sheri Dillon, stated Trump would "voluntarily donate all profits from foreign government payments made to his hotel to the United States Treasury." There is no evidence Trump ever followed through on this promise.

– **January 11, 2017** – Trump refused to divest from his real estate companies or place his assets in a blind trust, as encouraged by the U. S. Office of Government Ethics. The Government designates a Blind Trust for executive branch employees where the trustee has no relation to the government official. Previous presidents used this process. Before he was elected, Trump promised to do so, but no paperwork demonstrating he did so has been filed. Instead, he entrusted his business operations to his sons.

– **January 20, 2017** – On Inauguration Day, Melania Trump's biography on the White House's website promoted her jewelry line. Her site also claimed she had a degree in design and architecture, which was not true.

– **January 25, 2017** – After Trump won the presidential election, his Palm Beach resort, Mar-a-Lago, doubled its initiation fee to $200,000. Lobbyists, special interests, and foreign influencers signed up.

– **January 27, 2017** – Trump signed an executive order banning citizens from seven Muslim-majority countries from entering the United States. The ban exempted travelers from those Muslim countries where he had extensive business interest—Saudi Arabia and Turkey.

– **January 29, 2017** – Amid considerable backlash, Trump aggressively defended his travel ban, claiming that limiting immigration protected the U. S. from terrorists. He said, "This is not about religion—this is about terror." Since 9/11, terrorists killed ninety-four people in America. None of them came from the countries Trump banned.

– **January 30, 2017** – Trump fired acting Attorney General Sally Yates after she instructed Justice Department lawyers not to protect executive orders from legal challenges, as per the well-established custom of independence.

– **January 2017** – Two entities owned by foreign governments—the Industrial and Commercial Bank of China and the Abu Dhabi Tourism and Culture Authority —rented space in Trump Tower. Foreigners spent millions on Trump properties in Florida.

– **February 7, 2017** – Vice President Pence cast the tie-breaking vote to confirm Trump's appointment of Betsy DeVos as Secretary of Education. DeVos had no government experience and no background in public education. She was wealthy and a major contributor to the Trump campaign.

– **February 8, 2017** – Trump lashed out publicly at Nordstrom because it stopped carrying his daughter's retail brand.

– **February 9, 2017** – Senior White House counselor Kellyanne Conway promoted Ivanka Trump's retail brand while in her official capacity as an aide to Trump. On Fox News she said, "Go buy Ivanka's stuff is what I would tell you. I'm going to give a free commercial here. Go buy it today, everybody." Sales for Ivanka's products nearly tripled the next day.

– **February 22, 2017** – Trump International Hotel in D. C. received an estimated $50,000 for hosting an event for the Embassy of Kuwait. Since Trump never divested from his companies, he continued to benefit from such events.

– **February 26, 2017** – The Trump Organization had promised to donate profits from foreign governments to the U. S. Treasury. There was still no evidence this had been done.

– **March 3, 2017** – The government paid $1,092 of taxpayer money for a National Security Council official to stay two nights at Trump's Mar-a-Lago resort. This would have set the stage for future influencing if it weren't for an intense critical reaction denouncing the action.

– **March 9, 2017** – The Office of Government Ethics pressured the White House to reprimand Kellyanne Conway for endorsing Ivanka Trump's clothing line on television.

– **March 16, 2017** – Sixty-three Russians purchased around $100 million of Trump-branded real estate in Florida.

– **March 22, 2017** – The Secret Service requested $60 million more in funding to cover Trump and his family's protection. Included was protection of Trump's private residence at Trump Tower at a cost of $26.8 million yearly.

– **April 4, 2017** – A private Trump Organization trust (established to avoid the government recommended trust) was intended to prevent Trump from having financial access to his businesses. However, trust language allowed a lawyer to distribute income or principal to Trump at his request.

– **April 7, 2017** – Education Secretary Betsy DeVos received security at an unprecedented cost of $1 million per month.

– **May 1, 2017** – The Trump International Hotel in D. C. received $30,000 from a convention promoting Turkish-American relations. By retaining ownership in his businesses, such payments from foreign states violate the Emoluments Clause of the Constitution.

– **May 6, 2017** – Nicole Kushner Meyer, sister of Jared Kushner, solicited investments from the Chinese, promising American visas in return. She ran an ad in China that read, "Invest $500,000 and immigrate to the United States."

– **June 20, 2017** – Trump cut homelessness and low-income housing programs in his budget, but exempted his property—New York City's Sunset City housing complex.

– **July 18, 2017** – The U. S. military rented space in Trump Tower at $2.4 million annually to retain space should Trump decide to stay overnight. As of this date, Trump hadn't spent a single night in the Tower. This is in addition to $26 million the secret service spent to protect Trump's residence there.

– **August 21, 2017** – Only eight months into his presidency, the Secret Service used up its annual funding for agents to protect Trump's family members, mostly due to their extensive travels here and abroad.

– **August 21, 2017** – A report from the Government Accountability Office noted that each trip to Mar-a-Lago cost taxpayers $3 million. At two visits per month, over Trump's term, this would cost taxpayers $288 million.

– **August 21, 2017** – The Secret Service spent substantial sums of money at Trump's businesses, including at least $137,000 on eight months of golf cart rentals at Mar-a-Lago.

– **September 1, 2017** – Trump appointed Kansas Secretary of State, Kris Kobach, to lead an investigation into voter fraud in the 2016 election. (This was a futile effort to prove Trump received more popular votes than Hillary Clinton.) Kobach was a paid columnist for the alt-right Breitbart website while he performed that investigation.

– **September 6, 2017** – Members of Trump's private golf clubs included twenty-one lobbyists and fifty executives from corporations with federal contracts. In addition to providing money to Trump from $200,000 membership fees, the clubs provided members with significant opportunities for access to the president.

– **September 12, 2017** – Trump hosted Najib Razak, Malaysia's Prime Minister, at the White House, despite the Justice Department's ongoing investigation of corruption in his administration. Razak was accused of funneling $3.5 billion in Malaysian government money to the U. S. for personal items, including jewelry, real estate, and film rights. He and his entourage stayed in the D. C. Trump Hotel.

– **November 8, 2017** – Trump appointed numerous family members to government positions, more so than any predecessor. He also managed to circumvent security requirements for staff, including his daughter and son-in-law.

– **December 23, 2017** – Trump renewed leases for nickel and copper mining near Boundary Waters in Minnesota, a protected wilderness area. Parties with interests in the mining leases actively lobbied the Trump administration, and its head executive rented a house in D. C. to Ivanka Trump and Jared Kushner.

– **April 2, 2018** – EPA Administrator Scott Pruitt rented a condo from the lobbying firm William & Jensen at $50 per day which, according to the *New York Times,* was well below the market rate. William & Jensen represented Enbridge pipeline, a company awaiting approval from the EPA. Enbridge soon received approval from Pruitt's agency.

– **April 7, 2018** – EPA Administrator Scott Pruitt had a 20-person security detail that cost more than $3.5 million in just eleven months. His security team was three times larger than Obama's EPA Administrator. Unlike predecessors, Pruitt insisted on traveling first class with his detail, including on a family vacation to Disneyland. Outrage over excesses were a factor in him being ousted.

– **October 17, 2019** – Trump's attempt to profit from his presidency caused a stir when he announced the Trump Doral, Florida, resort would host the annual International G7 Summit in June 2020. The move, condemned from multiple sources, was soon reversed.

– **May 2020** – Trump appointed Louis DeJoy Postmaster General when Republican efforts to impair mail-in voting kicked in. DeJoy was a Trump contributor and had business interests that were in conflict with performing in this position. Shortly after taking over, he removed automatic sorting equipment and mail drop-off sites from post offices around the country. Citizens across the nation complained their mail delivery had severely deteriorated. Congress investigated and demanded DeJoy testify, after which mail delivery returned to near normal performance levels.

– **June 20, 2020** – Trump frequently dismissed government officials when they refused to do his bidding on unethical or illegal matters. He fired federal prosecutor Geoffrey S. Berman, the U. S. attorney in New York City whose office prosecuted Trump's lawyer, Michael D. Cohen, and who investigated Trump's lawyer, Rudolph Giuliani.

– **June 26, 2020** – Russia offered Taliban-linked militants bounties to kill American troops. According to the *New York Times*, Trump and his administration knew about these bounties for months from intelligence reports and did nothing to confront or punish Russia. Trump was indebted to the Russians for their help in the 2016 presidential campaign. Also, according to Cohen, at that time Trump had plans to build a Trump Tower in Moscow.

– **November 2020** – By not conceding the election to Biden, Trump used the time after his election day defeat to solicit donations from followers, supposedly to finance a fight against election corruption. He raised nearly $300 million The fine print in solicitations allowed him to spend most of the money in ways other than fighting election results, and he did so. Again, his supporters were scammed.

People are shaped by their associations—the groups in which they spend their lives and invest their time. Corruption begets corruption.

CORRUPTION

While testing the waters for a run for president back in 2000, Trump said, *It's possible that I could be the first presidential candidate to run and make money on it.* And make money he did. Duplicity, deceit, and unscrupulous graft were rampant in all facets of the Trump administration. He, his family, and cohorts blatantly demonstrated a degree and scope of corruption never before observed in the U. S. government. The Republican Party was spineless in the face of this. Maintaining that "no one is above the law," they proved just the opposite.

A citizen watchdog group, *Public Citizen,* filed ethics complaints regarding significant conflicts of interest for thirty-six appointees in Trump's administration. Detailed reports were attached to each complaint. There was no indication any vetting processes were used to select candidates. Many had no experience or credentials at all. The requirements for appointments appeared to be (1) total loyalty to Trump—not country—and (2) candidates made significant financial contributions to Trump's campaign. In spite of this information, a Republican Senate approved these nominations.

Trump used token and highly-publicized gestures of altruism toward charities, but he used them as his personal slush fund or, in many cases, he didn't pay pledges for donations once the spotlight was off.

Known for shady business dealing, he was notorious for not paying contractors on his building projects. Bankruptcies of six of his business left associates without payment for loans, work, or materials. According to Barbara Res, a Trump Vice President, his stories on these failures in his book, *The Art of the Comeback*, were fabricated.

Excessively litigious, an amazing abundance of messy lawsuits were always pending, a tactic Trump used to avoid obligations. According to USA Today, there were 3,500 of them. Trump was a plaintiff in 1,900 cases, a defendant in 1,450, and 169 were Federal. These are astounding numbers, which strongly suggest something aberrant was going on.

In the political arena, Trump didn't *drain the swamp* as promised. He created it. The examples below—which are nowhere near comprehensive—illustrate that fact. Trump wasn't good at very many things, but when it came to corruption, he was an aficionado. He spent more time scheming to enrich himself than governing.

– **November 18, 2016** – Trump agreed to settle Trump University fraud lawsuits for $25 million. Misleading marketing tactics were used to recruit participants.

– **December 2016** – Trump's senior adviser, Jared Kushner, and incoming National Security Adviser, Michael Flynn, met at Trump Tower with Russian Ambassador, Sergey Kislyak to establish a "line of connection" with Russia while the Obama administration was placing sanctions on the Russian government for interference in the election.

– **January 10, 2017** – Robert F. Kennedy, Jr. said Trump, a supporter of the extremist anti-vaccination movement, asked him about leading a vaccine safety investigation.

– **January 27, 2017** – According to FBI Director James Comey, Trump demanded loyalty from him and other government employees who were supposed to be independent. At a private dinner, Trump said, "I need loyalty, I expect loyalty." Comey replied he would always be honest with Trump but the Department of Justice and FBI must remain independent of the Executive Branch. Comey was fired from his position four months later.

– **February 13, 2017** – Less than one month after Trump took office, Michael Flynn resigned as national security adviser after misleading Vice President Pence about contact with Russian Ambassador Sergey Kislyak about lifting U. S. sanctions against Russia.

– **February 14, 2017** – A day after Michael Flynn resigned, Trump requested a meeting with James Comey, FBI Director, to talk about Flynn. Trump admitted to Comey that Flynn misled Pence, but claimed he was "a good guy." Trump said he hoped Comey could "let this go."

– **February 14, 2017** – After Flynn's resignation, Trump (more concerned about leaks than corruption) tweeted, "The real story here is why are there so many illegal leaks coming out of Washington?"

– **February 14, 2017** – The Republican House Ways and Means Committee rejected a request from Democrats for Trump to release his tax returns. Under federal law, the chairman of the committee, Republican Kevin Brady, could request tax information. He refused to do so.

– **February 15, 2017** – Vice President Pence had falsely stated no member of the Trump campaign, including national security adviser Michael Flynn, had contact with any Russian officials. This was not true. Pence publicly defended Flynn's phone calls to the Russian Ambassador, claiming Flynn did not discuss sanctions against Russia. Flynn later confessed to the FBI he had.

– **February 19, 2017** – The Federal Reserve projected a 1.8% increase in economic production. Trump pressured the Council of Economic Advisers to predict a 3.5% surge over ten years, which would allow the U. S. to borrow trillions of dollars.

– **March 1, 2017** – The Justice Department determined Attorney General Sessions met twice with Russian Ambassador Sergey Kislyak. Sessions did not mention these meetings in his confirmation hearings. He also claimed he knew of no contacts between Trump's team and Russia.

– **March 2, 2017** – After being drug into the Russian investigation, Attorney General Sessions recused himself from the Justice Department's investigation. Reports surfaced he had two undisclosed meetings with the Russian Ambassador. Trump needed Sessions to protect him from the investigation and tried to persuade him not to recuse himself.

– **March 3, 2017** – It was determined Attorney General Sessions used Trump campaign funds for plane travel to meet with Russian diplomats. During his confirmation hearing, he had sworn he didn't meet with Russians.

– **March 10, 2017** – Trump ordered the resignation of forty-six Obama appointed prosecutors, including New York City attorney, Preet Bharara, who was said to be investigating Trump's buddy, Rupert Murdoch, and Fox News executives.

– **March 11, 2017** – Before becoming national security adviser, Michael Flynn was paid around a half a million dollars (later determined to be $600,000) to lobby for the Turkish government. After assuming his government role, he stopped formally accepting payments from them but continued to promote policy that favored Turkey.

– **March 14, 2017** – Trump wrote off $100 million in losses and paid an effective tax rate of 25%, the rate paid by most individuals making $30,000, in his 2005 return.

– **March 17, 2017** – U. S. Attorney Bharara investigated Tom Price, Trump's head of the Department of Health and Human

Services, for purchasing $300,000 in healthcare stock while in a position that could influence the stock's performance.

– **March 22, 2017** – Republican Devin Nunes, chair of the House Intelligence Committee, was in possession of inside House information that Trump, his associates, and administration were to be investigate by an intelligence agency. The night before the House Committee was to announce this, Nunes paid a secret visit to the White House. Democrat Committee member, Adam Schiff said, "Nunes needs to decide if he's chairman of an independent investigation or a surrogate for the White House."

– **March 22, 2017** – Paul Manafort accepted $10 million per year for consulting with Russian billionaire, Oleg Deripaska, one of Putin's allies. Manafort served as Trump's campaign manager May through August 2016.

– **March 30, 2017** – James Comey said Trump asked him to "lift the cloud" off the Russian investigation because the investigation impeded his ability to make deals.

– **March 31, 2017** – Health and Human Services Secretary Tom Price purchased $90,000 of pharmaceutical stocks a month before the implementation of a bill that would allow drug companies to incentivize doctors.

– **April 1, 2017** – Michael Flynn received $45,000 from a Russian news station in exchange for speaking at their annual event. Flynn failed to disclose this on his financial disclosure to the U. S. Office of Government Ethics.

– **April 11, 2017** – It was reported that Trump, accustomed to total loyalty from associates, asked FBI Director Comey to publicly state that the FBI was not investigating him.

Trump's said, "Because I have been very loyal to you, very loyal; we had that thing, you know."

– **April 14, 2017** – Trump's administration announced the White House would no longer produce visitor logs, leaving Trump and White House officials free to hold private meetings without oversight on visitor identity or affiliation. Lobbyists and others had unfettered access. Previous presidents used logs and made them available for review.

– **April 24, 2017** – Michael Flynn, Trump's national security adviser, didn't disclose on his federal security clearance statement $33,000 paid to him by Russia.

– **April 25, 2017** – Michael Flynn's former client, Turkish businessman Ekim Alpetkin, had ties with both Russia and Putin. Alpetkin is the one who paid Flynn $600,000 shortly before Trump appointed him national security adviser.

– **May 17, 2017** – Shortly before Trump took office, Flynn discouraged White House officials from pursuing a U. S. military operation against Turkey. Flynn had been paid substantial amounts of money by the Turkish government.

– **May 17, 2017** – Flynn was under investigation over lobbying fees received from the Turkish government. Trump had been warned by Obama of issues with Flynn. Accustomed to unscrupulous business dealings, Trump appointed him anyway.

– **May 18, 2017** – *Reuters* news reported that during the 2016 election, the Trump campaign had numerous undisclosed contacts with Russian officials and individuals with close ties to the Kremlin, including six unreported contacts with Russian ambassador to the U. S., Sergey Kislyak.

– **June 1, 2017** – According to former State Department official Dan Fried, immediately after the inauguration Trump's administration tried to find a way to lift Russian sanctions the Obama administration imposed for their interference with the 2016 presidential election.

– **June 2, 2017** – White House lawyers ordered federal employees not to comply with information requests from Democrats for oversight of their agencies' activities.

– **June 11, 2017** – Trump endeavored to cultivate a personal relationship with a federal prosecutor, Preet Bharara, after the 2016 election. When Bharara reported this to Attorney General Sessions, he was fired the next day.

– **June 13, 2017** – Since the election, huge amounts of suspicious money flowed to Trump through his property sales. Seventy percent of real estate, much of it in Florida, purchased from the Trump Organization was reportedly sold to anonymous companies rather than identifiable people. Before the election, only two percent of Trump properties went to anonymous buyers.

– **June 19, 2017** – During a security clearance process, Flynn failed to disclose a business trip to the Middle East during which he represented both Russian and U. S. business interests. Flynn's omission was part of a pattern of behavior that included concealing foreign contacts, payments, travel, and work on behalf of foreign interests.

– **June 22, 2017** – Trump was accustomed to erasing the truth by creating his own reality. Two intelligence officials advised Mueller that Trump approached them and requested they publicly announce that the Trump campaign had not colluded with Russian operatives.

– **June 26, 2017** – Interior Secretary Ryan Zinke flew on a charter plane from Las Vegas to his hometown in Montana. The cost to taxpayers was $12,375. Zinke and his staff used private and military aircraft multiple other times.

– **June 2017** – Trump International Hotel in D. C. received $270,000 from Saudi Arabia for lobbying staff.

– **July 9, 2017** – The *New York Times* reported Donald Trump, Jr. "was promised damaging information about Hillary Clinton before agreeing to meet with a Kremlin-connected Russian lawyer during the 2016 campaign." Trump, Jr. admitted he went to the meeting because the Russian "might have information helpful to the campaign."

– **July 12, 2017** – To defend Donald Trump, Jr. for meeting with a Russian lawyer during the campaign, Trump repeated his "go to" line—the Russian investigation was "the greatest *witch hunt* in American political history."

– **July 31, 2017** – Trump lied in a public statement regarding the meeting between Donald Trump, Jr. and a Kremlin connected lawyer, stating the meeting "primarily discussed a program about the adoption of Russian children." The subsequent release of Trump, Jr.'s email clearly showed otherwise. The topic of the meeting was Hillary Clinton and Russian support for Trump's campaign against her. No repercussions resulted from this lie.

– **August 2, 2017** – During a meeting in the White House situation room, participants reported Trump complained about his NATO allies and contemplated how the U. S. could get a cut of Afghanistan's mineral wealth. He also stated that a top U. S. general "ought to be fired."

– **September 20, 2017** – Trump's campaign manager, Paul Manafort, offered a private briefing to Russian billionaire, Oleg Deripaska, weeks before the election. Deripaska, one of the wealthiest men in Russia, was a close Putin ally as well as a former client of Manafort.

– **September 29, 2017** – Health and Human Services Secretary Tom Price resigned after public outrage because he inappropriately spent over $300,000 on private jets.

– **October 5, 2017** – Treasury Secretary Steven Mnuchin spent $811,797 on seven trips on military aircraft.

– **October 9, 2017** – After National Football League players began kneeling for the national anthem, Trump interjected himself into the controversy by sending Vice President Pence to a Colts vs. 49ers game, specifically to leave the stadium as a public rebuke for the kneeling. Pence's trip cost taxpayers around $250,000.

– **October 18, 2017** – Trump thanked @TEN_GOP on Twitter for posting, "We love you, Mr. President." This was a Russian account. The group's profile was then removed.

– **October 18, 2017** – Trump promised the father of a fallen soldier $25,000 but didn't keep his promise. After *The Washington Post* reported this, a check for $25,000 was sent.

– **October 19, 2017** – At a security conference, CIA Director Mike Pompeo made a false statement: "The intelligence community's assessment is that the Russian meddling that took place did not affect the outcome of the election." The report did not speculate on that.

– **October 23, 2017** – To repair Puerto Rico's electric power infrastructure after hurricane Maria, the Trump administration awarded a $300 million contract to Whitefish Energy—a small Montana-based company with only two employees. Whitefish's CEO, Andy Techmanski, from the same hometown as Interior Secretary Ryan Zinke, confirmed they knew each other. A provision in the contract said the U. S. government couldn't "audit or review the cost and profit elements" of Whitefish's work. This would allow Whitefish to spend the $300 million with no oversight. The governor of Puerto Rico canceled the contract.

– **October 30, 2017** – Before the 2016 election, someone advised Trump aide George Papadopoulos the Russians had harmful information on Hillary Clinton. Papadopoulos pled guilty to lying when FBI investigators asked him about the conversation. Evidence revealed Trump's campaign knew of Russia's intention to sabotage Clinton's campaign. In fact, Trump invited Russian involvement in a speech.

– **November 17, 2017** – The FCC announced it would repeal regulations limiting media mergers from forming conglomerates and growing too powerful. This allowed Broadcast Group Sinclair, a radical right-wing media organization, to merge with Tribune Media to become the largest in the country. Sinclair now owns over 290 local television stations nationwide and requires they broadcast mandated right-wing news scripts and documentaries. Sinclair reaches 72% of American homes. The public is mostly unaware of the slanted reporting from these local stations that were objective and trustworthy in the past.

– **November 20, 2017** – Trump closed his charitable organization under investigation for "self-dealing," which means the owner funneled money from a charity into his personal bank accounts.

– January 17, 2018 – Adult film actress Stormy Daniels revealed she had an affair with Trump in 2006, four months before Melania Trump gave birth. A few weeks before the 2016 election, Trump paid Daniels through his lawyer, Michael Cohen, $130,000 to keep the affair quiet.

– January 18, 2018 – Trump appointee Carl Higbie, Chief of External Affairs at the Corporation for National and Community Services, resigned after it was revealed he aired racists, anti-Muslim, and anti-LGBT remarks.

– January 25, 2018 – Per White House Counsellor Donald McGahn, Trump ordered the firing of special counsel Robert Mueller back in June 2017. McGahn advised that firing Mueller would imply interference in the Russian investigation and refused to carry out the order. He threatened to step down if the president followed through.

– February 8, 2018 – White House secretary Rob Porter resigned amid convincing allegations of domestic abuse. It was reported White House Counsel McGahn and Chief of Staff Kelly knew about these allegations for months but did nothing about them.

– February 21, 2018 – The Southern Poverty Law Center reported an increase in hate groups in 2017. The largest growth was Nazi organizations. Twenty-two new chapters were formed across the U. S., and attacks on Jewish property increased substantially. It's harder to tie down Islamic and right-wing extremist numbers. They have become more discreet. Extremist leader Ben Daley advised followers to be covert and avoid the skinhead look. "It's time to reimagine the nationalist look and playbook." He also warned against using violent language on the Internet.

– **February 27, 2018** – Special counsel Mueller filed twenty-four U. S. charges of bank and tax fraud against Richard Gates, deputy chairman of Trump's campaign. Gates pled guilty to one count of conspiracy and one count of making a false statement to investigators.

– **February 27, 2018** – The Department of Housing and Urban Development planned to spend $31,000 on a dining room set and $165,000 for lounge furniture for Ben Carson's Washington office. This happened after Trump cut HUD's annual funding by $6.8 billion.

– **February 28, 2018** – After resigning from the White House, former communications director Hope Hicks testified to the House Intelligence Committee she had told what she called "white lies" on behalf of Trump.

– **February 28, 2018** – Jared Kushner's firm received a loan of $325 million shortly after he met with the CEO of Citigroup at the White House. Also, after meetings there with the CEO of Apollo Global Management (a massive wealth management fund), Kushner's companies were loaned $184 million to refinance a Chicago skyscraper.

– **February 28, 2018** – In 2017, two unidentified persons forged nominations for the Nobel Peace Prize on behalf of Trump. When the nominators were contacted, they claimed no knowledge of the submissions. Trump— critical of and envious of Obama's Nobel Peace Prize— often stated publicly that he should have one.

– **March 1, 2018** – The FBI investigated Russian oligarch Alexander Torshin, deputy governor of the Bank of Russia, who had close ties with the Kremlin, for funneling money through the NRA to the Trump campaign.

– **March 6, 2018** – The Office of Special Counsel announced Kellyanne Conway violated the Hatch Act regulation twice. This Act prohibits federal employees from publicly endorsing or criticizing candidates for high-level positions. Conway was an advocate for Roy Moore, an accused child molester, in an Alabama Senate race. She spoke on his behalf in two separate Fox News interviews.

– **March 7, 2018** – Tony Tooke, Trump's Chief of the Forest Service, resigned under allegations of sexual misconduct.

– **March 8, 2018** – The Interior Department planned to spend $139,000 on six doors for Secretary Ryan Zinke's office.

– **April 3, 2018** – Attorney Alex van der Zwaan pleaded guilty to lying to federal officials in the Mueller investigations about contacts with the Trump campaign as well as with a Russian intelligence operative.

– **April 6, 2018** – After an internet uproar over the hypocrisy of extreme right-leaning information, some of it classified as propaganda, Trump tweeted in defense of Sinclair, one of the largest media organizations in America, who mandates 290 stations across the country include misleading radical right-wing scripts on local television news shows without viewers realizing it. Some experts say Sinclair is in tune with Breitbart and covertly releases more disinformation than Fox News.

– **April 9, 2018** – The FBI raided Trump lawyer, Michael Cohen's, office in New York City. A furious Trump said, "It's an attack on our country in a true sense." Rumors circulated that Trump considered dismissing Robert Mueller and Rod Rosenstein, the U. S. Deputy Attorney General.

– **May 16, 2018** – The Senate Judiciary Committee released a 2,500-page document that included the testimony of Donald Trump, Jr. and top aides who met with Russian delegates at Trump Tower in 2016. The information provided evidence of collusion between the Trump campaign and Russia. Sen. Mark R. Warner stated, "The Russian effort was extensive, sophisticated, and ordered by President Putin himself for the purpose of helping Trump hurt Hillary Clinton." The Republican House and Senate took no action on the matter.

– **August 21, 2018** – Trump's former campaign manager, Paul Manafort, was convicted of five counts of tax fraud, two counts of bank fraud, and one count of failure to disclose a foreign bank account.

– **August 21, 2018** – Trump's former lawyer, Michael Cohen, pled guilty in federal court in New York to campaign finance violations for paying hush money to women who claimed to have had affairs with Trump as well as other charges.

– **November 29, 2018** – Michael Cohen, Trump's former lawyer, pled guilty to making false statements. He had testified that discussions about a Trump Tower project in Moscow ended in January 2016. Later he admitted discussions occurred well into Trump's presidential campaign.

– **January 25, 2019** – Roger Stone, a Trump advisor, was indicted on obstruction of an official proceeding, making false statements, and witness tampering in connection with Russia's involvement in the 2016 presidential election.

– **July 25, 2019** – At Trump's direction, U. S. Ambassador to the European Union urged Ukrainian President Volodymyr Zelensky to investigate democratic candidate

Joe Biden and his son Hunter. Days later, Trump blocked planned U. S. military aid to Ukraine after which he spoke by phone with Zelensky and said, "I need you to do me a favor" before agreeing to provide the funds. This led to a whistleblower complaint and Trump's impeachment.

– **August 12, 2019** – A whistleblower issued a complaint that Trump used his office to solicit interference in the 2020 presidential election. The report revealed a July 15, 2019 phone call between Trump and Ukrainian President Volodymyr Zelensky and Trump's cover-up efforts to restrict access to call records on the conversation.

– **October 3, 2019** – After being investigated for applying political pressure on Ukraine, Trump publicly called for China to investigate Joe Biden and his son, Hunter.

– **November 7, 2019** – A New York judge ordered Trump to pay $2 million to settle claims that the Trump Foundation misused charitable donation funds raised in a televised fundraiser for veterans during his 2016 campaign.

– **December 6, 2019** – The White House refused to cooperate with the impeachment trial and would not send representative counsel to hearings. Trump also prohibited officials from testifying or handing over documents.

– **December 18, 2019** – Trump became the third president to be impeached in U. S. history. He tweeted: "THIS IS AN ASSAULT ON AMERICA, AND AN ASSAULT ON THE REPUBLICAN PARTY!!!!"

– **July 6, 2020** – Companies linked to Trump's family and cronies applied for $21 million in Small Business Administration monies earmarked for businesses hurt by the pandemic. Those to benefit included his son-in-law, Kushner, and his son, Trump, Jr. There is likely substantial graft. Trump had fired key people on the watchdog team.

– **July 10, 2020** – Trump commuted the prison sentence of his friend and political adviser Roger Stone, who was convicted of obstructing a criminal investigation into Russian interference in the 2016 election.

– **August 14, 2020** – The Senate Intelligence Committee asked federal prosecutors to investigate former Trump advisor Stephen Bannon for lying to the committee during its inquiry into Russian interference in the 2016 election. Donald Trump, Jr., Jared Kushner, Paul Manafort, and Hope Hicks all gave conflicting testimonies.

– **August 20, 2020** – Stephen Bannon, Trump's former strategist, who claimed to be a man of the people, was arrested on a $35 million yacht owned by fugitive Chinese billionaire Guo Wengui. Bannon was charged with cheating hundreds of thousands of donors who were told their money would go toward building a wall along the Mexican border. The indictment claimed Bannon used almost $1 million for personal expenses. Trump pardoned Bannon.

– **August 22, 2020** – Trump was ordered by a California judge to pay adult-film actress Stormy Daniels $44,100 for legal fees related to a lawsuit she brought against him. Daniels had sued Trump to be released from a $130,000 nondisclosure agreement that required her to keep quiet about their sexual relationship.

– **August 22, 2020** – In a conversation recorded by Trump's niece, Mary Trump, his sister, Maryanne Trump Barry, a retired federal judge said, "You can't trust him. His goddamned tweet and lying, oh my God. I'm talking too freely, but you know. The change of stories. The lack of preparation. The lying. Holy shit."

– **August 24, 2020** – New York State's attorney general asked the State Supreme Court to compel Eric Trump to testify in an investigation into Trump for overstating assets to secure loans and obtain economic and tax benefits.

– **August 2020** — Postmaster General, Louis Dejoy, was subpoenaed to testify to Congress on slow mail delivery before the November election. Suspecting he colluded with Trump, House investigators required he release his calendar. He did so, with almost all of it redacted (blacked out).

September 17, 2020 – According to *The Washington Post,* Trump's club in Bedminster, New Jersey charged the government $1.1 million. Before assuming office, Trump committed to "completely isolate" himself from his businesses. He didn't. And, while in office, he visited his properties 274 times at significant cost to taxpayers.

– **October 8, 2020** – Top Trump fund-raiser and defense contractor Elliott Broidy was charged with conspiring to violate lobbying laws. He accepted $6 million from a foreign client to lobby Trump. Also, in 2018, Broidy was forced to resign as deputy finance chairman of the Republican National Committee after he paid a Playboy model $1.6 million to keep quiet about their affair.

– **October 10, 2020** – Trump promised to separate himself from the Trump Organization. The *New York Times* reported that in his first two years as president, he directed close to $12 million of business to his companies.

– **October 12, 2020** – When Trump's children visited Trump hotels and resorts, some of them overseas, the U. S. government had to pay for Secret Service agents to travel and stay with them. According to *The Washington Post*, in addition to the Trump Organization getting revenue from these Trump properties, it also earned at least $238,000 in taxpayer money by charging the government for protection.

– **October 2020** – The *New York Times* reported Trump maintains a secret bank account in China. During the 2020 campaign, Trump accused Biden of being too soft on China because his son Hunter had business dealings there.

– **October 20, 2020** – It's difficult to determine Trump's taxes since he refuses to release them. Trump bragged about paying taxes to other countries when he was criticized for speculation he paid none for many years in the U. S. It is known he paid $750 in U. S. income taxes in 2016, and he paid $188,561 to China three years before.

Throughout his term, Trump and his staff engaged in rampant corruption. It was reported he is now getting at the money he solicited from followers for political reasons by laundering it through cohorts. Per *Forbes*, after Trump was defeated in 2020, $2.8 million and $4.3 million of donations were transferred into his private business accounts. Also, $7 million was paid to Trump properties from his super PAC. The Trump Crime Syndicate is alive and well.

As far as anyone can tell, Trump contributed nothing to his campaigns, although in 2016, he lied when he announced his run for President: *I don't need anybody's money. I'm using my own money. I'm not using lobbyists. I'm not using donors. I don't care. I'm really rich.*

The New York Times reported he was $421 million in debt. *Forbes* claimed it was closer to $1 billion. It appears he spent none of his own money on campaigns. Instead he put campaign money into his personal accounts.

Interfering and *meddling* in the election are inadequate words to describe what the Russians did. In her book, *Cyberwar: How Russian Hackers and Trolls helped Elect a President,* University of Pennsylvania's Kathleen Hall Jamieson, showed through statistics how this tipped the scale to Trump. Russia purchase Facebook ads and set up phony accounts and groups, like "African-Americans for Hillary," and ground out fake information using persuasion and mind control tactics. It worked, I know. Some of my friends were convinced Hillary was dead set on starting a war.

Relations between Trump and Russian power mongers prove he put his interests over that of the United States. He is a Putin dupe, a Russian comrade, or perhaps a Russian asset. Mueller indicted 13 Russians, 3 Russian Companies, and 12 members of Russian military intelligence. Why Trump was not prosecuted for collaborating and why Russia was not severely punished for disrupting the 2016 election is a mystery—except that Trump controlled the attorney general and Republicans held the House and Senate for his first two years in office.

There is clear evidence Trump interfered with the Russian investigation. The Republican-led Intelligence Committee confirmed Russia's role, but Republican Congressmen were complicit by not holding Trump accountable. Getting by with this made him even more brazen. What else was he capable of? Lots.

Under Trump, the rich got richer and the poor got poorer. Perhaps Trump's most effective fleecing is of his followers. Howard Stern, a onetime Trump friend said, "The people who voted for Trump for the most part. . .he'd be disgusted with." Barbara Res said, "Trump has built a fierce loyalty amid a segment of the population he holds in contempt. . .Trump can't *stand* the common man." He called his followers "disgusting people." All indications are he disdains the lower class but hides his contempt. He even says at events that he loves them.

During my career, I was on an elaborate boat with well-off, politically-connected business people. Sunning on the deck, one of them said, "I wonder what the poor people are doing." Another responded, "I'm *not* wondering what the poor people are doing." That about says it all.

Working in corporate America for years, I concluded those companies could solve every problem in this country if they weren't so greedy and would invest in the American people. If executives did that with the enthusiasm with which they accumulated more wealth than they or their families could ever spend, this would be a wonderful country for all.

If they paid employees adequately, people would have more money to spend, government social programs could be reduced, and the economy would blossom. And if they sponsored and collaborated with educators to develop employees from the pools of hopeless rural and urban people, every person they hired would save an entire family.

A business I worked with in a major city consistently had over three-hundred much needed positions open at any one time while smart young urban kids in that city dropped out of high schools in droves. I proposed a program wherein the company would collaborate with educational institutions in the city to create courses targeted to save masses of young people by preparing them for company summer internships and jobs after graduation. I received no response. Greed prevails; hope fades. What are the poor people doing? Some struggle to feed their children. Others are shooting each other or taking opioids. Many are worshiping Trump.

LIES AND TRUTH DECAY

When a leader tries to bluff you with an alternate reality, remember political views are not facts. Opinions are not facts. Thoughts are not facts. Facts are facts. The truth resides in facts, not spin. Never underestimate the potent influence of thought manipulation and people's capacity for being duped into ignoring facts. Trump campaigned on a platform of lies, and many people bought them. And right-wing broadcasters, social media, and religious leaders channeled distorted news to a naive public unaware of mind-altering techniques. Viewers were led down a path to *truth decay* wherein conspiracy theories and fake news abounded. Followers respond to emotions rather than facts, and truth decay settled in as normal. A fake Trump persona was promoted.

Propaganda allowed him to capture a cult-like following that supported anything he said. Trump created *alternative realities* accepted by followers without question, including that he was a self-made man. Those believing he is a good businessman are ignoring facts and buying hype. His claim of starting his business on $1 million from his dad is false. He received $60 million and later inherited over $400 million. A plethora of bad business decisions and bankruptcies, including the Plaza Hotel, Trump Ice, Trump Steaks, Trump Shuttle, Trump Vodka, and three casino failures, plagued him. According to a New York Times reporter, he lost $1.17 billion between 1985 one 1994. A television show and Russian oligarchs rescued him when banks loans dried up.

Even his real estate success was a lie. Being an expert at branding, public relations, and self aggrandizement, he promoted a fake image. Without his father's connections and inheritance, he couldn't have gotten famous for real estate. His father taught him how to abuse tenants, ignore laws, cheat contractors, and mistreat workers. After mucking up in real estate, Trump turned to licensing his name. Many buildings with *Trump* on them are not his. Financial experts claim he would have made more money investing his inheritance in the stock market than he has made in real estate.

Trump's presidency is rife with lies. *The Washington Post* reported Trump made 1,318 false claims in his first 263 days as president, which equates to around five falsehoods per day. Radio Free Brooklyn, assembled a 50 x 10 foot mural displaying lies told by Trump. Thousands of ridiculous tweets full of misstatements, exaggerations, outright lies, and vitriol were posted at a New York site. The press reported lies daily.

It's wise to consider Trump is lying when his lips move or he tweets. Fact Checker's database tracked Trump's lies and misleading information. As of September 11, 2020, he had lied 23,035 times in 1,335 days. Other databases, even Wikipedia, have recorded his lies. Ridiculous big lies include: he would pay for his campaign, he won the 2020 election in a landslide, and he was a successful businessman. He continues to lie all day every day, and he always will. Following is a minuscule representation of his lies:

———————————

— **June 6, 2015** — Trump announced his run for president and said, *I don't need anybody's money. I'm using my own money. I'm not using lobbyists. I'm not using donors. I don't care. I'm really rich.* He lied. He did not spend his own money. In fact, he pocketed substantial amounts of campaign funds from followers, lobbyists, and other donors.

— **June 16, 2015** — Trump said, "I will build a great wall— and nobody builds walls better than me, believe me—and I'll build them very inexpensively. . .and I will make Mexico pay for that wall." Trump later lied about what wall was built. Per *Forbes*, of over 2,000 miles of border, taxpayers spent 15 billion on only 734 miles, about half of which was for replacement walls. Mexico has paid nothing.

– **October 7, 2016** – For thirty years, Trump, a racist, made false accusatory comments about the young black and latino men known as the "Central Park Five." Wrongly convicted of sexual assault, DNA evidence and a confession exonerated them. Trump inserted himself into the case again.

– **November 27, 2016** – Without evidence to support this claim, Trump tweeted, "In addition to winning the Electoral College in a landslide, I won the popular vote if you deduct the millions of people who voted illegally [for Clinton]."

– **January 21, 2017** – Sean Spicer emphatically stated the attendance at the National Mall for Trump's inaugural address, "was the largest audience to ever witness an inauguration, period." They also lied about the weather. Trump repeatedly made the same boast. Photos and other evidence clearly show otherwise.

– **January 22, 2017** – Kellyanne Conway said false statements about the crowd size at the inauguration were not lies, but "alternative facts." It's interesting she would use a cult-building technique in her defense of the lie.

– **February 7, 2017** – Trump stated the U. S. murder rate had reached a forty-seven-year peak. This was not true.

– **February 9, 2017** – Trump warned of terrorist attacks from refugees He tweeted that dangerous refugees were flooding in from countries outlawed by his travel ban. No attacks had been perpetrated by refugees from those countries.

– **February 11, 2017** – Trump and adviser Stephen Miller claimed three million illegal votes went to Hillary Clinton in the 2016 election. There is no evidence of this; there is evidence to the contrary. His preoccupation with Hillary winning the popular vote was puzzling. He couldn't let it go.

– **February 18, 2017** – The Department of Homeland Security drafted a proposal to mobilize the National Guard to arrest undocumented immigrants, but DHS never implemented the proposal. The White House denied it had ever existed in the first place. However, the proposal was documented in a memo leaked to the Associated Press.

– **March 4, 2017** – Without evidence, Trump again falsely accused Obama of wiretapping Trump Tower. President Trump's own Department of Justice rebuked his claim.

– **March 7, 2017** – Trump supported the House's "repeal-and-replace" healthcare bill, which would eliminate the Affordable Care Act (Obamacare). There was never any replacement plan, a violation of Trump's campaign promise to provide "insurance for everybody" without raising insurance premiums or cutting Medicaid. The Congressional Budget Office found the Republican bill would slash Medicaid, increase insurance premiums, and leave twenty-one million Americans uninsured. Cutting back on Medicare, Medicaid, and Social Security has been a long-time priority of Republicans —one many voters lacking critical thinking skills ignore.

– **April 4, 2017** - With no evidence, Trump blamed a gas attack in Syria on Obama administration's weakness.

– **April 16, 2017** – In response to demands to release his tax returns, Trump distracted with a tweet, "Someone should look into who paid for the small organized rallies yesterday." No evidence existed that protesters were paid.

– **April 20, 2017** – Trump promised within 90 days of his election he would appoint a team to investigate Russian election interference and protect against future hacking. No team was established and no plan was put in place to build one. Instead, Trump's administration focused on removing sanctions Obama had put in place against Russia for their interference and refused to fund investigations. Trump also refused to fund approved election fraud protections.

– **April 23, 2017** – Responding to ABC News, NBC News, *The Washington Post*, and *Wall Street Journal* polls that showed Trump had the lowest approval rating of any president since 1945, Trump tweeted, "New polls out today are very good considering much of the media is FAKE and almost always negative. Would still beat Hillary in a popular vote." He repeatedly called his popular vote loss "fake news."

– **April 29, 2017** – On *Face the Nation*, Trump falsely suggested the new Republican healthcare bill, which no one saw during his entire term, would protect health insurance for those with pre-existing conditions. No proposed replacement healthcare legislation by Republicans existed. This is why John McCain voted against the bill to reverse the Affordable Care Act (Obamacare), causing the bill to fail. Obsessed with undoing Obama's work, Trump's focus was on defeating the bill, the public be damned.

– **May 1, 2017** – Trump claimed Obama had illegally ordered surveillance of Trump Tower during the 2016 election. Trump's claim has been widely discredited and refuted by the FBI and the National Security Office.

– **May 11, 2017** – Trump was determined to show he got more popular votes than Clinton. He formed a task force to review purported voter fraud. Without evidence, he claimed voter registration and election integrity issues. All assertions of material illegal voting have been widely discredited.

– **June 6, 2017** – Scott Pruitt, EPA Administrator, claimed 50,000 jobs were added to the coal mining industry. The Bureau of Labor reported the number was closer to 1,400. Coal mining is down 15% since Trump took office.

– **June 22, 2017** – At a rally, Trump proposed a law that required all immigrants support themselves financially for five years before receiving government aid. This law already existed. Bill Clinton signed the Personal Responsibility and Work Opportunity Reconciliation Act in 1996 that restricted immigrants in the U. S. from benefiting from federal benefits for a period of five years.

– **June 25, 2017** – Trump tweeted, "Hillary Clinton colluded with the Democratic Party in order to beat Crazy Bernie Sanders. Is she allowed to so collude? Unfair to Bernie!" At the time, Trump was under investigation for colluding with Russia to influence the 2016 election.

– **June 27, 2017** – Trump falsely claimed he held the all-time record for being on Time Magazine covers. The Trump Organization displayed fake Time covers at Trump resorts.

– **August 2, 2017** – Trump claimed to *The Wall Street Journal* the Boy Scouts of America called him to say his speech to their organization was the "greatest speech ever made to them." Press Secretary, Sarah Sanders, admitted during a press conference the Boy Scouts of America never called the president to compliment his speech. In fact, critics had chastised Trump for making an inappropriate, adult-like comment in his speech to the boys.

– **August 30, 2017** – After Hurricane Harvey, Trump visited Texas and told a group there that recovery from the devastation would be "better than ever before" while his proposed budget significantly cut FEMA programs.

– **October 16, 2017** – Trump claimed Barack Obama didn't call families of fallen soldiers. This was untrue. Obama had long meetings with the families of fallen soldiers, as confirmed by both his staff and the soldiers' families.

– **October 20, 2017** – Trump tweeted, "Just out report: 'United Kingdom crime rises 13 percent annually amid spread of Radical Islamic terror.' not good, we must keep America safe!" The UK's Office of National Statistics did not attribute a rise in crime to Islam.

– **October 21, 2017** – The families of fallen American soldiers received rush UPS messages from Trump after he stated in a phone interview he had contacted "virtually all" Gold Star families. He hadn't.

– **October 26, 2017** – After Trump authorized the go-ahead for the Keystone XL pipeline project, he pledged the pipeline would be made of American steel. Foreign steel provided the primary material for the pipeline. The steel industry suffered under Trump. Imports of foreign steel rose 24 percent his first year as president.

– **November 29, 2017** – A Senate Republican claimed the tax bill Trump championed would not benefit the majority of Americans. It provided massive tax cuts to the wealthy. In tweets and speeches, Trump hyped benefits to lower income Americans. He claimed the bill was a way to "RESTORE AMERICAN PROSPERITY—and RECLAIM AMERICA'S DESTINY," which it did for the wealthy and corporations.

– **December 22, 2017** – Trump signed the Tax Cuts and Jobs Act. This legislation, which costs $1.5 trillion, cut the corporate tax rate to its lowest point since 1939 and assured a negative impact on the national debt, which increased $7.2 trillion during his term even though he inherited a vibrant economy. Only modestly, and in some cases temporarily, did this bill lower taxes for individuals. Goldman Sachs' chief political economist, Alec Phillips, said, "The effect for individuals in 2020 and beyond looks to be minimal and could actually be slightly negative."

– **December 27, 2017** – On December 27, 2017, Trump bragged he had signed more legislation than any president since Truman. This was a lie. He had no legislative agenda other than cutting taxes for the rich and eliminating the Affordable Care Act. In his first year in office, he signed the fewest pieces of legislation of any president since Eisenhower, even though Republicans held the House and the Senate. He did sign executive orders, most undoing Obama's actions.

– **October 2, 2018** – The *New York Times*, revealed Trump received $413 million from his father's real estate empire. The findings contradicted Trump's claims he was self made, that he built his multi-billion dollar empire on $1 million and his own hard work and deal-making.

– **October 9, 2018** – Protesters fought against the confirmation of Supreme Court Justice nominee Brett Kavanaugh. Trump put forth a conspiracy theory that leftist protestors were paid by Democrats. "The paid D.C. protesters are now ready to REALLY protest because they haven't gotten their checks—in other words, they weren't paid! The very rude elevator screamers are paid professionals only looking to make Senators look bad. Don't fall for it! Also, look at all of the professionally made identical signs. Paid for by Soros and others. These are not signs made in the basement from love! #Troublemakers" There is no evidence any of this was true.

– **October 31, 2018** – Trump tweeted a racist political ad about an undocumented immigrant convicted of murdering two police officers. The tagline said, "Democrats let him into our country. Democrats let him stay." The convicted criminal was originally released by Republican Sheriff, Joe Arpaio in Arizona. The immigrant then illegally re-entered the U. S. during George W. Bush's presidency.

– **November 6, 2018** – A class-action lawsuit challenged the government's detention of migrants, including children kept in cages at the border. Under Trump, more migrant children had been in government custody than at any time in American history. Due to a lack of transparency, the numbers are all over the place, but indications are over 6,000 children were separated from their parents—over five hundred of them are still not reunited to this day.

– **November 7, 2018** – A White House intern tried to wrestle away a microphone from CNN's Jim Acosta at a press conference because Acosta asked Trump challenging questions. The White House revoked Acosta's press pass and released a doctored video to justify their action. However, the original video of the incident on C-SPAN differed from the one released by the White House, which was altered to portray Acosta as the aggressor.

– **November 9, 2018** – Attorney General Matthew Whitaker became embroiled in the investigation of Russia's involvement in the 2016 election. Trump lied with his usual response in such matters, "I don't know Matt Whitaker." He had appointed him and had met him many times.

– **November 9, 2018** – When Democrats won the House, Trump suggested Florida voter fraud. He tweeted, "Law Enforcement is looking into another big corruption scandal having to do with Election Fraud." Florida's Department of Law Enforcement reported there were no legitimate allegations.

– **November 10, 2018** – Trump blamed the deadliest blaze in California's history on poor forest management and recommended raking forest floors as a solution.

– **November 20, 2018** – Trump said Saudi Arabia would invest $450 billion in the United States. This was not true.

– **November 25, 2018** – U. S. Border Patrol Agents sprayed tear gas at migrants at the Tijuana entry point. Trump said, "First of all, the tear gas is a very minor form of the tear gas itself. It's very safe." Tear gas, a war weapon, is caustic. There is no "minor form" of it that is "safe." An international Chemical Weapons Convention banned it in 1993.

– **December 6, 2018** – The *New York Times* exposed Trump for employing undocumented workers at the Trump National Golf Club in New Jersey. He also used undocumented workers for Trump building construction.

– **January 10, 2019** – Trump denied saying Mexico would pay for his border wall. Actually, he had said that many times. Very little wall was ever built, and Mexico paid for none of it.

– **January 17, 2019** – Trump's lawyer Michael Cohen admitted he rigged several online polls during the 2016 campaign, and he did so at the direction of Trump.

– **January 19, 2019** – The Trump administration's policy of separating children began months before it was ever made public. A government watchdog report revealed thousands more children were separated from their parents at the southern border than had originally been reported.

– **March 22, 2019** – Special Counsel Robert Mueller delivered to Attorney General William Barr a 448-page report on Russian interference in the 2016 election. Barr did not release the report. Instead he issued a four-page summary of it, downplaying and mischaracterizing Trump's culpability. When Barr finally released the full report, it was so redacted (blacked out) it was impossible to interpret. Mueller and others condemned the summary, which incorrectly absolved Trump of wrong doing. He said, "There is now public confusion about critical aspects of the results of our investigation." People close to Trump were indicted as a result of the investigation, but he was never held to account.

– **April 9, 2019** – Trump made a false claim that the Obama administration was responsible for child-separation policies at the Mexican border. Trump said he put an end to them. This was a lie. Trump created the policy of separation.

– **July 8, 2019** – The Trump administration had a history of rolling back environmental regulations. He lied when he said, "From day one, my administration has made it a top priority to ensure that America has among the very cleanest air and cleanest water on the planet." Actually, pollution had grown worse under Trump primarily because of substantial degrading of EPA regulations by his administration.

– **December 21, 2019** – Trump tweeted "the Obama Admin tried to limit Americans to the more-expensive LED bulbs for their home." George W. Bush's administration did that.

– **June 19, 2020** – Twitter put a warning label on a doctored video Trump tweeted that included a fake CNN headline that read, "Terrified toddler runs from racist baby."

– **August 4, 2020** – Trump claimed he didn't know about Russia's offer of bounties for American troops killed in Afghanistan. The bounties were reportedly brought to his attention in intelligence reports. White House insiders said Trump doesn't read the reports. Trump responded, "I read a lot. I comprehend extraordinarily well. Probably better than anybody you've interviewed in a long time." However, one White House source said that if you want to hide something from Trump, just put it in writing. If you want him to read something, put his name in it.

– **August 4, 2020** – Asked to comment on the death of civil rights leader John Lewis, Trump said, "I don't know John Lewis. . .He chose not to come to my inauguration."

– **September 13, 2020** – Trump boasted in a tweet he had received a "highly honored Bay of Pigs Award" from Cuban Americans. *The Guardian* noted there is no such award.

– **September 27, 2020** – Trump misrepresented financial data in many venues, so he refuses to release his tax returns. The *New York Times* claimed he was over $400 million in debt.

– **October 27, 2020** – At a Michigan rally, Trump boasted he won the state's "Man of the Year" award. There is no such award.

November 1, 2020 – Trump claimed at a Michigan rally that no new auto plants had opened in the state for decades. This was untrue. He also said five Japanese auto plants would be built in Michigan. This was not true, either.

– **November 5, 2020** – *The Washington Post* fact checker reported Trump told 29,508 falsehoods, including 4,000 in October while campaigning for president.

Lies and cheating were a defining feature of Trump's presidency. His niece, Mary Trump, in her book, *Too Much and Never Enough*, said he cheats "as a way of life." He believes there is no such thing as bad press and rarely suffers consequences for untruths. So he lies.

Trump campaigned on an infrastructure plan. Nothing was ever done. He promised to punish companies who sent jobs overseas but did not. He said he'd take the side of students on the issue of student loans. He did not. He spoke of a tax hike for the rich during his campaign but delivered massive tax cuts. Low income taxpayer cuts were minimal and some would expire while corporate cuts were forever. He claimed tax breaks would be offset with economic growth, but the deficit increased $1 trillion in 2019 alone.

He promised school vouchers for private schools, but didn't deliver. He lied about writing his books. He doesn't read, and he doesn't write, except in tweets. He promised lower drug prices but didn't deliver. He lied that he had a better healthcare plan to replace Obamacare—one that covered everyone and protected people from preexisting conditions. There was no plan.

Trump promised a border wall Mexico would pay for. They didn't. And he lied about how much wall was actually built. Only about 350 miles of new wall was built. Trump's original vision was for a concrete monument to him, costing almost $5 trillion. Eventually, $7.2 billion came from the military (including military housing and veteran benefits) and $1.3 billion from Congress. Forbes reported Trump eventually spent $15 billion on the border wall.

Trump lied about steel and auto plants opening up. He lied about NAFTA, NATO, and the European Union. He lied about a North Korea agreement. Profoundly ignorant on the economy, he lied that tariffs would improve the economy. But he didn't understand how they worked. China retaliated and the resulting trade war cost the country sorely. American manufacturers paid more for raw materials and consumers for products. Farm bankruptcies and a manufacturing slump followed. Farmers lost so much income that $28 billion in bailouts at taxpayer expense were required for Trump to keep their votes. And he lied again when he said dollars collected from China offset those costs. They did not.

Trump lied about being a good businessman and deal maker. He claims to be the top real estate person in NYC, but there are others more successful. He lied that Trump Tower has sixty-eight floors. It has fifty-eight. After 9/11, he bragged that he had the tallest building in New York, which was a lie. Barbara Res, who worked for him, said in her book, *Tower of Lies*, he didn't have the empire he claimed to have and his success came from not being limited by the truth. She said that without excessive PR, he would only be a footnote in New York's real estate history and that he is a publicity hound who believes his own lies.

Trump lied endlessly about the pandemic, including allowing the European Union to order 200M vaccine doses while ordering only 100M for the U. S. He funneled taxpayer and campaign dollars into his own pocket. He took credit for Obama's VA legislation. He lied when he promised to not golf like Obama did. He golfed more. He lies all day, every day. An aide said, "He lies like he breathes."

Most politicians don't lie. They spin. Lies can get them in trouble. Journalist S. V. Dáte nailed it when he said, " I have never encountered anyone who was as regularly and shamelessly dishonest as Donald Trump." He creates his own reality. After his defeat in the November 2020 election, he spread the notorious, outrageous lie he had won—and by a landslide no less. Nothing could be further from the truth. Over sixty legal opinions, two Supreme Court decisions, numerous state election officials, and the U. S. Congress said so.

FOURTH GRADE BEHAVIOR:
BULLYING, INSULTING, NAME CALLING

After evaluating his speech patterns and vocabulary in a study in 2018, Bill Frischling at *Factbase* reported that Trump speaks at a fourth-grade level. *The Boston Globe* also analyzed his verbal fluency based on debate speech. It showed that of all nineteen 2016 presidential candidates, Trump's verbal fluency was the least sophisticated. This analysis also rated his language as equivalent to that of a fourth grader. His doltish tweets reinforce the fact that he communicates at that level.

According to Tony Schwartz, ghost writer of *The Art of the Deal*, Trump wrote none of the book. This is no surprise. When comparing Trump's speaking and tweets to his books, it's obvious he didn't write them. Schwartz regrets writing it. He believes Trump has never read a book in his adult life and describes him as having no core values, no capacity for empathy, no emotion except anger, no regard for truth, and unable to admit he is wrong. He is guided by self-interest, getting noticed, and bullying and winning. Schwartz said Trump doesn't want his tax records made available because they will reveal he is a stone cold felon.

Trump's impediment is not limited to language. Emotional development issues drive behavior typical of an unpleasant, braggadocios, undisciplined child. Some described these immature behaviors as toddler tantrums. As President, he routinely, in fact, daily displayed nasty, socially unacceptable behavior, often with ranting and raving, and sorrowful pity-grubbing midnight tweets. This undignified behavior was from the president of our country—the supposed world leader of democracy—and it was embarrassing. The White House needed a time-out corner.

Trump's emotional immaturity and lack of discipline and common sense were exposed by his impetuous late night tweets, littered with lies, insults, and vindictive threats. Without any governmental acumen, no respect for rules or structure, no interest in learning, and little to no attention span, he bungled his way through diplomatic processes.

Trump has a thug mentality. He tramples on people with impunity. If he senses a weakness in a person, he pounces, although like most bullies, he is thin skinned and bellows at critics. Shocking name-calling and uncouth insults reflect his vitriol and lack of social skills. Influencers were Norman Vincent Peale, Tony Robbins, and Dale Carnegie who taught him tenacity and his father and Roy Cohn who taught him a *killer* mentality.

Sexual harassment and abuse abounded. He is generally an unpleasant, pompous-ass, obese fellow with squinty evil eyes rimmed in white within a fake orange complexion. With ridiculous, cartoonish hair plopped on his balding head, his appearance makes his deprecating comments and insults directed at women smirk worthy.

At rallies, he is a trite, inept, immature, amateur stand-up comedian only his rabid followers can appreciate. His constant demand for attention exacerbates other immature tendencies. He is stupidly transparent, and his thoughts, such as drinking bleach, are often batshit crazy. He projects his evil thoughts onto others. If he accuses a person of something, it's likely he's doing it or planning to do it himself.

Astoundingly, he conned his way into the position of president of the greatest democracy in the world and then tried to destroy it and become its fascist leader. Determined to dismantle it institution by institution, he and his goons created a mess so diabolical that citizens rose up en masse to defeat him in 2020 after one term. A second, lame duck term could have been disastrous. This monster has no decency or humility, and he will not go quietly into obscurity. If you are thinking, *Well, Nik, tell us what you really think,* let me say that I acknowledge my remarks are scathing here, but, well, just read on.

– **July 18, 2015** – Trump insulted Senator John McCain, a decorated Vietnam War veteran and POW, saying, "I like people who weren't captured." Trump was exempted from military service after receiving four student deferments and then for supposed foot spurs.

– **August 19, 2015** – In August of 2015, two of Trump's supporters beat a homeless Latino man with a metal pipe, and urinated on him. Trump said, "I will say, the people that are following me are very passionate. They love this country and they want this country to be great again." Peeing on someone is great? Really?

– **November 25, 2015** – At a campaign rally, Trump mocked *New York Times* reporter, Serge Kovasleski, who has a congenital joint condition. Trump imitated him at a rally by contorting his wrists and flailing his arms about.

– **November 25, 2015** – Trump claimed he had seen thousands of Muslims in New Jersey celebrating the September 11 attack on the World Trade Center. This claim was adamantly discredited by officials.

– **May 31, 2016** – Trump attacked Federal judge Gonzalo Curiel, who presided over the Trump University fraud case, which Trump lost, by claiming the judge represented a conflict of interest because "he was of Mexican heritage."

– **July 30, 2016** – Attack dog Trump, known for disrespecting Five Star families, belittled Khizr and Ghazala Khan—parents of a Muslim American soldier killed while serving in the Army—who spoke at the Democratic National Convention.

– **February 4, 2017** – Trump questioned the legitimacy of a federal judge who blocked his travel ban, calling Judge James Robart a "so-called judge" whose opinion took "law-enforcement away from our country." Justice Robart received the unanimous endorsement of the American Bar Association as "well-qualified" before his appointment to the bench by George W. Bush. Trump had appointed several Federal judges that the American Bar Association rated "not qualified."

– **February 9, 2017** – Trump attacked Senator John McCain after he raised objections to a botched Yemen raid conducted in collaboration with Saudi Arabia. One American soldier was killed and five others wounded. Around 35 innocents, including children, were reported killed. On his bully pulpit, Twitter, Trump said McCain had been "losing so long he doesn't know how to win anymore."

– **February 9, 2017** – In a meeting, Trump—a name-calling aficionado—said "Pocahontas" was the face of the Democratic party, referring to Elizabeth Warren.

– **March 3, 2017** – While Governor of Indiana, Vice President Pence used his personal email for state business. His office announced the account had been hacked, including confidential information too sensitive to release to the public. The Trump campaign attacked presidential candidate Hillary Clinton many times for using a private email address for government work. During the 2015 campaign and forever after Trump labeled her "crooked Hillary" and encouraged rally attendees to chant, "Lock her up!"

– **March 4, 2017** – Trump insulted Arnold Schwarzenegger, who responded, "When you take away after-school programs for children and meals on wheels for poor people, that's not what you call 'making America great again.'"

– **June 6, 2017** – In more than fifty cases nationwide, children were heard bullying classmates with calls for deportation, referencing Trump and using blatant racist language. For example, an eight-year-old in California said to a black classmate, "Now that Trump won, you're going to have to go back to Africa where you belong."

– **June 30, 2017** – MSNBC news anchors Joe Scarborough and Mika Brzezinski, who refused to be Trump's mouthpieces, alleged the White House tried to blackmail them with an article about their relationship in the *National Enquirer*. The newly engaged co-anchors claimed Trump's staff threatened to publish an *Enquirer* hit article if they did not contact Trump directly. (Trump is a friend of David Pecker, publisher of the *National Enquirer*. He frequently took advantage of this connection to intimidate people.) The *Enquirer* then published the hit piece on Scarborough and Brzezinski's relationship.

– **July 1, 2017** – Trump tweeted, "Crazy Joe Scarborough and dumb as a rock Mika are not bad people, but their low rated show is dominated by their NBC bosses. Too bad!"

– **September 23, 2017** – Trump suggested National Football League owners fire players who kneel during the national anthem and that owners should say, "Get that son of a bitch off the field right now, he's fired. He's fired!"

– **September 24, 2017** – Trump again publicly rebuked Football League players who knelt during the anthem.

– **April 18, 2018** – Trump tweeted, "There is a Revolution going on in California. Soooo many Sanctuary areas want OUT of this ridiculous, crime infested & breeding concept. Jerry Brown is trying to back out of the National

Guard at the Border, but the people of the State are not happy. Want Security & Safety NOW!"

– **August 13, 2018** – With the publication of Omarosa Manigault Newman's book, *Unhinged* about working in the White House—Trump went on a sexist, racist rant on twitter, calling her "a dog" and "a crazed crying lowlife."

– **September 28, 2018** – *The New York Times* reported thousands of migrant children were separated from their parents and held in a West Texas tent city.

– **October 15, 2018** – In an interview with Leslie Stahl on *60 Minutes*, Trump defended mocking Dr. Christine Blasey-Ford, research psychologist at the Stanford University School of Medicine, who testified in the Judge Brett Kavanaugh hearings. When asked by Stahl whether he thought he had treated Dr. Ford with respect, Trump said, "It doesn't matter—we won."

– **October 16, 2018** – The Trump administration showed support for Saudi crown prince Mohammed bin Salman, who was linked to the disappearance and murder of journalist Jamal Khashoggi, columnist for *The Washington Post*. Trump defended Salman in an interview with the *Associated Press*: "Here we go again with you're guilty until proven innocent." That day, Mike Pompeo, Secretary of State, arrived at the Saudi capitol grinning and shaking hands with the prince.

– **October 16, 2018** – After a federal judge threw out Stormy Daniels' defamation lawsuit against him, Trump tweeted, "Great, now I can go after Horseface and her third-rate lawyer in the Great State of Texas."

– **October 19, 2018** – At a rally in Missoula, Montana, Trump made American great again. He praised Republican Congressman Greg Gianforte for body-slamming *Guardian* reporter Ben Jacobs. To cheers, Trump said, "Any guy that can do a body slam—he's my kind of guy."

– **November 7, 2018** – Attorney General Sessions, who refused to protect Trump from investigations, resigned. Trump had mocked him for months after he recused himself from the Russia investigation.

– **November 19, 2018** – Ivanka Trump used a personal email account for hundreds of government-related emails, many in violation of federal records rules. Trump incessantly harped over Hilary Clinton's emails, which influenced her losing to him in 2016.

– **December 11, 2018** – Congress refused to provide funding for construction of his border wall. Trump threatened Democratic lawmakers that he would be "proud" to shut down the government. "I'll be the one to shut it down. I will take the mantle." He did.

– **December 22, 2018** – The government entered a partial shutdown as Trump blocked Congress over funding for his border wall. The shutdown lasted thirty-four days. This was the longest in the nation's history. Trump's action left about 800,000 federal workers without pay.

– **January 17, 2019** – House Speaker Nancy Pelosi planned to visit troops in Afghanistan. Trump canceled her use of military aircraft. This retaliatory action came after she requested he delay the State of the Union address because of the government shutdown and lack of security.

– **February 15, 2019** – Trump declared a national emergency in an effort to acquire $5.7 billion in funding for a border wall.

– **March 21, 2019** – A lawyer for Jared Kushner revealed Jared used private communications to discuss official matters. Trump had said Hillary Clinton's use of a private email server was "bigger than Watergate."

– **July 14, 2019** – Trump attacked four congresswomen of color, saying they should "go back and help fix the totally broken and crime-infested places from which they came." Ocasio-Cortez was born in New York, Tlaib in Detroit, and Pressley in Cincinnati.

– **July 17, 2019** – At a rally in North Carolina, Trump criticized Representative Ilhan Omar and encouraged the crowd to chant, "Send her back." To where? Who knows.

– **July 27, 2019** – Trump referred to Baltimore as "a disgusting, rat and rodent infested mess." And he called Representative Elijah Cummings a "brutal bully."

– **December 12, 2019** – Trump coveted the *TIME* Magazine Person of the Year award. When the magazine named Swedish climate activist, Greta Thunberg, Person of the Year, Trump tweeted: "So ridiculous. Greta must work on her Anger Management problem, then go to a good old fashioned movie with a friend! Chill Greta, Chill!"

– **May 7, 2020** – Refusing to be a president for all Americans, Trump called those who opposed him "dishonest, crooked people...They're scum—and I say it a lot, they're scum, they're human scum."

– **May 24, 2020** – As the nation met a sobering benchmark—100,000 killed by the coronavirus—Trump used Memorial Day to insult numerous women on Twitter. He called Stacy Abrams "Shamu," and said, "she visited every buffet restaurant in the State." He accused Nancy Pelosi of drinking "booze on the job" and referred to Hillary Clinton as a "skank."

– **May 29, 2020** – People in Minneapolis took to the streets to protest the killing of African American, George Floyd, by police. Trump tweeted the protesters were "THUGS" who condoned violence, "Any difficulty and we will assume control but, when the looting starts, the shooting starts." Reporters on site noted inciting of crowds, introduction of weapons, and property damage were done by members of extremist organizations that Trump supported.

– **May 30, 2020** – Trump again condemned people who protested the killing of George Floyd. He threatened them with "vicious dogs" and "ominous weapons." In a tweet suggesting a confrontation, he wrote, "Tonight, I understand, is MAGA NIGHT AT THE WHITE HOUSE???" Someone must have convinced him to calm his rhetoric. He later said he didn't mean to incite violence. "I was just asking. By the way, they love African-American people. They love black people." He lied.

– **May 31, 2020** – During days of conflict across the country, Trump praised extremists who counter protested. During a protest in D. C. that included counter protesters, he tweeted from within a White House bunker as fires raged outside. "Get tough Democrat Mayors and Governors," he wrote. "These people are ANARCHISTS. Call in our National Guard NOW." He respected the right to protest only when his supporters were protesting, like at the Capitol on January 6, 2021, when he remained silent and took no action for hours. When he did finally respond, he told the insurrectionists he loved them.

– **June 1, 2020** – To quell protesters demanding justice after the killing of Floyd and other black citizens, Trump threatened to summon "all available federal resources—civilian and military"—and referred to demonstrators as "an angry mob." On-site journalists reported radical right-wing groups were inciting rioting and damaging property. Trump praised and encouraged these violent actors during the protests while calling himself "your president of law and order."

– **June 1, 2020** – Leaving the White House bunker, Trump arranged a photo-op in front of nearby St. John's church. Peaceful protesters were sprayed with tear gas and projectiles to clear the way for him and his entourage. He stood in front of the church holding up a Bible as a prop.

– **June 2, 2020** – Trump's press secretary, Kayleigh McEnany, denied tear gas and rubber bullets were used to clear out protesters for Trump at St. John's church. Park Police, however, acknowledged firing "pepper ball" projectiles and "smoke canisters" into the peaceful crowd.

– **June 2, 2020** – Trump railed against protesters in New York City, where marches were largely peaceful. "NYC, CALL UP THE NATIONAL GUARD," he tweeted. "The lowlifes and losers are ripping you apart. Act fast!" As in other protests, radical right-wing rabble rousers were there.

– **June 3, 2020** – Trump lied and denied going into a bunker while protesters gathered outside the White House. Only after the press had evidence he was in the bunker did he acknowledged going there, but only for an "inspection." He said, "I went down during the day, and I was there for a tiny little short period of time, two, two and a half times."

– June 7, 2020 – Confronted with growing protests in Washington, D. C., Trump reportedly demanded the military deploy 10,000 active-duty troops to the city. The demand led to a heated exchange with Pentagon officials.

– June 8, 2020 – At a protest in Buffalo, New York, Martin Gugino, a 75-year-old peace activist, was hospitalized after two police officers shoved him backward to the ground, fracturing his skull. In a tweet, Trump baselessly claimed he "could be an ANTIFA provocateur," adding, "he fell harder than was pushed...Could be a set up?"

– June 17, 2020 – Trump railed against John Bolton, his former national security adviser, over publication of his memoir. It painted the president as an ill-prepared leader who curried favor with dictators and schemed to stop criminal investigations. Trump tweeted, "Wacko John Bolton's "exceedingly tedious" (*New York Times*) book is made up of lies & fake stories." He called Bolton "A disgruntled boring fool who only wanted to go to war. Never had a clue, was ostracized & happily dumped. What a dope!"

– June 28, 2020 – Trump proudly tweeted a video showing a supporter shouting "white power" at a Florida retirement community.

– July 1, 2020 – Trump promised to veto a $740 billion defense bill because of a provision to remove names of ten Confederate generals from military bases. He called the bill "the Elizabeth 'Pocahontas' Warren (of all people!) Amendment."

– July 4, 2020 – Trump attacked protesters: "We will never allow an angry mob to tear down our statues, erase our history, indoctrinate our children or trample on our freedoms. We are now in the process of defeating the radical left, the Marxists, the anarchists, the agitators, the looters. . ."

– July 27, 2020 – An hour before Dr. Anthony Fauci threw the opening pitch in the Yankees game, Trump announced he had been invited to throw out the ceremonial first pitch at an August Yankees game. The Yankees, however, stated they had never invited Trump to do so.

– August 28, 2020 – At a campaign rally in New Hampshire, Trump ridiculed protesters around the country. "Protesters, your ass. I don't talk about my ass. They're not protesters. Those aren't protesters. Those are anarchists, they're agitators, they're rioters, they're looters." No one needs a reminder of Trump's ass. The visual is traumatizing.

At a rally, Trump, The President of the United States called CNN reporters "dumb bastards." He called a football player "a son of a bitch." He called both a woman vice president and a world leader "nasty," and a staffer a "dog." He called a female broadcaster "dumb as a rock." He called a female politician a "skank." He called men who died in World War II "losers" and Marines who died "suckers." He called a revered legislator a "loser" and a military expert a "dope." He called his attorney general "mentally retarded." He called constituents "scum" and people at political rallies "disgusting people." What a guy, huh? I use his behavior as license to call him names—like my favorite, "dickwad." I'm no longer a nice person, but I consider myself no more flawed than the hypocrites who reconcile his rank behavior with their religion or conscience. Our poor country.

SEXUAL HARRASSMENT

Trump, a world-class objectifier and degrader of women, harbors a deep contempt and intense resentment toward them. In September 2018, when sexual misconduct allegations were raised against Supreme Court Justice nominee Brett Kavanaugh, Trump admitted he had been charged "by four or five women who got paid a lot of money to make up stories about me." He lied. Twenty-some women have come forward, none of whom got paid.

How many women are out there who haven't reported is unknown. Given his pattern of behavior, his associations with known sex traffickers, and his bragging about sexual mis-conduct, the real number is most likely even more shocking. And this does not include the countless numbers of uncouth, scathing insults he dished out publicly about women. This behavior should have disturbed all Americans in spite of their political affiliations. Apparently, it did not.

Trump, an insecure man-child, disrespects and loathes women. He calls them horrible names and makes nasty comments about them that are full of unseemly innuendos. During a notorious 2005 *Access Hollywood* tape, he bragged to Billy Bush about grabbing women's genitals without permission. He said, "I don't even wait. And when you're a star, they let you do it, you can do anything. . .grab them by the pussy." In response to public outcry, he later said, "I've never said I'm a perfect person."

One has to wonder how his wife, Melania, copes with this behavior. Stephanie Winston Wolkoff, author of *Melania and Me*, stated that Melania's response to Trump's unfaithfulness and rampant sexual advances to other women was, "Boys will be boys." After the Stormy Daniels scandal broke, she responded, "I know who I married."

According to Winston, Melania is emotionally distant and cocooned by wealth, so she is not bothered by anything—personal or political. Melania just says, "I really don't care." And she doesn't. She wore a coat with those exact words written on the back when flying to the southern border to visit a center housing children taken from their parents. According to Winston, other than Melania enjoying any occasion to "rile up the liberals," nothing fazes her. This makes her a good match for a self-described sexual predator, cheater, abuser, and narcissistic power monger.

If you have questions about the legitimacy of sexual harassment complaints and whether Trump is a predator, the scope and volume of the following list of formal, documented situations should resolve that issue. If not, you surely must conclude your President is, at very least, a disgusting, uncouth, creepy cad.

———————————

– **August 7, 2015** – Megyn Kelly called Trump out for telling a *Celebrity Apprentice* woman it would be a pretty picture to see her on her knees.

– **August 2015** – In a CNN interview, he said about Megyn Kelly: " . . .There was blood coming out of her eyes, blood coming out of her wherever."

– **April 2016** – Jill Harth accused Trump of sexual assault in a 1997 lawsuit.

– **May 2016** – Temple Taggart, Miss Utah in the 1997 Miss USA Pageant, said Trump sexually harassed her.

– **June 2016** – Cassandra Searles, Miss Washington in the 2013 Miss USA pageant, accused Trump of sexual misconduct.

– **October 11, 2016** – Tasha Dixon, a former Miss Universe contestant, accused Trump of sexual misconduct.

– **October 2016** – On the *Howard Stern Show*, Trump admitted: "I'll go backstage before a show and everyone's getting dressed and ready. . .and I'm allowed to go in because I'm the owner of the pageant. They're standing there with no clothes...I sort of get away with things like that."

– **October 12, 2016** – Miss Teen USA contestant Mariah Billado claimed Trump behaved inappropriately toward her during the pageant in 1997.

– **October 12, 2016** – Rachel Crooks claimed Trump sexually harassed her when she worked at Trump Tower.

– **October 12, 2016** – Jessica Leeds alleged Trump lifted the armrest and grabbed her breasts when she sat next to him on a plane.

– **October 12, 2016** – Mindy MacGillivray accused Trump of groping her without consent at a concert at Mar-a-Lago.

– **October 12, 2016** – Jennifer Murphy, a contestant on the *The Apprentice* said Trump kissed her without her consent and made several inappropriate remarks.

– **October 12, 2016** – Journalist Natasha Stoynoff, accused Trump of sexual harassment. She said he pinned her to a wall and kissed her. Trump (an overweight, orange, toupeed slug), responded, "Look at her...I don't think so."

– **October 13, 2016** – Lisa Boyne said Trump and modeling agent John Casablancas, known for his own sexual harassment scandals, paraded women in front of them at their table at an event and looked under their skirts to determine whether they were wearing underwear.

– **October 14, 2016** – Kristin Anderson said Trump groped her at a Manhattan club, reaching under her skirt and touching her, which "grossed out" her and her friends.

– **October 14, 2016** – Samantha Holvey reported Trump for sexual misconduct at the 2006 Miss USA pageant.

– **October 14, 2016** – Summer Zervos, a contestant on *The Apprentice*, accused Trump of assaulting her on several occasions, kissing, grabbing, and "thrusting his genitals."

– **October 15, 2016** – Cathy Heller accused Trump of sexual misconduct. She said he grabbed her, tried kissing her, and became angry when she twisted away.

– **October 21, 2016** – Karen Virginia accused Trump of groping her and touching her breast.

– **October 22, 2016** – Jessica Drake, an adult film actor and director, accused Trump of inappropriate sexual contact. She said he grabbed and kissed her without her consent at a golf tournament and made other unwanted advances. She declined an invitation to his suite, after which he asked, "What do you want? How much?"

– **October 27, 2016** – Ninni Laaksonen, former Miss Finland, claimed Trump groped her from behind.

– **January 17, 2017** – Summer Zervos filed a defamation lawsuit, claiming Trump tarnished her reputation by calling her and others, "liars who were telling their stories for ten minutes of fame."

– **March 28, 2017** – After a defamation suit was filed against Trump by *Apprentice* contestant Summer Zervos, Trump's lawyers invoked the Constitution's Supremacy Clause, which prohibits civil lawsuits against a president while he is in office. This suit might resurface after his term of office is over.

– **April 25, 2017** – At an event in Berlin, Ivanka Trump defended her father. She said, "I'm very proud of my father's advocacy...He's been a tremendous champion of supporting families and enabling them to thrive." The audience booed.

– **December 13, 2017** – Trump retaliated on Twitter after Senator Kirsten Gillibrand spoke out on behalf of women who accused Trump of sexual harassment. He tweeted: "Lightweight Senator Kirsten Gillibrand, a total flunky for Chuck Schumer and someone who would come to my office "begging" for campaign contributions not so long ago (and would do anything for them), is now in the ring fighting against Trump."

– **August 21, 2018** – In federal court, Michael Cohen, pled guilty of paying hush money to women for affairs with Trump.

– **June 21, 2019** – Journalist E. Jean Carroll accused Trump of rape in the 1990s. Trump denied ever meeting her. She released a photo of her with him. He said, "Take a look, you take a look. Look at her. I don't think so. . .I'll say it with great respect, number one, she's not my type." (Like he is anyone's type.)

– **July 12, 2019** – Trump's Labor Secretary, Alex Acosta, resigned after being accused of violating victims' rights in sex offender Jeffrey Epstein's 2008 case. Epstein and

Trump consorted together in both New York and at Trump's Palm Beach Mar-a-Lago resort.

– **August 10, 2019** – Trump admitted he knew Jeffrey Epstein, who was charged with sex trafficking women, for many years. He called him a "terrific guy." Trump said, "It is even said that he likes beautiful women as much as I do, and many of them are on the younger side."

– **July 22, 2020** – During a press briefing, Trump sympathized with Ghislaine Maxwell, who was arrested on charges of aiding sex offender Jeffrey Epstein. Trump said, "I wish her well, frankly. I've met her numerous times over the years, especially since I lived in Palm Beach, and I guess they lived in Palm Beach. But I wish her well, whatever it is."

– **September 17, 2020** – Model Amy Dorris said Trump sexually assaulted her in 1997 at the U. S. Open tennis tournament. He was 51; she 24. "He just shoved his tongue down my throat. I was pushing him off, and then that's when his grip became tighter and his hands were very gropey and all over my butt, my breasts, my back, everything."

———————————

It's humorous to women how Trump, an obese thug— with lizard eyes, a ridiculous orangutan-orange complexion, hair like a dead animal, and a face that looks as though it had been stung by a swarm of maniacal bees —dishes out insults on women's appearance as a defense to their complaints. Just thinking about a sexual encounter with him is like standing on the ominous precipice of an abyss. He is a boorish alpha-male who creeps women out to the point of shuddering. I mean, eeeewwww!

DISREGARD FOR MORES, TRADITIONS, PROTOCOL, AND ETHICS

Among the legal and corruption issues tied to the Trump presidency, there are also scores of examples of disregard for established American traditions, principles, and boundaries honored by past presidents.

This disregard—often revealed in Trump's own words—signals his desire to destroy democracy and become the authoritarian leader of a fascist state. His worship of the world's autocratic leaders and disrespect and alienation of democratic ally leaders validates this notion.

Trump's lack of discipline and the narcissistic tendency to project what he is thinking cause him to signal his ambitions. Threats to not leave the White House if defeated in an election made this clear in addition to numerous other statements of that sort. In his entitled opinion, it is only what he wants that matters. He respects no boundaries, no person, and has no sense of country or regard for its institutions and values.

– January 23, 2017 – After Trump took office, he didn't follow the advice of ethics experts to divest his assets.

– January 24, 2017 – As he launched a full-force attack on the Environmental Protection Agency's rules and regulations, Trump barred employees from posting on any social media or speaking with reporters.

– January 25, 2017 – Trump's executive order to build a wall and bolster deportation of immigrants also expanded deportation rules to include minor offenses, such as traffic violations, as reasons for exportation.

– January 25, 2017 – A Trump executive order directed the Departments of Justice and Homeland Security to withhold federal funds from "sanctuary cities" where local police don't always report undocumented immigrants to U. S. Immigration Customs Enforcement (ICE).

– January 26, 2017 – Trump tweeted that, if Mexico is unwilling to pay for the wall, it would be better to cancel the upcoming meeting with President Peña Nietos. In response, Nietos upped him and canceled the meeting.

– September 22, 2017 – Trump repeatedly used aggressive, insulting, and threatening language toward North Korea's Kim Jong-Un. He tweeted, "Kim Jong-Un of North Korea, who is obviously a madman who doesn't mind starving or killing his people, will be tested like never before!" Later, Trump, who was easily charmed by dictators, fell "in love" with Jong-Un.

– October 11, 2017 – Trump told military advisors he expected a tenfold increase in nuclear firepower. Every president since Ronald Reagan signed international disarmament agreements, which to this day legally restrict the U. S. from increasing nuclear stockpiles.

– March 26, 2018 – The Census Bureau announced it would add a citizenship status question to the 2020 U. S. Census form. Critics said the question would discourage undocumented immigrants from responding and thereby skew the data. California sued the Trump administration over the constitutionality of the question, and it was kept off the census form.

– August 27, 2018 – After the death of Senator John McCain, Trump issued no statement and refused to answer questions about McCain, who was a veteran who spent thirty-one years in the Senate. Flags at the White House were lowered to half staff on Saturday night after McCain's death and raised Sunday, the bare minimum required by law. Trump did post a tweet claiming deepest sympathy.

– **January 12, 2019** – Trump met with Vladimir Putin five times in two years. No records of the conversations exist— even in classified files. While previous presidents documented such talks, Trump went to "extraordinary lengths" to conceal what was discussed.

– **January 14, 2019** – The Clemson Tigers football team visited the White House after winning the national championship. Previous White House celebrations for sports teams featured elegant meals that highlighted the best of American cuisine. Trump served them a candlelit dinner of McDonald's fast food in paper wrappers.

– **May 8, 2020** – In a frenzy this day, Trump solidified his position as Commander of Tweets by battering the public with more than 100 posts in a single day. He posted over 46,000 during his term in office.

– **July 17, 2020** – The official portraits of former Presidents Bill Clinton and George W. Bush were taken out of the Grand Foyer of the White House, where portraits of recent presidents have long been displayed. Trump never did unveil the portrait of former President Barack Obama.

– **July 28, 2020** – Former Presidents Clinton, Bush, and Obama were scheduled to attend the funeral of civil rights leader and Congressman John Lewis. Trump declined.

– **August 20, 2020** – Federal Judge Victor Marrero rejected Trump's attempt to block the release of his tax returns. Marrero ruled Trump must submit them to the Manhattan district attorney, who was investigating his financial records. Trump told reporters, "This is a continuation of the witch hunt, the greatest witch hunt in history," Previous presidents and even presidential candidates released their tax returns to the public.

– **August 21, 2020** – Trump told Department of Homeland Security officials to watch Fox News broadcaster Lou Dobbs every night. Former DHS chief of staff Miles Taylor said, "The president would call us and...he would say, 'Why the hell didn't you watch Lou Dobbs last night? You need to listen to Lou. What Lou says is what I want to do.'" As a result, Taylor called Dobbs the department's "shadow chief of staff."

– **August 27, 2020** – Trump ignored the Hatch Act by using government property—the White House—for a political convention. Around 1,500 people attended. They sat close together, most not wearing masks. A White House official justified the absence of masks to CNN, "Everybody is going to catch this thing eventually."

– **August 27, 2020** – Past presidents avoided activities from which they might profit by their position. Trump took every opportunity to benefit from such activities. He visited his properties almost 300 times as president. As a result, the government and the Secret Service paid the Trump Organization more than $900,000. Also, each trip to Mar-a-Lago cost taxpayers $3 million. According to *The Washington Post*, Trump's business also brought in at least $3.8 million in fees from thirty-seven political events held at Trump's properties.

– **November 1, 2020** – Trump planned an election night party in the White House East Room with roughly 400 invited guests. Past presidents considered it inappropriate to use the White House for campaign activities.

– **November 9, 2020** – Ignoring protocol that Presidents don't call elections, Trump called the election and held an election night celebration at the White House, ignoring the time honored tradition of previous presidents not to do so.

– **December 2020** – After the election loss, White House staff had to contend with ten unmasked Trump parties by mid-month, and more were planned.

– **December 2020** – Trump ignored tradition and protocol surrounding the time-honored transition processes after a presidential election. He disappeared from the public for ten days during which more than 3,000 Americans died each day from the pandemic and millions suffered economic consequences. It was also disclosed Russia had penetrated numerous U. S. government computer systems, and still nothing from him except that it wasn't Russia. It was China.

– **December 2020** – Trump and his administration refused to cooperate with President Elect, Joe Biden, or his team on the transition or the inauguration in spite of Biden's desperate plea for coordination, especially on the pandemic.

– **December 23, 2020** – Trump left for Mar-a-Lago without approving a covid relief bill, which millions of citizens and businesses desperately needed. The people be damned. Finally, he did respond when chased down, but he threw a kink in the legislation, which Congress ignored.

OBAMA ENVY—AN OBSESSION

Trump's malignant jealousy of Obama spawned outrageous, destructive behavior that devastated American citizens; our ecosystem, democracy, and reputation in the international community; and the planet.

His unreasonable obsession with Obama—obviously sparked by extreme jealousy—suggests the degree of Trump's troubled mental condition. Intent on undoing everything Obama did, Trump's words, actions, and childish fits signaled a preoccupation with destroying Obama's legacy, rather than with doing the people's business. Trump turned executive order signings from dignified events in to pompous reality shows and public relations opportunities wherein he dramatically and gleefully, like a small child, held up his signature for all to see. Of fifty-eight executive orders, most of them reversed Obama's accomplishments.

Trump was fairly successful in this effort, to the detriment of the country. His actions revealed a disregard for anyone, including his own constituency. Trump left his mark, a sad, sorry one. His actions damaged and hurt people. He didn't care. His jealousy and vindictive, egocentric needs superseded obligations to the country and its citizenry. This was not a president for all Americans.

– **March 30, 2011** – Trump referred to "anonymous sources" in his fourteen-year battle to prove Obama was not born in the U. S. He's incapable of admitting he's wrong. Intent on creating an alternative reality, which he had been successful at doing all his life, he propagates that conspiracy theory to this day in spite of all evidence to the contrary.

– **January 20, 2017** – Immediately after his inauguration, Trump set out to dismantle the Affordable Care Act

(Obamacare), without installing a replacement, which would have left millions of Americans uninsured. He was unsuccessful in spite of his bullying of legislators and throwing fits about it for all four years of his term.

— **January 24, 2017** — Trump championed construction of the Keystone XL and Dakota Access oil pipelines— both blocked by Barack Obama.

— **February 1, 2017** Trump's White House withdrew the Mercury Effluent Rule, an Obama administration regulation assuring the safe use and disposal of mercury. Trace amounts of mercury can harm brain function and damage the nervous system.

— **February 1, 2017** — Trump and House Republicans rolled back an Obama administration regulation requiring petroleum companies to report minerals purchased from foreign governments. This regulation was designed to prevent government corruption.

— **February 2, 2017** — Trump tried to dismantle the Johnson Amendment, a law restricting churches and religious institutions from taking a public political stand while retaining their tax-exempt status. Being unsuccessful, he signed an executive order that provided leniency when enforcing the amendment.

— **February 3, 2017** — Trump rolled back an Obama Communications Commission agreement that provided affordable Internet access to low-income communities.

— **February 7, 2017** — With Trump administration's support, the Republican House eliminated education funds for low-income schools, a rollback of Obama's policies.

– **February 16, 2017** – Through the Congressional Review Act, Trump repealed the "stream protection rule," which prevented coal companies from dumping mining debris into rivers. Obama had implemented the regulation to ensure toxic materials, such as selenium, mercury, and arsenic were not released into rivers.

– **February 20, 2017** – Trump signed an executive order requiring the Bureau of Land Management to lift Obama's coal moratorium on new mining leases on federal lands.

– **February 22, 2017** – Trump signed an executive order halting an Obama administration directive allowing transgender students to use whichever school bathrooms were compatible with their gender identity.

– **February 23, 2017** – Attorney General Sessions announced renewal of contracts with for-profit prisons. This reversed Obama's efforts to phase out privatization of correctional facilities. The number of incarcerated people skyrocketed when private prisons were introduced.

– **March 28, 2017** – Trump signed a bill reversing Fair Pay and Safe Workplace regulations signed by Obama that protected workers against safety hazards.

– **March 30, 2017** – A tie-breaking Senate vote by Vice President Pence passed a bill to withhold federal funding from Planned Parenthood—monies that were in Obama's budget.

– **April 3, 2017** – Trump signed a bill eliminating Obama's rules that required Internet service providers to get consumers' permission before sharing or selling private information.

– **April 4, 2017** – Trump, in cooperation with the GOP, reversed an Obama requirement that employers keep accurate records of employee injuries.

– **April 12, 2017** – Education Secretary, Betsy DeVos, reversed Obama protections designed to help students with student loan payments.

– **April 12, 2017** – Budget Director Mick Mulvaney revealed *a rich people problem* when he proposed cutting spending approved during the Obama term. He said, "Any programs that redistribute money from rich to poor people, such as food stamps and Medicaid, constitute bad spending and misallocation of resources."

– **April 13, 2017** – Trump and a Republican Congress eliminated Obama's rule to automatically enrolled new federal employees in an Individual Retirement Account.

– **April 14, 2017** – Trump signed a bill allowing states to withhold funding from Planned Parenthood.

– **May 1, 2017** – Michelle Obama's "Let Girls Learn" initiative, which educated young women and girls in developing countries, was defunded.

– **May 1, 2017** – The Department of Agriculture terminated Obama standards that promoted healthy school lunches.

– **May 12, 2017** – Attorney General Sessions instructed federal prosecutors to apply mandatory minimum sentences that were against policy during Obama's term. Mandatory sentences caused federal prisoners to increase almost 30 percent in ten years. Trump claimed to be an advocate for prisoners. His actions generally showed otherwise.

– **June 16, 2017** – In a rollback of a signature policy of the Obama's administration, Trump partially reversed open diplomatic ties with Cuba, thereby installing a trade embargo and a ban on tourism.

– **June 16, 2017** – The White House tried to soften a bipartisan bill passed during the Obama administration designed to limit Trump's ability to alter sanctions against Russia for election interference.

– **July 26, 2017** – The Trump administration reversed an Obama rule that would have lowered the salary threshold for eligibility for overtime pay for 4.2 million people.

– **August 20, 2017** – Trump, the White Supremacist in Chief, ended a $400,000 federal grant for Life After Hate, an organization devoted to helping young people escape gangs, white supremacist groups, and Islamic extremist organizations. Originally founded in 2011 by Obama, this task force sought to combat a wide range of violent, extremist ideologies, and it is needed now more than ever.

– **September 5, 2017** – Trump ordered an end to Deferred Action for Childhood Arrivals (DACA), Obama's legislation that protected from deportation nearly 800,000 young people who arrived in the U. S. as children.

– **September 7, 2017** – Education Secretary Betsy DeVos called the Obama administration's Title IX guidelines on campus sexual assault protections a "failed system."

– **September 14, 2017** – Being unsuccessful at eliminating the Affordable Care Act (Obamacare), The Trump administration cut 92 percent of federal funding for the program, including grassroots efforts and communications. This ensured a lack of awareness of the program and how to enroll, which kept people from signing up.

– **September 22, 2017** – DeVos rescinded legal instruction for universities on how to handle allegations of sexual assault. Statistics showed that 1 in 5 women were victims of sexual assault while attending college. The Obama administration had required federally funded schools to improve reactions to such assaults.

– **October 6, 2017** – Trump mandated reversal of Obama's protection of employees' right to employer-provided birth control benefits under employee health care plans. Trump mandated that employers could use religious objection as grounds to withhold birth control benefits.

– **March 5, 2018** – The Trump administration allowed hunters to import African elephant trophies, thereby unleashing entitled, rich, white men on safari. The hunting practice was outlawed by Obama to protect elephants from becoming endangered.

– **March 7, 2018** – Trump and Republicans in the House and Senate used the Congressional Review Act with unprecedented frequency. This act allows the House, which was Republican controlled during Trump's first two years in office, to remove any regulation within sixty days of its enactment. This became the Trump administration's weapon of choice for rolling back Obama regulations. Before Trump, the Congressional Review Act had been used only once. When Trump took office, it was used fifteen times, with dozens more rules proposed for such removal.

– **August 21, 2018** – The Trump administration announced plans to cut back Obama's emission standards for coal burning power plants.

– **May 15, 2019** – Safety rules were changed under Trump that loosened Obama's restrictions enacted after the 2010 Deepwater Horizon explosion in the Gulf of Mexico. These petroleum companies donated substantial money to Trump's re-election campaign, and his changes saved them hundreds of millions of dollars.

– **June 19, 2019** – Under Trump, The Environmental Protection Agency eliminated power-plant regulations in the Affordable Clean Energy Rule enacted under Obama.

– **January 9, 2020** – Trump proposed changes to the National Environmental Policy Act, which allowed federal agencies to bypass environmental consequences of projects.

– **January 21, 2020** – At the World Economic Forum, Trump called climate change activists "prophets of doom."

– **January 23, 2020** – Under Trump, the EPA revised provisions protecting streams, rivers, and wetlands under the Navigable Waters Protection Rule.

– **June 26, 2020** – Trump requested the Supreme Court overturn the Affordable Care Act (Obamacare). This brief was submitted at a time when millions of Americans had lost their jobs and healthcare during the pandemic. No replacement plan existed. The Supreme court ruled against this request.

– **July 29, 2020** – The Supreme Court ruled against Trump administration's efforts to eliminate the DACA program—

which Obama championed. It protected young people from deportation. The Trump administration reacted by blocking new applications to DACA.

— **July 29, 2020** — The Obama fair-housing rule was revoked. Trump wrote on Twitter, "I have rescinded the Obama-Biden AFFH Rule. Enjoy!"

— **August 13, 2020** — The Trump administration EPA eliminated an Obama requirement that oil and gas companies repair methane leaks. This change is projected to result in the release of approximately 850,000 tons of planet-warming methane by the end of the decade.

— **August 13, 2020** — With considerable flair, Trump selectively took up the mantle on shower heads and flushing toilets in response, he said, to Obama administration's rules designed to reduce water usage. His Energy Department proposed eliminating such programs. Trump said at an event in July, as the pandemic raged across the nation, "So shower heads— you take a shower, the water doesn't come out. You want to wash your hands, the water doesn't come out. So what do you do? You just stand there longer or you take a shower longer? Because my hair—I don't know about you, but it has to be perfect. Perfect." Trump, President of the United States, groused at rallies about having to flush a toilet twice. Dignity be damned.

How history will interpret comparisons of the Obama and Trump administrations will most likely center around the outcome of The Trump Pandemic as compared to Obama's handling of the H1N1 and ebola crises. In addition, when it comes to lies and other misinformation, Obama is clearly on the opposite end of the intelligence and integrity spectrum from Trump's plethora of lies and the ridiculous and embarrassing fourth grade communications by The Commander of Tweets.

In spite of everything thrown at him by hostile Republicans, Obama will go down as more respected, more accomplished, and less encumbered from scandal. He inherited a devastating recession while Trump inherited from Obama the best economy in a decade and left it in worse shape for everyone but the most wealthy 1%.

Also, Trump will be forever known as the president who attempted to overthrow the United States government by inciting an insurrection. And, of course, there were two impeachments. His administration and campaign were teeming with criminals and scandal. Being a Nazi enabler, Russian comrade, and fake Christian are distinctions which set Trump apart from Obama and every other president in the history of the nation.

Most likely, Trump's greatest legacy will be his emboldening of extremist groups. In contrast, Obama funded a "Life after Hate" organization to help people exit violent extremist groups. Trump de-funded it. A disturbing documentary, *QAnon: The Search for Q* (on iTunes, Peacock, and *youtube.com*) illustrates the need for the Obama program. If the tide is not turned on the proliferation of extremism, the future is grim for America. Our country deserves better.

My already precarious faith in humanity has been shattered by extremist enthusiasts. No amount of Moscato Asti can soothe me. Every loyal American should worry about malignant extremist movements festering under Trump's leadership and stand against them. They have already sucker punched our country.

DEGRADATION OF
INTERNATIONAL RELATIONS

Betrayal of allies, weird relations with North Korea's Jung-Un and Putin, and the worship of other fascists leaders give away Trump's fascist ambitions. He is impressed by their totalitarian powers. Narcissists tend to admire other narcissists. In addition, his attack on democratic institutions and insults of ally leaders reflect his preference for dictatorships. Support of Nazis, supremacists, racists, and other extremist groups is a strong indication of his crazed dictator ambitions that require his collaboration with our country's worst internal and international enemies.

––––––––––––––

– **January 29, 2017** – Trump was cozy with Saudi Arabia. He ordered a raid in Yemen, a country at war with them. A Navy SEAL and thirty civilians were killed and five American soldiers wounded. U. S. officials and Senator John McCain noted that the raid was ill-advised and that America's interest and objectives in regard to the raid were unclear.

– **February 7, 2017** – The House Administration Committee, led by Republicans, amazingly voted to eliminate the Elections Assistance Commission, the only federal agency responsible for ensuring the integrity of voting machines so they are not hacked in future elections.

– **February 12, 2017** – North Korea fired a ballistic missile. A naive Trump and Japanese Prime Minister Shinzo Abe strategized about the situation in the presence of other diners at an event at Trump's Mar-a-Lago resort.

– February 15, 2017 - The Trump administration stated that Trump aide Mike Flynn did not discuss sanctions against Russia. Flynn later confessed to the FBI he had.

– May 8, 2017 – Trump withdrew the United States from NAFTA, the North American Free Trade Agreement.

– May 25, 2017 – During the NATO Summit in Brussels, Belgium, Trump visibly and rudely pushed world leaders out of the way so he could stand center front for a picture. He stood there, chin up, nose in the air, chest pumped out like a pompous ass ready for his shot as leaders looked on awestruck at this epitome of arrogance.

– June 1, 2017 – Trump withdrew the U. S. from the Paris Agreement. The U. S. and Syria were the only countries to reject the agreement. However, Syria eventually joined it.

– June 5, 2017 – The U. S. Ambassador to China resigned because of Trump's decision to leave the Paris Agreement.

– September 15, 2017 – After a terrorist attack in London, Trump interjected that those responsible were recruited online. British Prime Minister Theresa May corrected him.

– September 19, 2017 – In a speech at the United Nations, Trump called Kim Jong-Un "Rocket Man" and threatened to "totally destroy North Korea."

– October 13, 2017 – Trump announced plans to decertify the deal to curb Iran's nuclear program. The United Kingdom, France, and Germany remained committed.

– November 11, 2017 – Trump increased tensions with North Korea by tweeting, "Why would Kim Jong-Un insult me by calling me 'old,' when I would NEVER call him 'short and fat?' Oh well, I try so hard to be his friend—and maybe someday that will happen!" (It's interesting that Trump would consider calling someone fat.)

— **November 29, 2017** — Trump received worldwide condemnation when he retweeted three anti-Muslim videos from the hate group *Britain First*. UK Prime Minister Theresa May explained, *"Britain First* spreads hate-filled narratives and lies that stoke tensions."

— **January 2, 2018** — Trump tweeted, "North Korean Leader, Kim Jong-Un, just stated the 'Nuclear Button is on his desk at all times.' Will someone from his depleted and food starved regime please inform him that I too have a Nuclear Button, but it is a much bigger & more powerful one than his, and my Button works!"

— **May 8, 2018** — Trump acted on his threat to withdraw the United States from the Iran nuclear deal, a 2015 agreement reached by seven countries after years of negotiations. The deal granted sanction relief to Iran in exchange for its agreement not to develop or acquire nuclear weapons. After withdrawal, Trump reimposed sanctions on Iran.

— **June 9, 2018** — Trump left the 44th G7 international summit early and withdrew the United States' endorsement of a joint communique in which Canada, the U. S., the UK, France, Italy, Japan and Germany agreed on"free, fair, and mutually beneficial trade." The agreement also addressed fighting protectionism. Trump tweeted that Canadian Prime Minister Justin Trudeau was, "very dishonest & meek."

— **July 5, 2018** — In May, after negotiations on trade failed in Beijing, Trump introduced tariffs on $34 billion of Chinese products. China then retaliated with tariffs on U. S. imports. China's Ministry of Commerce charged the United States with launching "the biggest trade war in economic history."

– **August 23, 2018** – The U. S. and China installed a second round of tariffs on $16 billion of imports. China filed a complaint with the World Trade Organization.

– **September 23, 2018** – The U. S. and China Trade War escalated to a third level of tariffs worth a total of $250 billion of Chinese goods imported into the U. S. Tariffs on incoming goods were absorbed by the American people. Tariffs on exports hurt American companies, especially farmers. When China retaliated, the Trump Administration spent billions of taxpayer dollars on subsidies to American farmers to offset losses of crop sales and to assure Republican election support from them in the future.

– **September 25, 2018** – Trump was laughed at when he said in a speech at the United Nations, "In less than two years, my administration has accomplished more than almost any administration in the history of our country." When the audience laughed, Trump added, "So true." Creating his own reality again, he later said, "They weren't laughing at me, they were laughing with me."

– **April 26, 2019** – More than 100 countries agreed to an Arms Trade Treaty to promote peace and end illicit arms trade. At a NRA convention, Trump announced the U. S. would withdraw from that agreement.

– **June 25, 2019** – After the U. S. imposed sanctions against Iran's Supreme Leader Ayatollah Ali Khamenei, Trump increased tensions by posting a tweet, "Any attack by Iran on anything American will be met with great and overwhelming force. In some areas, overwhelming will mean obliteration."

– **August 2, 2019** – Trump withdrew the U. S. from a Cold War agreement with Russia—the Intermediate-Range Nuclear Forces Treaty, which limited the types of weapons the nations could possess. This change, favorable to Russia, could have unfortunate long-term repercussions for America.

– **September 1, 2019** – Trump's administration implemented 15 per cent tariffs on $112 billion of Chinese imports. More American consumers had to absorb more costs, and the trade deficit soared to $679 billion by 2021, a twelve-year high.

– **November 4, 2019** – Trump pulled the U. S. out of the Paris Agreement on climate change. Of 197 countries, 189 had ratified the agreement. This put the U. S. in the same league as other non-signers: Iran, Iraq, Angola, and Libya.

– **January 4, 2020** – Trump said if Iran retaliated for an American airstrike that killed their general Suleimani, the U. S. would target 52 sites "important to Iran & the Iranian culture. . .and HIT [them] VERY FAST AND VERY HARD." Targeting sites of cultural significance is in opposition to the 1954 Hague Convention as well as the Department of Defense's "Law of War" manual.

– **January 31, 2020** – Trump cancelled participation in the Mine Ban Treaty, an agreement that prohibited the use of anti-personnel landmines anywhere in the world.

Immediately after his inauguration, Biden and his administration began mending relations with foreign countries and reestablishing connections with allies and international organizations. And the world breathed.

THE SUBVERSION OF DEMOCRACY

In a quest for power, Trump set out to destroy the architecture of United States' institutions and, ultimately, American democracy. One tactic he used to do so was to put people in key positions in his administration who were committed to dismantling the government organizations to which they were appointed. These people were purposely selected because they were unqualified, incompetent, or in opposition to the missions of the organizations they led.

He also carelessly awarded positions to family, donors, loyalists, and lobbyists without consideration of qualifications. There were little or no vetting processes for appointments, and it is a challenge to find anyone in his administration qualified for their appointed post. If they were capable, he neutered them, and they were eventually fired, or they left. His reach was wide.

Additionally, Trump and his greedy spawn and cronies strategized to plunder the Federal Treasury, the country's resources, and its people. The antics of his team began with the corrupt 2017 inauguration event and continued until he was out of office. The scope of this corruption did considerable damage around the world.

Trump also endeavored to diminish public trust in the intelligence community. He used *loaded language* by giving them the negative tag of "the deep state." He attacked, fired staff, and put forth conspiracy theories. His reasons were twofold: (1) fear of agency investigations into Russian election tampering and conflicts of interest, and (2) fear of these agencies interfering with his ambitions to become the authoritarian leader of the country.

Aspiring to be a dictator, Trump showed blatant disregard for the values, mores, and institutions of the United States. His unbounded hypocrisy was staggering. With an uncanny ability to persuade followers to act against their own best interests, he used distraction and distorted emotional and political dogma to manipulate and pillage. This strategy fostered preparedness for deconstruction of the government in his second term so he could stay in power.

– **February 27, 2017** – Under Trump, Attorney General Sessions determined the Voting Rights Act—a landmark federal legislation that protected equal voting rights for all Americans—was "an intrusive act." The Justice Department dropped this long-standing law, opening up opportunities for a plethora of laws and regulations that prevent citizens from voting.

– **March 3, 2017** – Rather than banning lobbyists from official offices entirely, as Obama had done, the Trump White House welcomed such visitors and eliminated the policy previous presidents had followed of keeping a daily visit sign-in record. This change made access by lobbyists, special interests, and opportunists covert. Also, former lobbyists were hired for internal staff positions in agencies they had lobbied against. These acts violated ethics rules.

– **March 3, 2017** – Trump eliminated an ethics course for White House staff that instructed new staffers on ethical methods of interaction with Congress, private companies, and officials. The Trump administration showed no respect for ethical boundaries honored by previous presidents.

– **March 7, 2017** – To fund the border wall with Mexico, Trump considered cutting the budget for airport security and the Coast Guard.

– March 15, 2017 – Trump's first Executive Order travel ban of Muslim countries had been struct down in court. U. S. District Judge Derek ruled against Trump's second travel ban, saying it was derived from "religious animus," and its purpose was "to disfavor a particular religion."

– March 28, 2017 – Trump sought to slash $18 billion of federal funding for mental health support, foreign aid, and public housing and to funnel those funds to military spending and the border wall.

– March 16, 2017 – Trump's budget proposal included a twenty percent budget cut to the National Institutes of Health—an agency that funded medical research. The dean of Baylor's biomedical research school responded that the proposed cuts would bring American biomedical science to a standstill, leaving our country vulnerable to pandemics and other medical crises.

– April 2, 2017 – A Kentucky federal judge ruled Trump may have incited violence against protesters at his 2016 campaign rally in Kentucky.

– April 4, 2017 – In a blatant assumption of power, Attorney General Sessions put consent decrees on permanent hold. These decrees allowed federal officials to institute criminal justice reform in situations in the country where police misconduct occurred, such as in Ferguson, Missouri. This included requiring body cameras for police officers, a police training program on racial bias, and establishment of a Civilian Review Board to independently review claims of excessive police force.

– April 6, 2017 – To break a Democratic filibuster in the Senate, Republicans altered a well-established Senate voting procedure to force confirmation of Trump's Supreme Court nominee, Neil Gorsuch. Before the change, Senate rules required 60 votes to confirm a new justice. With the change, Republicans were able to overcome Democratic objections with only 51 votes.

– **April 7, 2017** – An anonymous Twitter user, perhaps a government employee, had been critical of Trump. The Department of Homeland Security ordered Twitter to reveal private information on him. Twitter refused, and filed a lawsuit. DHS then dropped the request.

– **April 24, 2017** – The Anti-Defamation League reported that six month into Trump's administration, anti-Semitic attacks rose 86 percent, including bomb threats, assaults, and grave desecrations. Nazis, white supremacist, racist, and other extremist group memberships and activities also increased.

– **April 24, 2017** – Trump ordered White House aides to draft a tax plan to slash the corporate tax rate from 35% to 21%. Many corporations pay no taxes and nothing was done to close those loopholes. Trump told his aides cutting taxes for businesses must take priority over decreasing the federal deficit, which escalated from $19.92 trillion when he took office to $27.72 trillion when his term was up. Still, Trump bragged about the economy, one of many efforts to create his own reality.

– **April 26, 2017** – Trump criticized the 9th Circuit Court for blocking efforts to deny federal funding for "sanctuary cities" and threatened to break up the three-judge panel.

– **April 30, 2017** – Trump demonstrated a fascination with fascist leaders. He invited the authoritarian leader of the Philippines, Rodrigo Duterte, to the White House.

According to a Human Rights Watch group, Duterte's death squads carried out more than 12,000 murders of citizens who were supposedly drug dealers and users. After the meeting, Trump said the pair had a "great relationship."

– **May 2, 2017** – Trump railed against constraints on his power. He called the U. S. system of checks and balances between legislative, executive, and judicial branches an "archaic" system. He said, "Maybe at some point we'll have to take those rules on, because, for the good of the nation, things are going to have to be different." That might be good for Trump, but it would not be good for the nation.

– **May 2, 2017** – Trump tweeted that the country needed a good government 'shutdown'. Back when Democrats held the Senate, he suggested rules should be changed in order to lower the number of votes needed by Republicans to break a filibuster. Later, with Republicans in control of the Senate, he never mentioned this prospect again.

– **May 9, 2017** – Trump fired FBI Director James Comey, leader of a federal investigation into Trump's potential collusion with Russia during the 2016 election. Trump didn't advise Comey, who learned of his dismissal while speaking to a crowd of Bureau agents. Contrary to his image on *The Apprentice*, Trump was a coward when it came to firing. He either did it by tweet or had someone else do it.

– **May 10, 2017** – Trump told the Russian Ambassador and the Russian Foreign Minister to the United States, "I just fired the head of the FBI. He was crazy, a real nut job... I faced great pressure because of Russia. That's taken off."

– **May 11, 2017** – In an interview, Trump admitted he had the Russia investigation on his mind when he fired FBI

Director Comey. He said, "And, in fact, when I decided to just do it, said to myself, I said: This Russia thing with Trump and Russia is a made-up story, it's an excuse by the Democrats for having lost an election that they should've won."

– **May 12, 2017** – After Sarah Sanders, Sean Spicer, and President Trump each gave conflicting reasons for Trump dismissing James Comey, Trump tweeted, "Maybe the best thing to do is cancel all future "press briefings" and hand out written responses for the sake of accuracy????"

– **May 12, 2017** – Trump tweeted, "James Comey better hope that there are no "tapes" of our conversations before he starts leaking to the press!" After that tweet, Comey was quoted as responding, "Lordy, I hope there are tapes."

– **May 12, 2017** – Trump foolishly shared classified and highly sensitive information with the Russian foreign minister and Russian ambassador at a White House meeting. This jeopardized the identity of an intelligence source that had infiltrated the Islamic State. A U. S. official said Trump "revealed more information to the Russian Ambassador than we've shared with our own allies."

– **May 31, 2017** – The White House granted ethics waivers to seventeen senior officials, including Kellyanne Conway and Steve Bannon. The waivers allowed Bannon to interact with Breitbart News. Conway was allowed to interact with lobbyists and private clients.

– **August 1, 2017** – The Trump campaign selected white nationalist William Johnson to serve as a California delegate for the next presidential election.

– **August 2, 2017** – Secretary of State Rex Tillerson decided not to spend the $60 million allocated to the

State Department for battling foreign propaganda (disinformation campaigns from countries like Russia and China). R. C. Hammond, Tillerson's aide, suggested this decision was because the Trump administration was concerned about offending the Russians.

− **August 12, 2017** − During the "Unite the Right" rally in Charlottesville, Nazis and Ku Klux Klan members carried tiki torches and shouted slogans including, "The Jews Will Not Replace Us." James Fields, Jr., a white nationalist, drove his car into a crowd of counter-protesters, killing Heather Heyer and injuring nineteen. Trump refused to rebuke the white nationalists, revealing publicly his loyalty to that group. Instead, he placed partial blame for Field's attack on the counter-protesters themselves.

− **August 14, 2017** − After Trump refused to condemn a Virginia white nationalist rally, Kenneth Frazier, African American CEO of Merck Pharmaceuticals, resigned from the American Manufacturing Council. He said, "America's leaders must honor our fundamental values by clearly rejecting hatred, bigotry, and group supremacy, which run counter to the American ideal that all people are created equal."

− **August 15, 2017** − At a news conference about the white supremacists rally in Virginia, Trump doubled down and said, "There were very fine people on both sides" of the violence. This may have been when many Americans realized they had voted for a white supremacist enabler.

− **August 15, 2017** − After more CEOs resigned from his American Manufacturing Council, Trump said he had executives waiting to take their place. He tweeted, "For every CEO that drops out of the Manufacturing Council, I have many to take their place." Perhaps not.

– **August 16, 2017** – Without explanation, Trump abruptly dissolved the American Manufacturing Council as well as the Strategy & Policy Forum, tweeting only "thank you all!"

– **November 2, 2017** – When asked about the number of vacant leadership positions in the State Department, Trump responded, "I'm the only one that matters, because when it comes to it, that's what the policy is going to be. You've seen that, you've seen it strongly."

– **January 29, 2018** – The Anti-Defamation League reported that white Supremacist propaganda on college campuses tripled in 2017—Trump's first year in office.

– **January 31, 2018** – Trump's State of the Union Address generated public praise from white supremacists, including David Duke and Richard Spencer.

– **March 3, 2018** – Chinese President Xi Jinping altered the Chinese constitution to abolish term limits, allowing him to retain power indefinitely. Trump said, "[Xi's] now president for life. President for life. . .I think it's great. Maybe we'll have to give that a shot someday."

– **March 4, 2018** – The State Department was issued $120 million to combat Russian election meddling. With midterm elections looming, none of the funds had been spent.

– **May 25, 2018** – Trump signed executive orders related to federal employees. J. David Cox, Sr., of the American Federation of Government Employees said, "President Trump's executive orders do nothing to help federal workers do their jobs better. In fact, they do the opposite by depriving workers of their rights to address and resolve workplace issues such as sexual harassment, racial discrimination, retaliation against whistleblowers, improving workplace health and safety, enforcing reasonable accommodations for workers with disabilities, and more."

– **July 15, 2018** – Trump sided with Putin over American intelligence at a joint press conference in Helsinki. Asked about Russian collusion in the 2016 election, Trump said, "They said they think it's Russia; I have President Putin, he just said it's not Russia. I will say this: I don't see any reason why it would be. I have great confidence in my intelligence people, but I will tell you that President Putin was extremely strong and powerful in his denial today." This comment caused quite a stir in the U. S. since it reinforced that Trump was a Russian asset.

– **September 19, 2018** – When interviewed by *The Hill,* Trump criticized Attorney General Sessions for recusing himself from the Russian investigation. "I don't have an attorney general. It's very sad," Trump said. He called Sessions "weak" and "disloyal." Trump demands total loyalty and did not accept that the Attorney General was accountable to the American people to protect the constitution rather than being an employee there to protect the president from scandal.

– **December 17, 2019** – Trump denounced his impeachment as "an unprecedented and unconstitutional abuse of power." He said those accused in the Salem witch trials were afforded more due process than him. He forbade his administration and staff to participate in the process, nor did he do so.

– **December 23, 2019** – Rudy Giuliani admitted involvement in removing the U. S. Ukrainian Ambassador Marie Yovanovitch from office after she refused to cooperate in a smear campaign against Biden. "I believed I needed Yovanovitch out of the way," Giuliani told *The New Yorker*. "She was going to make investigations difficult for everybody." Giuliani most likely "took one" for Trump by admitting this.

– **December 28, 2019** – Trump violated the requirement that whistleblowers remain anonymous. He brazenly retweeted a post containing the name of an alleged whistleblower whose complaint had sparked his impeachment inquiry.

– **February 7, 2020** – After the Senate's failed to convict the president once the House impeached him, Trump retaliated by firing the U. S. European Union Ambassador Gordon Sondland and Lt. Col. Alexander Vindman who testified in the House impeachment trial.

– **September 1, 2020** – Per Stephanie Winston Wolkoff, a former senior adviser to Melania Trump, the first lady used private email accounts while in the White House. Trump had said many times his opponent, Hillary Clinton, should have been imprisoned for using a private email server.

– **September 10, 2020** – The Trump administration secretly withheld about $4 million from a program dedicated to helping New York City first responders who suffered from illnesses related to the September 11 terrorist attacks. Public reaction was swift once this was discovered.

– **October 19, 2020** – Republicans in the Senate refused to consider Obama's nomination of Merrick Garland for the Supreme Court in 2016 "because Obama was *eleven months* from the end of his term." Republicans reversed direction and ignored that precedent and allowed Trump to nominate Amy Coney Barrett in 2020 *three months* from the end of his term—a double standard, indeed.

– **November 5, 2020** – *The Washington Post's* FactChecker Glenn Kessler reported Trump told 29,508 lies with 4,000 in October of 2020 alone. In one day, November 2, before the Presidential election, he and his cohorts told 504 falsehoods. Indications are his cult members believed them all.

– **January 24, 2021** – Glenn Kessler, *The Washington Post* fact checker, revealed Trump made 30,573 false statements during his term. This included 6 per day in his first year, 16 per day in his second, 22 in his third, and 39 in his fourth.

Trump and his supporters implemented a sustained effort to attack our country's democracy. On January 6, 2021, he incited an insurrection to hunt down and kill legislators and the Vice President to overturn an election. He will never abandon his quest for unlimited power. He will never go away. Americans cannot just move on now that Trump is out of office. Unless Republican leaders acknowledge the future threats from this cunning, diabolical power monger and act accordingly, our country and their party are in serious jeopardy.

Without a doubt, the insurrection would not have happened without Trump. A Senate conviction with a resolution to prevent Trump from running for office again would have secured democracy. Why wouldn't Republicans do that? Are they afraid a vindictive Trump will prevent their re-election? Are they loyal to religion over country? Are they members of *The Family* who consider Trump an imperfect leader, but their powerful, "chosen" Wolf King? Did they simply lose their moral compass? Or were they co-conspirators? Who knows? The Senate impeachment trial suggests: If you ever commit a crime, you better hope the people who helped you are on the jury.

APPOINTMENTS INTENDED TO DESTROY INSTITUTIONS

Strangely, assuring conflict of interest between appointees and the institutions they led was standard practice in the Trump administration. The primary criteria for appointments was loyalty and financial contributions to Trump and, in many cases, a willingness to disrupt, destroy, or plunder financially and administratively the institutions to which appointees were assigned. This was in line with Trump advisor Steven Bannon's strategy of deconstruction of the administrative state. He is a propagandist who champions radical, disruptive social change as a path to fascism.

Many appointees lacked experience and were ill equipped to effectively administer the business of the agencies to which they were assigned. Most had no experience in government or in the fields for which they were responsible. Lobbyists, family members, loyal friends, and campaign donors were given key positions. Competency was not a requirement; vetting processes were nonexistent.

Conflicts of interest were common. *The Daily Beast* reported that 63 Trump appointees had lobbied actively in the industries they were to oversee, and 11 received direct payments from companies in the industries they were to regulate. The Republican Senate approved the nominations anyway.

Following are some of the many situations where Trump selected people (and the Republican Senate approved them) who were not qualified or who were ideologically opposed to the missions of those organizations. They were prepared to disrupt and even dismantle them. Citizens watched in disbelief as purveyors of deconstruction were installed in positions of power. As frightening as this was, the real damage would have occurred if

Trump had won a second term, at which time his pack could attack institutions with abandon.

———————————

– **February 29, 2017** – Of the 341 nominations for government positions made by Trump, 63 had actively lobbied in the industries they were to oversee. And 11 received payments from companies in the industries they were to regulate.

– **February 2017** – Rick Perry, ex-governor of Texas, a denier of global warming and a proponent of coal and oil, was selected for Secretary of Energy. When running for president twice, he repeatedly proposed eliminating the Department of Energy. He resigned this position in 2019 after being sucked into the Ukraine impeachment situation.

– **February 17, 2017** – Trump chose Betsy DeVos for Secretary of Education. She had no experience in government, education, or public schools, but had made generous donations to the Trump campaign. Proving to be a champion of religious education, she severely disadvantaged public schools. Federal funds intended for public education were funneled to private and religious schools.

– **March 2, 2017** – The Senate confirmed Ben Carson, a retired neurosurgeon and loyal Trump supporter, as the new Secretary of the Department of Housing and Urban Development. The department's budget of about $30 billion supports public housing for around 2.1 million people. Carson had no experience in governing or overseeing an organization on the scale of HUD, nor had he ever worked in any capacity on urban development or housing.

– **April 14, 2017** – Candice Jackson, who criticized Stanford University for a tutoring program that helped minorities, was appointed by Betsy DeVos as acting head of the department's Office of Civil Rights.

– **May 2, 2017** – Trump appointed Teresa Manning, a former anti-abortion activist, to lead Title X for the Department of Health and Human Services. This program allocates funds for family planning for America's low-income citizens. Manning was a lobbyist for the National Right to Life Committee, the nation's oldest and largest pro-life, anti-abortion organization.

– **June 15, 2017** – Trump selected Lynne Patton, an event planner who planned golf events and Eric Trump's wedding, to run federal housing for New York City. Patton would control a multi-billion-dollar budget to manage housing for thousands of New Yorkers.

– **June 21, 2017** – Department of Education Secretary Betsy DeVos selected the CEO of a private student loan company to lead the Federal Student Aid program, which handles $1.3 trillion in federal student loans.

– **June 30, 2017** – For senior adviser in the Office of Gender Equality and Women's Empowerment, Trump appointed activist, Bethany Kozma, a woman who led a campaign to restrict transgenders access to bathrooms.

– **September 4, 2017** – Trump appointed Representative Jim Bridenstine to lead NASA. Bridenstine said repeatedly he doesn't believe humans cause climate change. Among NASA's projects were twenty-seven missions that monitored climate change. Bridenstine had been a Navy pilot, had run Tulsa's Air and Space Museum, and had served on the House Science, Space, and Tech Committee, but he had no other credentials related to science or space and had no experience administering such a massive organization.

– **October 4, 2017** – EPA director Scott Pruitt's schedule showed he held many meetings with oil lobbyists, automobile executives, and other industry leaders, while making almost no time for environmental advocates. He immediately and aggressively set about reversing Obama administration policies, especially those related to the environment. He also advanced policies favorable to the oil, gas, coal, chemical, and manufacturing industries.

– **October 5, 2017** – Trump nominated Andrew Wheeler, a coal lobbyist and legal counsel for the largest coal mining companies in America, to the second most powerful position at the Environmental Protection Agency.

– **October 13, 2017** – Trump selected climate change skeptic, Kathleen Hartnett White, for chair of the Council on Environmental Quality. She wrote: "Whether emitted from the human use of fossil fuels or as a natural (and necessary) gas in the atmosphere surrounding the earth, carbon dioxide has none of the attributes of a pollutant."

– **November 2, 2017** – Trump nominated Sam Clovis, a former radio host and Trump campaign aide, for chief scientist at the Department of Agriculture. Clovis had almost no scientific or agricultural experience. He taught Business Administration at Iowa's Morningside College. Later, Clovis bowed out of consideration after contacts with Russia swept him into Robert Mueller's investigation.

– **November 2, 2017** – When criticized for the fact that seventy-five percent of State Department positions remained unfilled, Trump said, "I'm the only one that matters, because when it comes to it, that's what the policy is going to be. You've seen that, you've seen it strongly."

‒ **November 8, 2017** ‒ Trump appointed Eric Trump's brother-in-law chief of staff at the Department of Energy.

‒ **January 30, 2018** ‒ Brenda Fitzgerald, Trump's appointee for Director of the Center for Disease Control, profited from investments in the tobacco industry.

‒ **March 2, 2018** ‒ William G. Otis, Trump's appointee for the Sentencing Commission, which sets policy for punishing federal prisoners, had supported abolishing the agency. He also had a history of making racially charged statements.

‒ **March 8, 2018** ‒ The AP reported one-third of 59 people appointed to the EPA had ties to fossil fuel companies as registered lobbyists. And some were lawyers or associates of chemical manufacturers.

‒ **July 5, 2018** ‒ Trump appointed Andrew Wheeler Deputy Administrator of the EPA. A lobbyist and critic of limits on greenhouse gas emissions, he was a supporter of fossil fuels. In March 2018, Wheeler complained to CNN that the EPA was "brainwashing our kids."

‒ **March 8, 2019** ‒ Trump nominated David Bernhardt to Secretary of Interior, a role responsible for the conservation and management of federal lands and natural resources. As a former oil lobbyist, Bernhardt had been a champion of rolling back protections of endangered species.

‒ **August 17, 2020** ‒ Trump appointed Louis DeJoy as Postmaster General in spite of conflicts of interest. And DeJoy had donated $1.2 million to Trump's election campaign.

‒ **September 14, 2020** ‒ The Environmental Protection Agency had recognized carbon dioxide as a greenhouse gas and an air pollutant for many years. Trump removed Michael Kuperberg, head of the program, and replaced him with David Legates, a climate-change skeptic who wrote: "carbon dioxide is plant food and is not a pollutant."

– November 2020 – A lame duck after losing the election, Trump made the most bizarre appointments of all in regard to destroying institutions. He blatantly and provocatively appointed two white supremacists to government roles: Preservation of Holocaust Museums and the Preservation of American's Heritage abroad. And he says he doesn't kid.

Deliberately impairing established institutions—especially political, educational, and messaging ones—is a powerful tool brainwashers use to assure another set can be installed in their place. This is the stealth approach to thought control as opposed to a coercive one. Since this process is covert, followers—who have already been influenced to not question their charismatic leader's actions —go along without any thought of what might fill the resulting void. In a political situation, that is the path to totalitarianism, which requires a compliant public.

To preserve our nation's institutions, citizens must challenge any person or organization destroying it. An awareness of methods used to accomplish that destruction is vital to maintaining our democracy. Compliance and complicity are not options.

America came precariously close to becoming an authoritarian state like many across the world that have *fake elections*. By discrediting our election, Trump sought an unfettered second term, during which he would have unleashed a wave of demolition. By the end of that term, he might have mustered an extremist army and gained enough power and influence to realize his fascist goals.

AUTHORITARIAN AMBITIONS

Narcissists are known for grandiose ambitions, and are undisciplined about keeping thoughts to themselves. It's wise to take Trump at his word when he suggests becoming the authoritarian, permanent leader of the country.

If his behavior as President was not enough to conclude Trump wanted to destroy democracy, consider his fascination with and admiration of facist leaders. His relationships with them contrasted sharply with his lack of respect for democratic leaders, whom he called weak. He made it clear with whom he wished to align himself—dictator role models, many from countries that held fake elections.

Trump's pattern of challenging the Constitution, laws, regulations, and traditions of the United States was well established, and Republican Congressmen supported him. He respected no boundaries, repeatedly claimed "total authority," and bristled over limits or restrictions of power. He surrounded himself with "yes men," and demanded unconditional loyalty, although he did not give it. This culture was so prominent in his world, it even infected doctors who sold out their ethics and fawned over him. Ethical staff coped by "yessing" him, but not following through.

Trump had no understanding of the Constitution or regard for government. He constantly undermined requirements, probably both intentionally and out of ignorance. Reporting by the press and backlash from politicians and loyal government employees were the only things standing between him and absolute control.

Trump—foolishly transparent about what was going on in his mind—telegraphed his intentions. Following are just a few of his comments that signal his aspiration to be the authoritarian leader of the United States of America. Some of them are redundant but are repeated here to emphasis this point.

Trump talked openly about getting rid of the two-term limitation for president.

After Chinese President Xi Jinping successfully abolished term limits, Trump said, "[Xi's] now president for life. President for life. . .Maybe we'll have to give that a shot someday."

Trump said, "When somebody is the president of the United States, the authority is total, and that's the way it's got to be." Constitutional experts and governors disagreed.

At a press briefing, Trump threatened to adjourn the House and Senate in order to make appointments without approval. He said, "If the House will not agree to that adjournment, I will exercise my constitutional authority to adjourn both chambers of Congress. Perhaps it's never been done before, nobody is even sure if it has, but we're going to do it."

Several times Trump used the pandemic to justify staying in office. He proposed cancelling the 2020 election, leaving him in power for who knows how long. The president has no power to cancel an election or he surely would have done so.

Trump tweeted, "With all of the Fake News coming out of NBC and the Networks, at what point is it appropriate to challenge their Licenses?"

Trump referred to the system of checks and balances between the legislative, executive, and judicial branches as an "archaic" system. He said, "Maybe at some point we'll have to take those rules on, because, for the good of the nation, things are going to have to be different."

Trump said repeatedly he might not accept the results of the 2020 presidential election—if he loses. Once he lost, he kept his word and refused to accept the election results.

Trump predicted many times the 2020 presidential election would be rigged. Delegitimizing elections before they happened positioned him to claim the presidency permanently. Accustomed to creating his own reality, he predicted, "The only way we're going to lose this election is if the election is rigged."

By his actions after the 2020 election, it is clear that, in his authoritarian mindset, Trump considered himself the determiner of whether or not it was rigged—that neither evidence nor the electoral authority of other institutions applied.

Trump said if he lost the election, he wouldn't commit to a peaceful transfer of power. "Well, we're going to have to see what happens," he said. What happened was he lost by more than 7 million popular votes and 77 electoral votes (the same spread as the 2016 election he won), but he refused to give up the presidency or assist in the transition of power.

Instead of conceding, in the post-election transition period, he instigated an all-out attempt to steal the election by inciting an insurrection at the Capitol by his extremist followers while he ripped them off for more than $300 million in donations and then betrayed them.

Trump's blatant actions—corruption, attacks on the press, destroying government institutions, unwillingness to accept election defeat, and disregard for the rule of law and the Constitution—supported his pursuit of a grandiose dream of becoming an authoritarian leader of this country.

Dr. Kathleen Taylor said, "Often the degree to which freedom is trumpeted reflects the degree to which it is actually being restricted." Trump told the crowd gathered to raid the Capitol on January 6, 2021, they were fighting for their freedom when they were really fighting for his totalitarian rule. When he was tried for inciting the insurrection, he denied these followers and abandoned those who encountered criminal legal actions.

Trump's toxic mix of grandiose arrogance and ignorance is why he believes he should be in charge. He said: "It would take an hour-and-a-half to learn everything there is to know about missiles....I think I know most of it anyway." John Kelly tried to get him to consult with generals, but Trump said, "I know more than anybody else."

Consider this scenario. If a run for president in 2024 is not viable, Trump will run for governor of Florida, entice followers (voters) to join him there, win the election, establish cohorts in key positions, amass an army of extremists, take over the government as an authoritarian leader, install his goons in positions of power, and seek Florida's succession from the Union. Members of his family will show up in politics to carve out a piece of his power pie. He can then be the autocratic leader of his own little kingdom.

If you consider this outrageous, just look at his past nefarious behavior. One thing is certain. Trump won't go away. His narcissistic cravings, vindictiveness addiction, and histrionic and insatiable need for pity, attention, and power are impulses not to be controlled—or denied.

ATTACKS ON THE FREE PRESS

The free press is known as the Fourth Estate because of its independence from the three government branches—executive, legislative, and judicial. The press is protected in the constitution and has an obligation to inform on political issues and to advocate for the public through news and the media. This includes the duty to uncover corruption. To be in control, authoritarian leaders depend on controlling all public communications. In America, the free press is what prevents this from happening.

Trump made every effort to control or to destroy the free press in this country. He controlled Fox News, Breitbart, Sinclair, and numerous other radical right-wing channels, as well as social media and evangelistic outlets. The mainstream U. S. press, however, was having none of his interference in their reporting, Their commitment to the truth played a key role in preserving our democracy as Trump tinkered wildly with reality through media messaging.

Trump, constantly frustrated with his inability to control messaging in the free press, lashed out with a vengeance. While right-wing broadcasting organizations regularly disseminated his propaganda, which was outrageously sold as "no spin," Trump could not manage the free press. So he used loaded language—the label of *fake news*—to discredit them. Many people bought it, which is a testament to the effectiveness of indoctrination processes propagated by radical right-wing cult strategists.

Throughout his term, Trump rarely participated in press conferences as previous presidents had done. Not being quick on his feet, he was so incompetent that he became confrontational and rude to objective news sources while favoring right-wing ones who pandered to him. He preferred to communicate directly with the public through tweets and rallies where he could "perform" to adoring crowds and satisfy his urge for attention and crowd worship while spewing unchallenged lies with abandon.

As President of the United States, Trump turned politics into a reality show. Performing was his forte. Administration and governance were not. Not competent in either of these two areas, he bungled his way through.

– **February 17, 2017** – In what was a constant attack on the free press, Trump tweeted: "The FAKE NEWS media (failing @nytimes, @NBCNews, @ABC, @CBS, @CNN) is not my enemy, it is the enemy of the American People!"

– **February 24, 2017** - At a Conservative Political Action Conference, Trump declared major media outlets "FAKE NEWS." Press Secretary, Sean Spicer, barred the *New York Times*, CNN, and *Politico* from White House briefings while Fox News and Breitbart News were allowed.

– **February 25, 2017** – Trump announced he wouldn't attend the White House Correspondents' Dinner. The last president to skip the dinner was Ronald Reagan, who was recovering from an attempted assassination.

– **February 28, 2017** – To stop a long string of press leaks, Trump approved a rule allowing White House senior staff to examine cell phones of White House workers. Aides and junior staffers were required to relinquish mobile devices to be searched. Spicer forbade staffers to speak to the press about this; however, the story was leaked to the press.

– **May 9, 2017** – Dan Heyman, a West Virginia journalist, was arrested after questioning Health and Human Services Secretary Tom Price. As a result, Heyman spent seven hours in jail for "willful disruption of governmental processes." Later, a state prosecutor found Heyman broke no laws and refused to prosecute him.

– **August 22, 2017** – During an Arizona rally, Trump blamed the American news media for vehement public reactions to a white supremacist "Unite the Right" rally. He declared, "It's time to expose the crooked media deceptions... the only people giving a platform to these hate groups is the media itself and the fake news."

– **October 5, 2017** – Because of a lack of understanding of duties of the Senate Intelligence Committee or perhaps in an attempt to deflect attention from the Russia investigation, Trump tweeted, "Why Isn't the Senate Intel Committee looking into the Fake News Networks in OUR country to see why so much of our news is just made up-FAKE!"

– **October 11, 2017** – Trump threatened the broadcasting licenses of NBC and other media stations, saying on Twitter, "With all of the Fake News coming out of NBC and the Networks, at what point is it appropriate to challenge their License? Bad for country!"

– **November 27, 2017** – Trump tweeted, "We should have a contest as to which the Networks, plus CNN and not including Fox, is the most dishonest, corrupt and/or distorted in its political coverage of your favorite President (me). They are all bad. Winner to receive the FAKE NEWS TROPHY!"

– **December 20, 2017** – As of this date, Trump had tweeted about "fake news" or "fake media" 176 times—on average, once every two days for a year.

– **January 2, 2018** – After months of lambasting journalists, attacking the press, and calling their reporting "fake news," Trump suggested in a tweet there should be "THE MOST DISHONEST & CORRUPT MEDIA AWARDS OF THE YEAR," where "subjects will cover Dishonesty & Bad Reporting in various categories from the Fake News Media."

– **July 17, 2020** – Press reporters revealed Federal officers in military gear descended on Portland, Oregon, wounding demonstrators and taking some away in unmarked vans. Governor Brown called the arrests "a blatant abuse of power." Trump defended their actions and said of the protestors, "These are not protesters. These people are anarchists. These are people that hate our country. And we're not going to let it go forward." Trump tweeted similarly about other protests. He endorsed white supremacists and radical groups' protests and their attacking peaceful protesters, inciting riots, and engaging in property destruction, which he blamed on Democrats. The press called him out.

Trump's ineptitude is the primary cause of his many failures in business and politics. He didn't even engineer his Presidential victory. The press exposed the delusion of his capabilities. As Pulitzer Prize winning author David Cay Johnson said in *The Making of Donald Trump* and *It's Even Worse than You Think,* Trump told people what they wanted to hear while picking their pockets. The free press —the anchor that defends the Constitution and protects democracy—stood between our government and an aspiring, nefarious, fascist maniac; his self-serving cohorts; and a mass of manipulated, subjugated victim followers. And democracy as we know it held. The Fourth Estate of our government prevailed as we stood on the precipice of losing our freedoms and values.

ATTACKS ON SCIENCE
AND THE ENVIRONMENT

(See "Obama Envy—an Obsession" for more instances of such attacks.)

With no respect for science or preservation of the environment, Trump strategically placed individuals in charge of science, health, environment, and education agencies who were opposed to policies and missions of those organizations. Appointments rewarded unqualified family members, cronies, and donors who were charged with ravaging and desecrating the very organizations they should have protected and nurtured.

Why would Trump do this? The approach is consistent with his advisor Steve Bannon's philosophy of government, which included destruction of institutions and destabilization of the government structure in order to rebuild it with a fascist government. Bannon's approach to government was "to smash things." And smash them Trump did. So much so that, no doubt, with a second term, he would have been postured to destroy democracy as we know it.

— **February 16, 2017** — Department of Agriculture staff were furnished a list of terms they could no longer use in scientific research, such as "climate change."

— **February 27, 2017** — In his proposed budget, Trump increased defense and security spending by $54 billion and cut spending on science, education, poverty, and the environment by nearly the same amount. Even with this defense funding, his housecleaning of the Department of Homeland Security left the country vulnerable and him free to collaborate with Russia and whatever else.

– **March 3, 2017** – Trump's budget significantly cut the National Oceanic and Atmospheric Administration (NOAA) budget and de-funded programs that monitored climate change.

– **March 9, 2017** – Environmental Protection Agency Administrator Scott Pruitt stated he didn't believe carbon dioxide was a primary contributor to global warming. This statement contradicted substantial scientific evidence, here and world-wide, which included EPA studies that determined carbon emissions were a leading cause of global warming.

– **April 5, 2017** – Under the EPA proposed budget, a program that educated the public on the dangers of lead exposure and trained construction workers how to remove toxic lead-based paints was cut.

– **April 14, 2017** – EPA Administrator Scott Pruitt announced the U. S. should withdraw from the Paris Agreement—a global initiative to address climate change. About 200 countries signed the Agreement.

– **April 28, 2017** – The EPA removed or altered all information about climate change on its website and other public information sources and added the anti-global warming views of Trump's administration.

– **May 8, 2017** – The EPA announced it would not continue employment for half the scientists on its advisory board. These academics advised the government on scientific issues and their implications and evaluated whether scientific studies met a sufficient standard of rigor.

– **May 12, 2017** – The Environmental Protection Agency announced it would withdraw mining restrictions on Alaska's headwaters, which allowed mining facilities into the area. This came after an EPA study concluded mining could decimate salmon populations in that area and harm Alaskans who depended on salmon.

– **May 19, 2017** – Four months after Trump's inauguration, the Center for Disease Control was down almost 700 administrative and scientific positions. This left the Center ill equipped to deal with medical and biological issues, including a pandemic.

– **June 19, 2017** – Department of Energy Secretary, Rick Perry, said he didn't believe carbon dioxide caused climate change, a view contradicted by numerous scientific studies conducted by NASA, the EPA, and the National Oceanic and Atmospheric Administration as well as scientists and experts around the globe.

– **June 20, 2017** – The Trump administration planned to cut 1,200 jobs from the EPA, reducing the workforce 15 percent and shrinking the budget 31 percent.

– **June 27, 2017** – The EPA rolled back all of Obama's protections and policies that ensured drinking water was clean and safe.

– **August 2, 2017** – Sam Clovis, Trump's nominee for top scientist at the Department of Agriculture, called progressives "race traders" in his blog—whatever that means.

– **August 14, 2017** – Obama had put into place an initiative to raise fuel efficiency standards for cars. The Trump administration rolled them back.

– **October 3, 2017** – Trump's administration denied protection for 25 endangered species.

– **October 9, 2017** – Trump and EPA Administrator Scott Pruitt decided to repeal the Clean Power Act introduced by Obama, which was designed to lower carbon dioxide emissions 32 percent by year 2030.

– **October 9, 2017** – At the Kentucky Farm Bureau, EPA Administrator Scott Pruitt announced he would remove tax credits for wind and solar energy. Pruitt refused to answer questions about the $20 billion in annual federal tax subsidies for fossil fuel industries. Is it possible we are incentivizing the wrong industry?

– **October 16, 2017** – The EPA revised criteria used to determine dangerous levels of radiation. The threshold established under Trump's criteria was ten times that set by the Obama administration.

– **October 20, 2017** – The EPA deleted information on its website that listed resources for educating local governments on ways to address climate change.

– **October 22, 2017** – The EPA canceled speaking engagements for agency's scientists who were scheduled to present findings on climate change.

– **October 2017** – Trump promised to create jobs for coal miners. During his term in office, employment in the industry grew only four percent. The coal mining industry employs around 65,000 people.

– **December 28, 2017** – Trump rolled back offshore drilling regulations put in place after the British

Petroleum oil spill in 2010, an incident that killed eleven people and released millions of barrels of crude oil into the gulf. Trump's decision to eliminate regulations will save drilling companies around $288 million over the next decade. Petroleum companies were major supporters of Trump's Campaign. In return, they received billions in United States government subsidies and tax breaks.

– **January 4, 2018** – The Trump administration drafted a proposal to open 94% of protected American shorelines for offshore drilling. 94%! Obama's administration spent years and hundreds of millions of dollars protecting the Arctic and Atlantic Seaboards. Director of Federal Affairs at the National Resources Defense Council called the Trump proposal, "the most extreme fossil fuel assault on our nation's public oceans—ever."

– **April 18, 2018** – Trump stopped funding the NASA Monitoring System that measures carbon dioxide and methane and verifies compliance with emission cuts agreed to in the Paris climate accords.

– **March 11, 2019** – Trump submitted a 2020 budget providing $8.6 billion for a border wall and a thirty-one percent cut to the Environmental Protection Agency.

– **June 4, 2020** – Trump signed an executive order to expedite projects by weakening environmental review requirements. Inexplicably, he claimed the pandemic made it necessary to override such regulations.

– **June 10, 2020** – After relaxing regulations on drilling off the Florida coast, Trump's Interior Department planned for offshore drilling in the area.

– **August 17, 2020** – Trump's administration announced it intended to sell leases for drilling oil and gas in Alaska's Arctic National Wildlife Refuge. The Center for American Progress said this would release more than 4.3 billion metric tons of carbon dioxide into the atmosphere.

– **October 28, 2020** – Trump eliminated Clinton Administration's protections banning logging and development on 9.3 million acres of the Tongass National Forest in Alaska. This allowed loggers to down trees in one of the largest temperate rainforests on Earth.

Trump's four-year attack on science and the environment was part of his deconstruction of institutions and his nonsensical interpretations of science and medicine. When faced with the challenges of a pandemic and environmental issues, his approach was mostly denial and avoidance. The country and its citizens paid dearly for that.

Unfortunately, cult leaders often harbor beliefs that are far removed from reality. Trump is notorious for creating his own made-up alternative realities, many of them unrealistic if not downright ridiculous. In addition to his extreme, unfortunate beliefs about science and the environment, he has become more extreme since "not winning" re-election.

The willingness of Trump's violent extremist army to "stand by" combined with his impulses and incompetence set the stage for an insurrection, the final atrocity of his administration, one that had many people questioning, "Is this America?"

The following account of atrocities will have you asking that question.

ABUSE, CRUELTIES, AND ATROCITIES

The scope of cruel actions, collusions, lies, crimes, and corruption propagated by Donald Trump, his cronies, dysfunctional family members, rabid racists, and complicit minions is astonishing. Abhorrent behavior and a lack of humanity ran rampant throughout the administration. This circle could aptly be described as The Trump Crime Syndicate. Although arrests, convictions, and legal admonishments of him and his cohorts' confirm that this label is apropos, many unseemly actions were ignored. This was primarily because of a Republican Congress, a compliant attorney general, and so much corruption that it became normalized. Lies, of any sort, were acceptable.

Trump's policies disenfranchised minorities and anyone not totally loyal to him. He surrounded himself with "yes men" but gave no loyalty to anyone, often leaving destroyed people in his wake. With no respect for anyone's rights or thoughts, any inkling a person did not support him unconditionally caused the unleashing of intense vitriol, including name-calling, insults, tweet shaming, and if possible, firing or undoing of the person in some manner.

Trump was shameless. He unleashed the power of the presidency and manipulated and crushed poor, destitute families. He mismanaged the pandemic and separated migrant children from parents. Information on that dastardly nightmare is beyond the scope of this book, but the timeline and magnitude of these actions are recorded at the following Southern Poverty Law Center site:

www.splcenter.org/news/2020/06/17/family-separation-under-trump-administration-timeline.

Trump's attack on the middle class enriched him and his cronies through tax legislation and a multitude of other actions, including exploitation through solicitations for donations.

And in an insane obsession to destroy the legacy of Obama, he desecrated natural resources and nearly left millions with no health insurance and no replacement plan. And he didn't care. Revenge was the driving force behind many of his actions. The man is missing the sensitivity gene and has zero capacity for empathy.

With no decency or conscience, Trump marginalized anyone not a natural-born, white, Christian, heterosexual male in relatively good health. Supporters were fooled by this master manipulator in to believing he was doing a good thing when he took advantage of them. Shockingly, nearly one-third of the people in this country are so thoroughly gaslighted and cult-like that they are okay with that and continue to support him no matter what. They listened to what he said rather than watching what he did.

The most puzzling of devotees are Christians. Now, many are fake Christians, who have lost their moral compass and are complicit or outright supportive of the subjugation of others and even themselves. A cult is characterized by members who are exploited by a charismatic, self-serving leader and who view those outside their unit as the enemy. They accept that those people can be treated abusively.

Beliefs are not damaging if they drive good behavior. Many religious leaders are compassionate. Some are not. Today, much of the Christian religion has been reimagined— highjacked actually. It's disturbing so many evangelicals support Trump's self-serving behaviors that hurt people. Religious behavoirs can be good or bad, and the bad has blossomed during the Trump era.

The depth and scale of Trump's mental impairment and his cruelty are extensive. With over fifty-some years of failed business experience, his pattern of behavior paints a picture of a shyster, notorious for unscrupulous business dealings and legal wrangling that ripped off contractors, business associates, and employees, leaving devastation in his wake. A con man and opportunistic scammer, he plunders indiscriminately those he encounters. Betrayal is his game.

Trump is not sharp or shrewd, but he is cunning. Any one of the abhorrent incidents below should have taken him down politically. If calling soldiers who lost their lives in World War II "losers" won't do it, nothing will. For a country that was once a beacon of democracy, this is humiliating. Our country has lost credibility and its leadership role in the international community. Instead, we have become a laughingstock among world leaders, a spineless puppet to Russia, and an embarrassment to citizens not in the Trump cult.

While attempting to become the fascist leader of our country, Trump had no limits. He was both a perpetrator of abuse and a whiney victim craving pity. Daily wrongdoings and ridiculous incidents ran into the thousands. Only a few are included here. Any one of the following should have stopped the madness. None did.

– **May 21, 2017** – In his budget, Trump proposed slashing $1.7 trillion from low-income programs, including food stamps ($193 billion) and Medicaid ($800 billion). Forty-two million Americans depended on food stamps and 68 million on Medicaid for healthcare. A significant number of them resided in Republican states where people enthusiastically voted against their own best interests.

– **May 22, 2017** – The Trump Administration failed to get rid of the Affordable Care Act through legislation, so they worked hard to sabotage it. Their policy caused insurance providers to raise premiums and deprived uninsured citizens of information on how to sign up.

– **May 24, 2017** – Housing Secretary Ben Carson said, "poverty was a state of mind," but proposed no solutions.

– **May 28, 2017** – Trump lied in a tweet, "I suggest that we add more dollars to Healthcare and make it the best anywhere!" In spite of campaign promises, he did nothing to improve healthcare and did plenty to impede it. He proposed cutting Medicaid by $800 billion and eliminating Obamacare.

– **July 26, 2017** – Trump tweeted, "The United States Government will not accept or allow... Transgender individuals to serve in any capacity in the U. S. Military." Two judges blocked this discriminatory action.

– **October 5, 2017** – Attorney General Sessions announced the Civil Rights Act would no longer protect transgender workers from employer discrimination.

– **October 6, 2017** – FEMA's website presented statistics on the slow recovery in Puerto Rico after Hurricane Maria. Only 50 percent of Puerto Ricans had access to drinking water and 98 percent were still without electricity. The next day, the statistics were deleted from the site. Trump blamed the Governor of Puerto Rico for the slow recovery.

– **October 12, 2017** – Trump eliminated a healthcare subsidy that covered out-of-pocket medical expenses for poor Americans. Scrapping subsidies drove up insurance premiums even further to cover the difference. Insurance premiums had already risen since Trump took office.

– **October 12, 2017** – Five months after Puerto Rico was hit by Hurricane Maria, 400,000 Puerto Ricans still didn't have power. Trump responded on Twitter: "We cannot keep

FEMA, the Military & First Responders. . .in P.R. forever!"
Again, he blamed the Governor of Puerto Rico.

– **October 24, 2017** – Vice President Pence broke a
Senate tie to defeat legislation that made Wall Street
accountable to consumers through class-action lawsuits
against large financial institutions. The Director of the
Consumer Bureau responded, "Companies like Wells Fargo
and Equifax remain free to break the law without fear of legal
blowback from customers." No explanation was given on
why financial businesses should be exempt from laws.

– **February 6, 2018** – The Trump administration awarded
a $156 million contract to Tribute Contracting LLC to
provide 18.5 million emergency meals to victims of the
hurricane in Puerto Rico. Just 50,000 meals were
delivered on the contracted date. There was no watchdog
observation of the use of these funds.

– **May 7, 2018** – Within two months after the 2017
inauguration, U. S. Mexican border patrol began quietly
separating families. Asylum seekers were imprisoned and
children under eighteen handed over to the U. S.
Department of Health and Human Services (DHS).

June 15, 2018 – DHS publicly acknowledged separating
nearly 2,000 children from their families at the Mexican
border from April 19 through May 31, inciting public
outcry. The separation was done without a plan on how to
reunite families later, and adequate records were not kept.
By the end of the 2020, 545 children had still not been
reunited with their parents, many of them too young to
know their names or the names of their parents.

– June 17, 2018 – Homeland Security Secretary, Kirsten Nielson falsely tweeted: "We do not have a policy of separating families at the border. Period." In December 2018, she lied again: "I'm not a liar. I've never had a policy for family separation."

– June 20, 2018 – CBS reported that 2,342 children had been separated from their parents at the border. Trump blamed the courts and previous administrations for the separations. He lied that Obama had started the policy. Responding to public pressure, he signed an executive order to stop separations, but they continued.

– June 26, 2018 – The ALCU filed a class action suit after which U. S. District Judge, Dana Sabraw prohibited further separations and ruled families were to be reunited within thirty days. This did not happen.

– July 13, 2018 – In a court filing, the Trump administration admitted 2,551 families remained separated. Parents were deported without their children.

– October 11, 2018 – After the Trump Administration took intense flak over separating families at the border, they said they had stopped the process. *The New Yorker* reported the administration had doubled down and was still separating them "in the cover of night." Amnesty International reported 6,022 families had been separated with the children being held in tents and fenced cages.

– December 2018 – Trump administration officials lied repeatedly, minimizing reported numbers of separated children and claiming separations had stopped.

– July 12, 2019 – The House Committee on Oversight and Reform stated the administration was not transparent about border separations, and that the nightmare of separating families continued.

– August 21, 2019 – A Trump administration's rule allowed indefinite detention of migrant families who cross the border without authorization.

– January 18, 2020 – Wildly inconsistent numbers were reported over the course of the fiasco of children removed from their parents at the border. *The Los Angeles Times* reported the official government count was 4,368. Flaws in tracking suggest the number was even higher.

– October 6, 2020 – When U. S. attorneys expressed concerns about separating immigrant children from parents, Attorney General Sessions dismissed their concerns, stating, "We need to take away children—regardless of how young they are."

– October 21, 2020 – Of the 545 children still separated at the Mexican border, a report revealed that roughly 60 children were under age five when taken from their parents, who were most likely deported. These orphaned children now live in privately run detention centers.

––––––––––––––––––––––

Voltaire said, "Anyone who can make you believe absurdities can make you commit atrocities." Trump's followers—people who are in a cult who don't know they are in a cult—will likely continue to be exploited and manipulated into endorsing bad behavior. In some ways, that is more disturbing than anything Trump can dish out.

Trump's intelligence is a self-delusion. He bragged: "I'm highly educated. I know words. I have the best words. [Words like bigly.]" Truth is, his vocabulary is limited. He uses the same words over and over. Asked who he goes to for advice, he said, "I'm speaking with myself because I have a good brain." He calls himself a genius. So does Kanye.

Trump implies he has a degree from Wharton graduate school and ranked at the top of his class. Truth is, he was an undergraduate and not a steller student. (Michael Cohen admitted threatening legal action against schools that would reveal Trump's records.) Trump is incapable of realizing his limitations. Apathetic about learning and averse to detail, he spent his whole life faking it. Steve Bannon said Trump's strategy when challenged is to *flood the zone with shit*. This is exactly what he did when responding to criticism, when dealing with a pandemic, and when protesting the 2020 election. This explains 3,000 law suits and 50,000 tweets. In general, the *flood the zone* tactic has worked well for him.

My initial intent was for the scope of this book to run through the end of 2020, but the Trump-induced insurrection on January 6, 2021—when his unhinged followers ravaged the People's House—was an atrocity requiring acknowledgment. The event raised the consciousness of some of his supporters who, finally, recognized the extent of his dastardly intentions. But, as expected, loyal Trump followers continue to support his sustained effort to attack our democracy. These rebels include extremists, radical right-wing evangelicals, and many legislators—some in *The Family*.

On *Good Morning America* the day after the insurrection, Oklahoma Representative Markwayne Mullin disagreed that Trump had fanned the fires. Taking a tactic from the Trump playbook, he said, "We are all to blame. The media is to blame. The left and the right are to blame." Sometimes, it's hugely embarrassing to be from Oklahoma.

A stunned, George Stephanopoulos responded, "We didn't do it. The mobsters did it, the rioters did it, and the President encouraged it."

INEPTNESS OF A PRESIDENT
AND HIS ADMINISTRATION

Trump is no genius, and if he is tweeting and talking like an idiot, it is because he is an idiot. His presidency was marked with clumsy, blundering, amateurish, incompetent, and often corrupt behavior and cartoonish episodes the scope of which has never been seen before in this country, which was nothing less than astounding. He is an unstable, pompous know-it-all who doesn't listen and doesn't learn.

Because Trump appointees were not screened or vetted, they were generally incompetent in governance and matters of business, administration, and common sense management. This stunning lack of qualifications and capabilities was staggering and disturbing. In addition, many were greedy and exhibited a total disregard for ethics. Some were criminals.

Trump was equally inept. His skill set did not include finesse, diplomacy, or fiscal oversight, and his mis-management is reflected in the need to constantly reverse-engineer policies to match his false statements. The turnover in his administration far exceeded any experienced in previous ones—eight were the result of criminal charges. Also, with a dismal reality show mentality, he enjoyed firing people and did so with abandon. A coward, he did it in tweets or had someone else do it for him. In 2020, voters fired him.

– **May 29, 2017** – CIA Director Mike Pompeo said top-secret daily briefings had to be kept short and filled with "killer graphics" to hold Trump's attention.

– **June 1, 2017** – At the onset of hurricane season, leadership positions remained vacant for NOAA and FEMA, agencies responsible for monitoring weather patterns of incoming natural disasters and addressing recovery from them.

– **June 6, 2017** – White House Press Secretary Sean Spicer announced Trump's tweets—which ran as high as more than 100 a day and were full of name-calling, vitriol, and uncouth insults—were official statements from the president.

– **July 27, 2017** – White House Chief of Staff, Reince Priebus, was fired by tweet. On July 30, *The Atlantic* wrote, "Everyone who works for Trump has to know their turn in the barrel can come at any time, that the slavish loyalty he demands will be repaid only in abuse." Critics said Priebus, who was previously Chairman of the Republican Party, was the man who "sold his party out" to Trump.

– **August 7, 2017** – By August of his first year, Trump had confirmed only 45 percent of his nominees to executive branch roles, a substantially lower pace than his three predecessors. Per the Partnership for Public Service, only 20 percent of the 577 "essential" executive branch positions were filled. His focus was on seeking attention, gaining power, scheming on ways to make money, and undoing Obama's accomplishments. No legislation was put forth.

– **August 8, 2017** – After Kim Jong-Un's regime tested an intercontinental ballistic missile capable of reaching the United States, Trump said he would unleash fire and fury like the world has never seen if North Korea threatened the United States with nuclear action. This warning of catastrophic nuclear action caused Secretary of State Rex Tillerson to downplay Trump's "bellicosity," saying, "I think Americans should sleep well at night and have no concerns about this particular rhetoric of the last few days."

– **August 18, 2017** – After Steve Bannon scored a Time Magazine cover, Trump fired him, claiming Bannon had been a "staffer" and "had very little to do with our historic victory," despite the fact that Bannon, an expert on cult-building and thought reform, was a top aide throughout the campaign and a key influencer in early White House days. These two men with enormous egos and cravings for attention were bound to clash eventually.

– **August 21, 2017** – In a televised speech on strategy in Afghanistan, Trump was vague on American objectives and gave no indication of how many troops the U. S. would commit to the war effort. Nor did he introduce criteria for evaluating the effectiveness of those operations.

– **August 25, 2017** – Sebastian Gorka, White House Deputy Assistant, was fired. No reason was given.

– **August 25, 2017** – Trump pardoned former Arizona sheriff, Joe Arpaio. An Arizona judge had convicted Arpaio of criminal contempt of court for "flagrant disregard" of a court order to cease and desist the racial profiling and incarceration of Latinos jailed in tents in the hot Arizona desert. District Judge Murray Snow stated that Arpaio made "multiple intentional misstatements of fact while under oath." Arpaio told news reporters he would ignore the injunction and keep on doing what he had been doing.

– **September 21, 2017** – In a speech at the UN, Trump cited the exemplary healthcare system of a place called Nambia. Praising this nonexistent African nation, he stated, "Nambia's health system is increasingly self-sufficient." Did he not take his medication that day, or what?

– September 21, 2017 – Twenty-two of Trump's appointees to the Department of Agriculture had no prior agricultural experience and some lacked college degrees. However, all 22 did work on the Trump 2016 campaign.

– September 26, 2017 – Acting head of the Drug Enforcement Administration, Chuck Rosenberg, resigned. He stated that he didn't believe Trump had a moral grasp of justice. This was after Trump spoke to an audience of New York police officers, saying, "When you see these thugs being thrown into the back of a paddy wagon—you just see them thrown in, rough—I said, please don't be too nice. Like when you guys put somebody in the car and you're protecting their head, you know, the way you put their hand over? Like, don't hit their head, and they've just killed somebody—don't hit their head. I said, you can take the hand away, OK?" White House Press Secretary Sarah Sanders claimed the president's statement was a "joke."

– October 4, 2017 – ISIS killed four U. S. soldiers. When asked at a press conference why he still hadn't spoken about the fallen soldiers by October 16, Trump claimed he had written the families personal letters, which would "go out either today or tomorrow." He insinuated President Obama had not called the families of fallen soldiers. This was untrue. Obama called Gold Star families throughout his presidency, as confirmed by his staff and the families. The next day, Trump placed a condolence call to Myeshia Johnson, widow of fallen serviceman Sgt. La David Johnson. Mrs. Johnson said Trump forgot her husband's name on the call. Trump shamefully accused the Gold Star widow of lying.

– October 12, 2017 – White House Chief of Staff John Kelly was often overheard in shouting matches with Trump, which reinforced reports of chaos in the White House.

– **November 9, 2017** – The U. S. Foreign Service lost an unprecedented number of diplomats after Trump's inauguration. Five high-level diplomats resigned. Fourteen out of thirty-three lower level career diplomats resigned as well. The Foreign Service also experienced a steep drop in young people applying for government positions—over 17,000 applied in 2015. Half that many applied in 2017.

– **November 15, 2017** – After a mass shooting in California, Trump tweeted about the wrong city. The shooting occurred in Rancho Tehama, California. He tweeted, "May God be with the people of Sutherland Springs, Texas."

– **January 11, 2018** – In an immigration meeting with Congress, it was reported Trump referred to El Salvador, Haiti, and African nations as "shithole countries."

– **January 14, 2018** – Taylor Weyeneth, a twenty-four-year-old whose only professional experience was as a staffer in Trump's campaign, was assigned the position of Deputy Chief of Staff for the Office of National Drug Control Policy, an agency whose role included the arduous and expansive task of resolving the opioid epidemic.

– **March 3, 2018** – In an impulsive, spur-of-the-moment action and ignoring advice from economic advisors, Trump unilaterally, without the approval of Congress, introduced steep tariffs on steel and aluminum imports. White House officials expressed concern this would result in a trade war.

– **March 7, 2018** – Trump's son-in-law, Jared Kushner, met with Mexican President Enrique Peña Nieto without consulting the current U. S. Ambassador to Mexico, Roberta Jacobson. Kushner had almost no experience in international diplomacy, or any other government functions for that matter. Sending someone with no experience in Mexican relations was an example of unprofessional diplomacy typical of the administration.

– **March 7, 2018** – Former Communications Director Hope Hicks revealed two of her email accounts were hacked.

– **March 12, 2018** – Head of the Department of Education, Betsy DeVos, admitted during a *60 Minutes* interview she hadn't visited any underperforming schools in the country and didn't know about any public school statistics in her home state of Michigan.

– **March 13, 2018** – Trump fired Secretary of State Rex Tillerson and replaced him with CIA Director Mike Pompeo, whom the president described as having "a very similar thought process [as himself]."

– **June 10, 2018** – *Politico* reported Trump routinely tore up papers. Government officials taped them together for archiving purposes to ensure Trump didn't violate the Presidential Records Act, which requires the White House preserve all memos, letters, emails, and papers the president touches and send them as historical records to the National Archives. Trump showed a general disdain for tradition, the law, protocol, and paperwork. Staff members complained that he didn't read.

– **July 29, 2018** – Trump threatened a government shutdown over financing of the wall at the Mexican border. He tweeted, "I would be willing to "shut down" government if the Democrats do not give us the votes for Border Security, which includes the Wall!"

– **September 5, 2018** – An anonymous correspondence from a White House insider published in the *New York Times* reported chaos in the Oval Office. It described Trump as an "impetuous, adversarial, petty, and ineffective president. Meetings with him veer off topic and off the rails. He engages in repetitive rants, and his impulsiveness results in half-baked, ill-informed, and occasionally reckless decisions that have to be walked back."

– **September 11, 2018** – Bob Woodward published his book, *Fear*, an inside view of the instability of Trump's White House. He wrote, "The reality was that the United States in 2017 was tethered to the words and actions of an emotionally overwrought, mercurial, and unpredictable leader. Members of his staff joined to purposefully block some of what they believed were the president's most dangerous impulses. It was a nervous breakdown of the executive power of the most powerful country in the world."

– **August, 2020** – Trump—an uncouth, orange, cartoonish, sofa stuffing-haired, tubby traitor—called Kamala Harris nasty, unlikeable, a communist, and a monster.

Who is the nasty, unlikable, monster—and a Russian enabler, Nazi sympathizer, and racist white supremacist? Look no further. Trump supporters put into the White House a man born to wealth with little knowledge of government, the country, or the world. And he had no interest in learning. He had mastered the art of the swindle, respected no boundaries and no person, and created an existential crisis in his party and the country. The idea that he is a self-made businessman and a great dealmaker is a lie. He is the least prepared and capable of any president. His solution to problems was to *flood the zone with shit.*

THE DIABOLICAL AND ABSURD

Once a person studies Trump through the lens of mental illnesses, it's obvious his behavior, though bizarre beyond belief, is highly predictable. Even actions that at first blush seem absurd, bewildering, and foolish are foreseeable if one understands his mental state.

An article in *Politico* by James Kimmel, Jr. at Yale University School of Medicine, December 12, 2020, might explain some of Trump's outrageous behavior. A study of brains as observed through imaging reveals the brain image of a person preoccupied with grievances and vindictiveness is similar to that of a person addicted to drugs. This suggests Trump's victim mentality and the resulting compulsion to rabidly lash out at perceived enemies is an addiction. The study calls this *revenge addiction*. This might explain his constant attack mode and the vindictiveness he spews daily.

One might conclude Trump's top priority is greed and power. But it is actually the need for pity, which is at the root of his behavior. All day, every day, he is a victim. That's what drives his acrimonious, vindictive reactions. It is why he constantly whines and displays infantile behavior. It is what he uses to rally his followers. In almost every tweet, Trump casts himself as a victim. Even his pursuit of attention is a reaction to his quest for pity. Thus, the absurd.

– **June, 2017** – Praise is oxygen to Trump. With the press present at Trump's first cabinet meeting, each cabinet member fawned over Trump—knowing to stay in his good graces, one must do so. In a roundtable fashion, each one took turns praising and honoring him, except for General Matis, who took a pass and praised his troops.

– **November 2, 2017** – In a statement during *Meet the Press*, Energy Secretary Rick Perry, an oil and gas guy from Texas, absurdly implied fossil fuels could lower rates of sexual assault.

– **November 18, 2017** – Trump was obsessed with Hillary Clinton. In the first year of his presidency, he tweeted about her seventy-seven times, an average of once every 4.7 days. In spite of the corruption in his administration, not to mention his business failures and crimes, he tweeted, "Crooked Hillary Clinton is the worst (and biggest) loser of all time." (Name-calling is his forte.)

– **December 4, 2017** – Following allegations that Roy Moore, candidate for Alabama senator, was a racist and had sexually abused teenage girls, Trump endorsed Moore's campaign for the Senate. Moore lost.

– **December 29, 2017** – In 2017, Trump spent nearly one-third of his time, at considerable cost to taxpayers, at properties that bear his name or that his company owned.

– **January 16, 2018** – A predictor of the insurrection on January 6, 2021 would be this: *The Daily Stormer*, a virulent white supremacist website, wrote that the publication found Trump's policies "encouraging and refreshing," and "Trump is more or less on the same page as us with regard to race and immigration." Trump's declared support of QAnon, Nazis, and Proud Boys further validate this conclusion.

– **January 19, 2018** – The Trump administration's turnover rate set records in his first year in office. According to the Brookings Institution, 34 percent of high-level White House aides resigned, were fired, or transferred.

– January 20, 2018 – During Barack Obama's presidency, Trump repeatedly chastised him for golfing. In his campaign, Trump promised not to do that. In his first year in office, Trump played golf 35 times—three times a month on average. Trump spent nearly one-third of his time (94 days his first year) at his properties and playing golf. By 2020, he had golfed a total of 228 times and visited his properties almost 300 times. Obama played golf only once a month on average during his presidency.

– February 25, 2018 – After harassing North Korean's leader Kim Jong-Un for a year with name-calling, insults, and bullying, Trump, in his own words, "fell in love" with him on a visit to that country. (Authoritarian leaders tend to admire other such people. Trump's ambitions cause him to admire, worship, or "fall in love" with such leaders while disrespecting the democratic leaders of our allies.)

– March 10, 2018 – Trump announced the U. S. military would stage a military parade in D. C., an event that could cost up to $30 million. The public and many military and government staff were horrified at the prospect.

– June 15, 2018 – Following the Trump administration's policy that separated migrant children from their parents, Trump blamed Democrats, tweeting, "The Democrats are forcing the breakup of families at the Border with their horrible and cruel legislative agenda." He also blamed Obama.

– July 24, 2018 – Trump had made unpopular statements denying Russia's meddling in the 2016 election. Strangely, he switched gears and tweeted the startling and absurd accusation that Russia would help Democrats win the 2018 midterm elections. "I'm very concerned that Russia will be fighting very hard to have an impact on the upcoming Election. Based on the fact that no President has been tougher on Russia than me, they will be pushing very hard for the Democrats." This was most likely desperate posturing to distract from investigations of Russian meddling in support of Trump in 2016. Trump was not "tougher" on Russians. He was a Russian asset.

– **August 30, 2018** – In spite of his boasts about the country's economy, Trump announced he was canceling an automatic 2.1 percent pay increase for federal employees. Delaware Senator Chris Coons reacted, "It is unacceptable that, after last year signing a Republican tax bill that gave away tens of billions in corporate tax cuts and added more than $1 trillion to the national debt, President Trump cites the need for government belt-tightening in his decision to slash a planned pay increase."

– **February 8, 2019** – Trump backtracked on insults to Kim Jong-Un in an in-person meeting since he had "fallen in love" with him. He tweeted that North Korea would become an "economic powerhouse. I have gotten to know him & fully understand how capable he is. North Korea will become a different kind of Rocket–an Economic one!"

– **February 28, 2019** – After a meeting with Kim Jong-Un, Trump was asked if he confronted Jong-Un about the death of Otto Warmbier—an American college student detained in North Korea in 2017 who died soon after returning home. Trump said, "He tells me that he didn't know about it, and I will take him at his word." Jong-Un had taken a tactic from the Trump playbook—ignorance.

– **March 2, 2019** – In a rambling two-hour speech at the Conservative Political Action Conference, Trump hugged an American flag, called Robert Mueller's investigation "bullshit," and mocked renewable energy saying, "When the wind stops blowing, that's the end of your electric. Let's hurry up. Darling—Darling, is the wind blowing today? I'd like to watch television, darling." Trump fancies himself a comedian. After this absurd drama, an observer wondered if he had taken his medication that day.

– **July 24, 2019** – Trump cancelled food assistance through the Supplemental Nutrition Assistance Program, stating that a robust economy and low unemployment meant assistance was no longer needed. Around forty-million Americans relied on this supplemental program for food; many of them were among his base, especially in the South where, interestingly, voters had a propensity to vote against their own best interests.

– **August 1, 2019** – Trump demonstrated his tendency toward grandiosity when he told a Cincinnati crowd at a rally: "We will be ending the AIDS epidemic shortly in America and curing childhood cancer very shortly."

– **August 20, 2019** – Trump suggested the U. S. purchase Greenland. Denmark's prime minister Mette Frederiksen responded: "Greenland is not for sale." Trump canceled a planned visit to Denmark and called Frederiksen "nasty."

– **August 21, 2019** – After several mass shootings, Trump blamed mental illness, not guns, for the violence. He said, "Mental illness and hatred pull the trigger, not the gun." The National Rifle Association spent more than $30 million on his 2016 election campaign.

– **September 1, 2019** – Trump tweeted that Hurricane Dorian would hit Alabama. The National Weather Service corrected him. Never one to admit he was wrong, he doubled down and held up a Weather Service map for the press, obviously altered with a Sharpie to include Alabama.

– **September 2019** – Trump proposed hurricanes be destroyed in their infancy by nuclear bombs off the coat of Africa.

– **December 20, 2019** – Mark Galli, editor in chief of *Christianity Today*, called for Trump's removal from office based on "moral deficiencies." In a harshly worded tweet, Trump lambasted the publication and called it a "far left magazine."

– **February 18, 2020** – Trump commuted the sentence of former Illinois Governor Rod Blagojevich, who was convicted on corruption charges in 2010. He had appeared on Trump's reality show, *The Celebrity Apprentice.*

– **February 24, 2020** – Trump lashed out at Supreme Court justices Ruth Bader Ginsburg and Sonia Sotomayor. In an unusual action for a president, he suggested they "recuse themselves for anything Trump or Trump related."

– **February 26, 2020** – Mike Pence had been criticized for his health policy, which had worsened Indiana's HIV outbreak while he was governor. Nevertheless, Trump appointed him to lead the United States' response to the coronavirus outbreak. Pence had no medical background. The response to the virus did not go well.

– **April 12, 2020** – In tweets, Trump blamed China, the World Health Organization, and Obama for the pandemic.

– **May 3, 2020** – In his usual victim mode, Trump pointed to a statue of Lincoln and said, "They always said nobody got treated worse than Lincoln. I believe I am treated worse." Trump enjoys his victim status.

– **May 12, 2020** – During a pandemic that killed tens of thousands of Americans, Trump took time to promote a conspiracy theory that Joe Scarborough of MSNBC committed murder. "When will they open a Cold Case on the Psycho Joe Scarborough matter in Florida," Trump tweeted, "Did he get away with murder? Some people think so." *Some people* was often Trump's authoritative source when creating an alternative reality.

– **May 26, 2020** – Trump continued spreading a conspiracy theory that MSNBC's Joe Scarborough had committed murder. Police in Florida had ruled there was no sign of foul play in the 2001 death of intern Lori Klausutis, who died when hitting her head in a fall after a heart attack. That didn't stop Trump. He said, "It's certainly a very suspicious situation. Very sad, very sad and very suspicious."

– **May 27, 2020** – Twitter fact-checked two of Trump's tweets claiming mail-in ballots were fraudulent. In response, he threatened to shut down Twitter, his favorite social media platform on which he had posted more than 50,000 tweets during his term in office.

– **June 18, 2020** – Certain Trump campaign posts and advertisements featured an inverted red triangle used by Nazis to single out political opponents. Facebook removed them under its company policy on hate-group symbols. Trump's campaign defended the symbol, claiming the red triangle was just an emoji.

– **July 9, 2020** – Victim Trump blasted the Supreme Court after it ruled he couldn't block the release of his financial records. He tweeted, "This is all a political prosecution. Courts in the past have given "broad deference." BUT NOT ME!"

– **July 10, 2020** – Trump bragged that he "aced" a simple, cursory mental acuity test he took at Walter Reed Medical Center. On Fox News, he boasted in a disjointed tweet in his fourth grade voice, "I actually took one when I—very recently, when I—when I was—the radical left were saying, is he all there? Is he all there? And I proved I was all there, because I got I aced it. I aced the test."

– **July 10, 2020** – Oddly, Trump said he educated people that Abraham Lincoln was a Republican. It is not unusual for him to assume his lack of knowledge is common among the general public. He said, "Like people don't remember, nobody ever heard of it until I came along, nobody remembered it for a long time, or they didn't use it at least, I use it all the time: Abraham Lincoln was a Republican. You know you say that and people say, 'I didn't know that,' but he was Republican, so we're doing a great job." Who knows who Trump is hanging out with, but most people do know Lincoln was a Republican.

– **July 14, 2020** – When asked in an interview with CBS News why African Americans are "still dying at the hands of law enforcement in this country," Trump replied, "So are white people. What a terrible question to ask."

– **July 15, 2020** – Employees of the executive branch are prohibited from using public office "for the endorsement of any product, service, or enterprise." After a boycott of Goya because the company's CEO praised Trump publicly, Ivanka posted a surreal, ludicrously incongruent image on social media of her holding a can of Goya beans.

– **July 16, 2020** – White House press secretary Kayleigh McEnany said science should not stand in the way of schools reopening during a pandemic. When the media shared her comment, she stated the coverage was a "case study in media bias."

– **July 28, 2020** – Twitter, Facebook, and YouTube removed a video both Trump and Trump, Jr. shared of people in white medical coats dismissing the importance of masks and touting the benefits of hydroxychloroquine. Pundits suggested the Trumps were somehow invested financially in the drug since they promoted it with impunity in spite of a lack of empirical evidence and the fact that medical experts advised against it and called it dangerous.

– **July 29, 2020** – Trump said that, contrary to what had been reported, he reads his daily intelligence briefings. "You know, I read a lot. They like to say I don't read. I read a lot. I comprehend extraordinarily well, probably better than anybody that you've interviewed in a long time. I read a lot."

– **July 29, 2020** – Trump said the reason he didn't ask Putin about reported bounties on U. S. troops during a call with the Russian leader was because it was "fake news."

– **August 8, 2020** – An aide to Trump inquired of the South Dakota governor's office what it took to have a president added to Mount Rushmore. In 2018, Trump told future Governor Kristi Noem, "Do you know it's my dream to have my face on Mount Rushmore?"

– **August 9, 2020** – A reporter asked Trump why he repeatedly took credit for a veterans' healthcare bill signed into law by Obama. The reporter told him, "It was passed in 2014." Trump answered, "OK. Thank you very much, everybody," and immediately walked away.

– **August 19, 2020** – At a news briefing, Trump commented on QAnon, "I don't know much about the movement other than I understand that they like me very much, which I appreciate." A reporter told Trump QAnon supporters believed Trump is "secretly saving the world from this satanic cult of pedophiles and cannibals." They are the organization that ridiculously claimed Hillary Clinton ran a sex-trafficking organization out of the basement of a pizza restaurant in D. C. The president replied: "I haven't heard that. But is that supposed to be a bad thing or good thing? If I can help save the world from problems, I'm willing to do it. I'm willing to put myself out there." It's a bad thing, and he knows it.

– **August 19, 2020** – After Goodyear Tires enforced a company policy of not allowing political messaging on clothing at work, which included MAGA attire, Trump called for a boycott of their tires and threatened to have Goodyear tires removed from the presidential limousine. Based in Ohio, Goodyear employed roughly 63,000 people. Goodyear clarified that political campaign restrictions applied to all parties. Employees held a rally with signs that said, "2020 is a good year to dump Trump."

– **August 20, 2020** – Wildfires displaced more than 100,000 Californians. Trump blamed the state and threatened to withhold federal emergency funds. At a rally, he said, "I said, you gotta clean your floors, you gotta clean your forests— there are many, many years of leaves and broken trees and they're like, like, so flammable, you touch them and it goes up." He added, "Maybe we're just going to have to make them pay for it because they don't listen to us."

– **August 31, 2020** – Trump said police officers can make mistakes when using deadly force, the same way golfers sometimes miss putts. "They choke. Just like in a golf tournament, they miss a three-foot—" Fox News host

Laura Ingraham interrupted the president. "You're not comparing it to golf. . ." she said.

– **September 2, 2020** – Trump publicly encouraged his followers to vote twice in November by mailing in an absentee ballot, then voting in person on Election Day.

– **September 2, 2020** – Trump signed a memo listing cities with Democratic leaders as "anarchist jurisdictions" that should have their federal funding cut.

– **September 3, 2020** – Trump canceled a visit to an American World War I cemetery in France, saying, "Why should I go to that cemetery? It's filled with losers."

– **September 3, 2020** – Trump said he didn't go to the Aisne-Marne American Cemetery in Belleau, France, as scheduled to honor American veterans there. The *Atlantic* reported Trump said the Marines were "suckers" for getting killed. Trump had avoided serving in the Vietnam war because of a supposed bone spur in his foot.

– **September 14, 2020** – Trump dismissed climate change and drought as factors in the ferocious, record-breaking wildfires sweeping across California and Colorado. "It will start getting cooler, just you watch," he said. He failed to consider the drought. State Natural Resources Agency Secretary Wade Crowfoot spoke of the importance of relying on science, to which Trump responded, "I don't think science knows, actually."

– **September 14, 2020** – Michael Caputo, Trump's top communications official at the Department of Health and Human Services, falsely accused CDC scientists of "sedition." Speaking at an event, he made this inane statement: "there are hit squads being trained all over this country" to keep Trump from winning a second term. "You understand that they're going to have to kill me, and unfortunately, I think that's where this is going."

– **September 2020** – *The Washington Post* reported that during his term in office, Trump visited his properties 274 times at considerable taxpayer expense. His family members traveled the world at taxpayer expense as well.

– **October 1, 2020** – According to Stephanie Winston Wolkoff, Melania Trump's former friend, Melania belittled the fate of thousands of migrant children taken from their parents at the Mexican border. Melania said in a recording, "Give me a fucking break. Were they saying anything when Obama did that?" (Obama didn't do that.) She boarded a plane to visit children separated from their parents at the border wearing the "I really don't care. Do you?" coat. She doesn't care. Winston Wolkoff revealed in her book that "I really don't care" was Melania's coping response to anything bothersome, including unfaithfulness and sexual harassment claims against her husband.

– **October 1, 2020** – Melania complained about having to work during the holidays. "I'm working like a—my ass off at Christmas stuff," she said. "You know, who gives a fuck about Christmas stuff and decoration?"

– **October 2020** – At a town hall forum, Trump refused to disavow QAnon, an extremist conspiracy-theory group that supported him. Two months later, they participated in an insurrection at the Capitol instigated by Trump.

– **November 2020** – The stock market immediately rose after Biden was elected. Trump took credit for it. Absurd.

As stated earlier, Trump appointed two white supremacists to government roles: (1) preservation of Holocaust Museums and (2) the Preservation of American's Heritage abroad. I repeat this information here because these appointments are so outlandishly *absurd*.

Another absurdity was Trump's claim that under his administration the economy was strong. This may be true for the wealthy, but millions of Americans suffered unprecedented economic trauma from lost jobs, housing, and food, much of this because of a grossly mis-managed pandemic. For most citizens, the economy was a disaster. Many of them were his followers, who without question, bought off on the *alternative reality* he sold them of a strong economy.

In addition, a $2 trillion tax cut favoring the rich, excessive spending, wasteful fiscal insanity, and his policies promoted an outrageously blossoming increase in the national debt of $7.2 trillion. Yes, trillion.

Trump repeatedly proffered the great economy falsehood rather than acknowledge the facts of the plight of the masses and the national debt increase. Both were contrary to his artificially created reality, which he probably believed. He celebrated the economy. One has to wonder if he had forgotten to take his medication or took too much of it. Or, perhaps he is just a liar and a schemer.

American citizens deserved better than a blow hard, incompetent president who "floods the zone with shit," as Bannon would say, anytime things got rough. They did not deserve the bizarre, the absurd, and certainly not the diabolical of separating children from their parents, the gross mismanagement of The Trump Virus, the impertinent fleecing of taxpayers, and the entitled exploitation of followers.

THE PANDEMIC AND POLITICS

Unfortunately for mankind, when science is mixed with politics, you get politics. Trump likes to call the coronavirus the *China Virus* or the *Kung Fu Virus*. Some call it *The Trump Virus* for two reasons: (1) He wants his name on everything, and (2) He has done more to propagate the virus than anyone else in the entire world. This was one thing he could not get out of with wild claims on Twitter or invented facts. The virus was real.

When it comes to Trump and the pandemic, or anything else, actually, it's all about him when things are good and all about someone else when things are not. He spent more time on the appearance of beating the virus; avoiding accountability; and dishing out blame, insults, and vindictiveness than on actually dealing with it. At its peak, he gave up and ignored it.

On the march to taking 560,000 lives—more than 4,300 Americans a day in January 2021—the pandemic killed more Americans than all the wars in the last 120 years. Trump and his minions politicized the pandemic. Donald used daily briefings to talk about Donald while obsessively monitoring his ratings. When his performances were so awful that his ratings crashed, he stopped the briefings and ignored the pandemic. What did Trump do or not do that allowed the virus to ravage our country so severely? A lot.

––––––––––

– **May 2018** – Obama formed a pandemic team under the National Security Council in 2016 after successfully managing the H1N1 flu and holding the ebola epidemic to only two cases. Trump disbanded the team and slashed the budget for the Center for Disease Control. He also left hundreds of positions vacant there. Timothy Ziemer, head of the Obama team, was not replaced and team members were disbursed. Obama's team had produced a pandemic playbook, which was disregarded by Trump and his administration.

– **January 22, 2020** – Trump said, "We're not at all worried about the virus. We have it totally under control." He avoided briefings and told Fox News, "It's all taken care of."

– **February 28, 2020** – Trump—accustomed to creating his own alternative reality—said, "It's going to disappear. One day—it's like a miracle—it will disappear." He said cases would soon be "down to close to zero."

– **March 4, 2020** – In spite of warnings from the World Health Organization (WHO), Trump disputed the deadliness of the coronavirus. He said so on a *hunch (*Trump bragged he made decisions based on hunches): "So, if we have thousands or hundreds of thousands of people that get better just by, you know, sitting around and even going to work—some of them go to work, but they get better."

– **March 5, 2020** – In spite of advice from the WHO, Trump said he intended to continue to shake hands, hold rallies, and host gatherings at the White House and Mar-a-Lago. And he did, clear through to the end of his term in office.

– **March 10, 2020** – Trump said, "Stay calm. It will go away."

– **March 13, 2020** – Trump said an Obama rule was why his administration could not provide coronavirus tests more expediently. No such rule existed. (He didn't follow Obama rules. Why would he follow this one if it did exit.)

– **March 18, 2020** – Though the WHO warned Trump his words could encourage racial profiling, he defended his use of the term "Chinese virus." As the virus swept across the U. S., some called it The Trump Virus. Other citizens began attacking Asian Americans throughout the country.

– **March 20, 2020** – Republican Senators Kelly Loeffler and Richard Burr resigned after selling millions in stocks ahead of a stock market decline due to the pandemic.

– **March 20, 2020** – Republican Richard Burr, chairman of the Senate Intelligence Committee, warned an inside group to prepare for economic turmoil while publicly supporting Trump that the virus was being blown out of proportion.

– **March 21, 2020** – Trump publicly endorsed a combination of two drugs, hydroxychloroquine and azithromycin, to treat the coronavirus. This was in spite of no testing or backing. The FDA, CDC, and medical professionals warned the drugs could be dangerous.

– **March 23, 2020** – Trump vowed "America will again and soon be open for business—very soon." At a press conference, he compared the alarming increase in deaths to automobile fatalities. "You look at automobile accidents, which are far greater than any numbers we're talking about. That doesn't mean we're going to tell everybody no more driving of cars."

– **March 24, 2020** – Trump told Fox News he "would love to have the country opened up and just raring to go by Easter." He tweeted, "THE CURE CANNOT BE WORSE (byfar) THAN THE PROBLEM!"

– **March 26, 2020** – Although health experts around the world had been warning about a pandemic for years, Trump claimed the coronavirus crisis caught the U. S. by surprise. He said, "This was something that nobody has ever thought could happen to this country. Nobody would have ever thought a thing like this could have happened." Obama had thought it could, and he had established a pandemic team, which Trump disbanded, and a playbook he ignored.

– **March 27, 2020** – Trump accused the governors of Michigan and Washington of not being sufficiently grateful for federal pandemic assistance. "I want them to be appreciative. If they don't treat you right, I don't call."

– **March 27, 2020** – Trump lied, "We've now established great testing....We've now tested more than anybody."

– **March 29, 2020** – Trump bragged that as many as 2.2 million Americans could have died "if we didn't do what we're doing." He added that if the U. S. was able to limit coronavirus deaths to between 100,000 and 200,000 people, "we altogether have done a very good job." At the end of his term, 400,000 Americans had died as the virus raged forward toward more than 520,000.

– **March 31, 2020** – Trump blamed his impeachment for diverting his attention from dealing with the pandemic. "Did it divert my attention? I think I'm getting A-pluses for the way I handled myself during a phony impeachment. Okay? It was a hoax. But certainly, I guess, I thought of it."

– **April 1, 2020** – On CNN, Pence said Trump never "belittled" the coronavirus threat. Trump made the same argument at his daily virus briefing with, "I knew how bad it was." Both statements contradicted what Trump said on many occasions in the past. He claimed on January 22, 2020, "We are not at all worried about the virus." He had even declared victory over the illness and moved on.

– **April 2, 2020** – Governors were desperate for PPE and crying out for ventilators. Jared Kushner said the Strategic National Stockpile of ventilators and medical supplies was "supposed to be *our* stockpile—it's not supposed to be states' stockpiles that they then use." Journalists at a Kushner news conference pointed out the program's website said differently. The next day, it was changed.

– **April 4, 2020** – Anthony Fauci, the nation's top infectious disease expert, said there was no evidence hydroxychloroquine could fight the coronavirus, nor that it was safe. Trump argued he was considering it for himself. "I may take it, OK? I may take it. And I'll have to tell my doctors about that, but I may take it."

– **April 5, 2020** – The U. S. stockpiled 29 million hydroxychloroquine pills, though health experts warned of dangerous side effects and no evidence of efficacy. Trump continued to push for it as a treatment for COVID-19. "What do I know? I'm not a doctor. But I have common sense."

– **April 6, 2020** – Trump advisor Peter Navarro warned Trump the coronavirus posed a great threat to the country: "The lives of millions of Americans could be imperiled by the pandemic." Trump continued to downplay the threat. "Now, this is just my hunch, and, but based on a lot of conversations with a lot of people that do this, because a lot of people will have this, and it's very mild. They will get better very rapidly."

– **April 7, 2020** – Trump blamed the World Health Organization for a slow response to the pandemic. He said, "They called it wrong. They really, they missed the call." Actually, the WHO warned of a "public health emergency of international concern" long before Trump took it seriously.

– **April 7, 2020** – A watchdog panel was established to oversee Trump administration's distribution of $2 trillion in coronavirus relief, but Trump ousted its chairman as well as head of the Pandemic Response Accountability Committee. Whistle-blower Michael Atkinson was also fired. Later, numerous incidents of relief fraud were uncovered.

— **April 9, 2020** — Trump defied health experts and rejected their advice that more people needed to be tested before the U. S. economy could restart. "Do you need it?" he asked about testing. Then he answered his own question, "No."

— **April 12, 2020** — "Time to #FireFauci" read a message Trump tweeted after the top infectious disease expert in the country said fewer Americans would have died had the country gone under lockdown earlier.

— **April 13, 2020** — Trump attacked the press at a news conference. He told a reporter, "You know you're a fake. Everything we did was right." He also incorrectly said the power to reopen the country rested solely with him, not governors, "When somebody is the president of the United States, the authority is total, and that's the way it's got to be." Governors disagreed, especially with the void of a national strategy to deal with the pandemic.

— **April 13, 2020** — The Treasury Department put Trump's signature on stimulus checks. No IRS disbursement had ever carried a president's name. Anonymous officials said it was Trump's idea to print his name on the checks. Trump also had his name printed on notes in food distributions.

— **April 14, 2020** — Trump announced he would cut U. S. payments to the World Health Organization, claiming they engaged in a coverup of the coronavirus outbreak in its early days in China. He presented no evidence of this.

– **April 15, 2020** – CNN reported Trump said, "Nobody needs ventilators anymore."

– **April 17, 2020** – Trump used Twitter to urge protesters to challenge governors' stay-at-home orders. He posted, "LIBERATE MICHIGAN!" "LIBERATE MINNESOTA!" when they enacted social-distancing restrictions.

– **April 18, 2020** – Trump proposed less testing and at times refused to fund it, but he faulted Democratic governors for not doing enough to test. "They don't want to use all of the capacity that we've created. We have tremendous capacity."

– **April 20, 2020** – The U. S. confirmed it had more coronavirus cases per capita than any other country.

– **April 21, 2020** – Hotels across the country suffered from a sharp decline in business. Trump asked his administration for a break on lease payments on Trump International Hotel in Washington, D. C. He also asked Florida's Palm Beach County if he must keep making $88,000 monthly lease payments for the Trump International Golf Club.

– **April 22, 2020** – Trump called warnings by experts of a second wave of the pandemic "fake news."

– **April 22, 2020** – Dr. Rick Bright, Director of the Biomedical Advanced Research Authority, was outside when he questioned the use of hydroxychloroquine.

– **April 23, 2020** – To the horror of experts, Trump speculated at a coronavirus briefing about ingesting bleach or disinfectants to fight the virus. He said, "Because you see it gets in the lungs and it does a tremendous number on the lungs, so it would be interesting to check that. Supposing we hit the body with a tremendous—whether it's ultraviolet or just very powerful light. And I think you said that hasn't been checked, but we're going to test it?" Health officials and manufacturers of household cleaners warned Americans not to follow Trump's advice.

– **April 25, 2020** – Trump tweeted. "I never said the pandemic was a Hoax! Who would say such a thing?" On February 28, at a South Carolina rally he said, "Now the Democrats are politicizing the coronavirus. And this is their new hoax." On another occasion he said the virus had become his critics' latest hoax. Healthcare providers said patients called the virus a hoax as they were dying of it.

– **April 26, 2020** – In late night tweets, Trump complained about a *New York Times* article on his work ethic and golfing, in light of the pandemic. He said, "Then I read a phony story in the failing @nytimes about my work schedule and eating habits, written by a third rate reporter who knows nothing about me. I will often be in the Oval Office late into the night & read & see that I am angrily eating a hamburger & Diet Coke in my bedroom. People with me are always stunned."

– **April 27, 2020** – States reported people were ingesting disinfectants after Trump's comments. Trump took the position it was not his fault.

– **April 27, 2020** – Trump ignored classified briefings in January and February calling the coronavirus an imminent threat. Officials anonymously complained Trump seldom reads or listens to oral summaries of the daily briefs and he allows fewer sessions than previous presidents.

– **April 29, 2020** – When states were still under lockdown and virus cases increasing, Jared Kushner predicted: "A lot of the country should be back to normal by June. The hope is that by July the country's really rocking again." The virus escalated in June and really took off in July.

– **April 30, 2020** – Administration officials pressured U. S. spy agencies to dig up evidence the coronavirus originated in a lab in Wuhan—a theory that had been widely discredited—rather than from a water market. This was Trump's attempt to blame China for "creating" the virus.

– **April 30, 2020** – Trump said, "Nobody's thinking about the coronavirus more. Nobody has spent more time, late in the evening, thinking about what's happened to this country in a short period of time." He must have been thinking how to lie about it. *The Washington Post* noted at least 44 incidents from March to May in which Trump downplayed the threat. He called it "very well under control" again and again.

– **May 3, 2020** – At a Fox News town hall, Trump said the coronavirus death toll could reach 100,000. The figure was double what he predicted two weeks earlier. Still, he said the country should reopen its economy. As a side note, he called his predecessor, Obama, "foolish" and "stupid" and bragged he, Trump, had "done more than any other president in the history of our country."

– **May 4, 2020** – The White House banned members of its pandemic task force from testifying before Congress. Specifically, Dr. Anthony Fauci was prohibited from testifying before a House committee.

– **May 6, 2020** – The Centers for Disease Control and Prevention produced a seventeen-page report on when America should reopen its economy. An anonymous official claimed the Trump administration disagreed with its conclusions and prevented its release, stating, "It would never see the light of day."

– **May 8, 2020** – Commemorating the 75th anniversary of the Allied victory in Europe, Trump met with seven World War II veterans, all in their 90s. He refused to wear a mask, telling reporters, "The wind blew so hard and such a direction that if the plague ever reached them, I'd be very surprised. It could have reached me, too. You didn't worry about me, you only worried about them, but that's OK."

– **May 11, 2020** – Trump's staff unveiled banners at a Rose Garden briefing that read, "AMERICA LEADS THE WORLD IN TESTING." This was far from the truth.

– **May 14, 2020** – Trump boasted, "We have the best testing in the world. Could be that testing's, frankly, overrated. Maybe it is overrated." The U. S. didn't have the best testing.

– **May, 15, 2020** – Trump said of the pandemic, "At some point, it'll go away." He also said, "This is a flu. This is like a flu. . .One day, like a miracle it will disappear."

– **May 15, 2020** – The coronavirus stabilization law Congress passed included money for *public* education institutions that were hurt by the pandemic. Trump's Education Secretary DeVos directed $180 million away from public schools and to private and religious ones.

– **May 18, 2020** – Trump confirmed he was taking hydroxychloroquine, a drug medical experts warned could be dangerous and was not shown to combat the virus. He said, "I started taking it, because I think it's good. I've heard a lot of good stories." His enthusiastic promotion made people question whether he, his family, or cronies had some financial stake in the drug. They also suspected he was lying about taking it.

– **May 21, 2020** – In spite of company policy and state law, Trump did not wear a mask while touring a Ford Motor Company factory. He said, "I didn't want to give the press the pleasure of seeing it." Michigan Attorney General Dana Nessel called him a "petulant child who refuses to follow the rules." Trump responded via tweet: "Do nothing A. G. of the Great State of Michigan, Dana Nessel, should not be taking her anger and stupidity out on Ford Motor."

– **May 22, 2020** – By labeling houses of worship "essential," Trump advised governors to reopen them, in spite of the pandemic. Medical experts had previously identified church services as super spreaders.

– **May 22, 2020** – Trump's approval ratings dropped during the pandemic. He questioned whether the nation's death toll was as high as health departments reported, claiming it could be "lower than" that. Experts said it was, no doubt, higher than the count as reported.

– **May 29, 2020** – Trump resigned the U. S. from the World Health Organization.

– **June 11, 2020** – After three months of no rallies, Trump scheduled one in Tulsa, Oklahoma. Rally attendees were required to sign a waiver forbidding them to sue the campaign if they contracted Covid-19. Many did get it.

– **June 15, 2020** – Trump blamed the increase in coronavirus cases on testing. In a tweet, he said, "Our testing is so much bigger and more advanced than any other country (we have done a great job on this!) that it shows more cases. Without testing, or weak testing, we would be showing almost no cases. Testing is a double-edged sword—Makes us look bad, but good to have!!!" Evidence suggested the U. S. lagged significantly behind other developed countries in testing, and Trump had refused to fund proposed testing.

– **June 16, 2020** – Officials in Tulsa asked the Trump campaign to cancel his rally because it could be a virus "super spreader." Trump blamed the media for opposition to his rallies, accusing them of "trying to Covid shame us."

– **June 18, 2020** – Trump often spread misinformation about testing. In a *Wall Street Journal* interview, he said too much testing for the coronavirus "made the U. S. look bad. I personally think testing is overrated, even though I created the greatest testing machine in history."

– **June 19, 2020** – Trump threatened those involved in planning demonstrations at his Tulsa rally. He tweeted, "Any protesters, anarchists, agitators, looters or lowlifes who are going to Oklahoma please understand, you will not be treated like you have been in New York, Seattle, or Minneapolis. It will be a much different scene!" His threat caused considerable concern among Tulsa citizens.

– **June 2020** – At his Tulsa rally, Trump called the coronavirus the "kung flu" virus. As post-rally infections spiked, Tulsa citizens called it The Trump Virus.

– **June 20, 2020** – Trump said, "When you do testing to that extent, you're going to find more people, you're going to find more cases. So I said to my people, 'Slow the testing down, please.' They test and they test."

– June 21, 2020 – Trump's Tulsa rally attracted only 6,600 people. Much of the 19,000-capacity arena was empty. Trump's staff had predicted one million attendees.

– June 23, 2020 – Trump aides maintained he was joking when he told his administration to slow coronavirus testing. Trump contradicted them, saying, "I don't kid."

– June 24, 2020 – At least six advance staffers, including two Secret Service employees, tested positive for COVID-19 after working Trump's rally in Tulsa.

– June 26, 2020 – At the first briefing of the coronavirus task force in almost two months, Pence referenced "remarkable progress" in the fight against it. Truth was, the virus was marching at a record rate across the country.

– June 27, 2020 – Staffers at Tulsa's arena for Trump's June rally reported his campaign staff removed "DO NOT SIT HERE, PLEASE!" signs on seats to create social distancing.

– July 4, 2020 – COVID-19 killed 130,000 Americans, but Trump bragged that ninety-nine percent of the virus cases were harmless. By the end of the year, close to 400,000 COVID deaths were reported. By February, just weeks after Trump left office and had ignored the pandemic after his November election defeat, deaths exceeded half a million.

– July 6, 2020 – At least forty lobbyists connected to Trump obtained around $10 billion in federal coronavirus aid monies for their clients. The watchdog group Public Citizen who reported this included five former Trump administration officials who potentially violated an executive order restricting lobbying activities. Who knows where all the money went? Trump had banished or severely weakened the watchdog organizations. Some companies were forced to return monies.

– July 8, 2020 – A health official in Tulsa said Trump's rally on June 20 likely caused a spike in virus cases in Tulsa county. Record-high numbers were reported.

– July 14, 2020 – Trump directed that all data about patients with the coronavirus be sent by hospitals to a central database in Washington, D. C. rather than to the Centers for Disease Control. This meant information could be manipulated by the White House and might be unreliable or possibly even unavailable to the public. Outrage ensued and the directive was never enforced.

– July 18, 2020 – The Trump administration fought to keep states from getting billions of dollars of coronavirus relief money to conduct testing. Contact tracing was also inhibited. The Trump administration also tried to block billions of dollars of funding the Senate wanted to go to the Center for Disease Control and Prevention.

– July 19, 2020 – During an interview, Trump said the United States' coronavirus mortality rate was "one of the lowest" in the world. This was not true. He added his prediction that the pandemic would come to an end: "It's going to disappear, and I'll be right. Because I've been right probably more than anybody else." Really?

– July 30, 2020 – Herman Cain, Republican presidential primary candidate, died from COVID-19 complications. Cain attended Trump's June rally in Tulsa where he was seen among the masses gleeful and not social distancing. Nor did he wear a mask. Four weeks later, he was dead.

– **August 3, 2020** – Dr. Deborah Birx, White House coronavirus coordinator, said the pandemic was "extraordinarily widespread." Trump called her "pathetic."

– **August 4, 2020** – Jonathan Swan of *Axios* asked Trump how the coronavirus was "under control" when 1,000 Americans died every day. Trump's response, "They are dying. That's true. It is what it is." By December of 2020, more than 21 million cases had been reported and over 360,000 people had died—ultimately reaching a peak of over 4,300 people dying each day in January 2021.

– **August 5, 2020** – The United States reported 1,380 coronavirus deaths in one day, but Trump said, "This thing's going away. It will go away like things go away."

– **August 10, 2020** – In 2014, Trump said Obama should resign for his response to the Ebola outbreak during which two people died in the United States. By December 2020, 360,000 Americans had died on Trump's watch.

– **August 10, 2020** – Trump bragged about his response to the pandemic. "I think it's been amazing what we've been able to do. We understand the disease. Nobody understood it because nobody's ever seen anything like this. The closest thing is in 1917, they say, right? The great pandemic. Certainly was a terrible thing where they lost anywhere from 50 to 100 million people. Probably ended the Second World War, all the soldiers were sick." The pandemic Trump spoke of occurred in 1918-1919 during the First World War, and 675,000 people died in the U. S. The Second World War occurred 26 years later, ending in 1945.

– **August 16, 2020** – Trump said an extract from the oleander plant was a cure for the coronavirus and the Food and Drug Administration "should be approving" it. MyPillow CEO Mike Lindell—a major Trump donor who was invested in the company that makes the extract—persuaded Trump to endorse it. There was no evidence the extract, Oleandrin, was effective.

– **August 23, 2020** – Without proof, Trump claimed the Food and Drug Administration intentionally delayed vaccine trials. He tweeted, "The deep state, or whoever, over at the FDA is making it difficult for drug companies to get people in order to test the vaccines and therapeutics. Obviously, they are hoping to delay the answer until after November 3rd. Must focus on speed, and saving lives!" Now, Trump has added the FDA to his loaded language creation: *the deep state.*

– **August 26, 2020** – The White House's task force changed advice posted on the CDC website. The revised version said people without symptoms do not need a test. The new guidelines came after months of Trump stating he was opposed to more testing because it revealed more cases.

– **August 31, 2020** – Trump retweeted a conspiracy theory that coronavirus killed only 9,000 people in this country.

– **August 2020** – Talk about yes men and Trump's ability to intimidate, on CNN, Dr. Stephen Haun, FDA administer refused to refute Trump's claim the coronavirus was "99% harmless." It's better American's die than contradict Trump? On March 3, WHO reported a 3.4% death rate, and many patients who lived suffered long-term health effects.

– **September 1, 2020** – After a congressional investigation revealing "evidence of fraud, waste, and abuse," a $646.7 million deal for ventilators was cancelled.

– **September 7, 2020** – In his book, *Rage*, Bob Woodward reported Trump knew about the dangers of coronavirus but downplayed them in public. "This is deadly stuff," Trump said in a February 7 call with Woodward. In contrast, on Feb. 26, Trump said at a press conference: "You know, in many cases, when you catch this, it's very light; you don't even know there's a problem. Sometimes they just get the sniffles."

– **September 10, 2020** – Trump said, "I didn't lie," in response to an ABC reporter asking him why he downplayed the pandemic to the public.

– **September 11, 2020** – Trump appointees at the Department of Health and Human Services interfered with Center for Disease Control coronavirus reports. *Politico* reported a Trump Administration spokesman, Michael Caputo, from the Department of Health and Human Services, claimed CDC reports were used to "hurt the president." He wanted to edit reports and accused the Center for Disease Control scientists of sedition.

– **September 14, 2020** – Trump appointee to HHS, Michael Caputo, promoted the idea of a conspiracy theory that "hit squads" were being trained around the country to create opposition to Trump.

– **September 15, 2020** – Referring to "herd immunity," in an ABC town hall meeting, Trump said the coronavirus would disappear. "You'll develop, you'll develop herd— like a herd mentality. It's going to be, it's going to be herd-developed, and that's going to happen."

– **September 17, 2020** – Attorney General William Barr argued that stay-at-home orders were similar to house arrest. "It's—you know, other than slavery, which was a different kind of restraint, this is the greatest intrusion on civil liberties in American history."

– **September 17, 2020** – Vice President Pence's former adviser, Olivia Troye, claimed that in a meeting Trump said, "Maybe this covid thing is a good thing. I don't like shaking hands with people. I don't have to shake hands with these disgusting people."

– **September 22, 2020** – With the nation's death toll from the coronavirus climbing at an alarming rate, Trump said at one of his rallies that the virus "affects virtually nobody."

– **October 2, 2020** – Trump announced in a Tweet that he and Melania tested positive for the coronavirus. The announcement followed months of him downplaying the virus that had at that time killed more than 200,000 Americans and caused an economic crisis. Soon after, more than a dozen people attending events at the White House contracted the virus and even more at Trump rallies.

– **October 2020** – After recovering from the virus, Trump bragged about receiving special treatment and attention at Walter Reed Hospital where he received care not available to most Americans with the virus. He continued with messaging that discouraged masks and social distancing. Neither were required at the White House. Soon it became known as a super spreader. Once he realized he could not control the pandemic, he did what he always does in such situations, he turned it over to someone else, governors, so he could blame them for the outcome. No national strategy existed.

– October 7, 2020 – The White House outbreak climbed to 34 known people and it was labeled a super-spreader. Trump ignored the pandemic in campaign activities.

– October 26, 2020 – A federal judge rejected Trump's policy to cut billions in food aid to low-income Americans during the pandemic. He appealed the judgment. Still, he added his signature to notes in food distributions.

– November 2020 – After his election loss, Trump said little about the pandemic for the rest of his term in office. He focused on challenging election results from his defeat, soliciting $300 million in donations from supporters, hosting parties at the White House, and playing golf.

– December 10, 2020 – The Trump Virus (on a march toward a half a million total deaths) reached a daily death number of 3,124—more each day than incurred on 9/11. It was more than Katrina, Maria, and Pearl Harbor combined.

– December 25, 2020 – Limited vaccinations began in December, but without federal leadership, states struggled to coordinate and administer them. More than 3,500 Americans died on Christmas Day.

– January 27, 2021 – Dr. Birx, coronavirus consultant to the President, said she was often surprised by charts and graphs she had never seen before presented at briefings. She wondered who was producing them and what was the source of the data.

Numbers reflect the hideous momentum of this virus. No doubt, it would have ravaged our country no matter who was in charge, as it did the world. But the numbers show the United States compared unfavorably with other developed countries in its intensity. Trump's incompetence profoundly contributed to that. He inspired and championed the behavior of non-maskers and undisciplined citizens.

It didn't have to happen this way. We could have had the German experience. In August 2020, 111 people per million died there compared to 547 per million in America. If Trump hadn't denied the virus initially, the production of personal protective equipment, hospital preparations, respiratory equipment needs, testing, and contact tracing and monitoring could have been ramped up sooner. The public could have been put on guard sooner and encouraged to respond rather than being told the virus was a hoax. If Trump had not eliminated the pandemic response infrastructure established by Obama, it would have made a difference as well.

In the absence of national leadership, each governor went his own way. A patchwork of responses resulted. When Trump did react, he used daily public briefings to campaign, brag, propose ridiculous ideas, insult pandemic experts, blame Obama, Pelosi, and Biden and star in a reality show about himself while acting foolishly and wondering why his ratings were plummeting.

After his election defeat, Trump hunkered down at the White House, partying, scheming to overthrow the government, and exploiting followers for money while ignoring the pandemic and not governing. During this time, four people I was close to died. I thought: Who's next? A son? A daughter? Oh, God, no-o-o.

Hate is derived from fear. I and many others are afraid. And a surprising number of good, caring people now hate for the first time in their lives. Considerable hate is derived from pandemic-related behavior. I suggest we've had all the Make America Great Again we can stand.

(See more about the pandemic in the following section on the 2020 Presidential election.)

THE 2020 PRESIDENTIAL ELECTION FIASCO

Actually, the election was not a fiasco. The system worked, but Trump did everything he could to make it chaotic. Refusing to acknowledge his loss, give up his position, or facilitate a smooth transition of power, he threw tantrums and disrupted government processes, causing some loyal supporters to abandon him. Not all did so. The cult survived. After his defeat, he blustered and whined his way through an embarrassing mess of alternative reality nonsense while exploiting his base by soliciting money, inciting rebellion, and attempting to disenfranchise 81 million voters. You could say, *he flooded the zone with shit.*

Trump creates chaos and conflict wherever he goes, and he does so on a daily, perhaps I should say, hourly or minute-by-minute basis. The 2020 campaign was no exception, but it did accomplish two important things: (1) It put an end to Trump's aspirations to destroy democracy and become an authoritarian leader of the United States—at least for now—and (2) It took the constant mayhem around Trump out of the White House. I and many others can once again rest in the cradle of politics and democracy—at least for four years.

Once the election was called for Biden, Trump became increasingly unhinged and, as predicted, immediately set about disputing the election results and using an arsenal of dubious tactics to rally his calvary and engineer a coup so he could stay in office. After creating The Big Lie that the election was rigged and he had won by a landslide, his legal team filed over sixty lawsuits and appeals in a frantic effort to overturn the election. All failed, even two cases that went to the Supreme Court. Our systems worked, democracy prevailed, and our country redeemed itself in the eyes of rational constituents, our allies, and the world. However, Trump's army of raging extremist supporters were convinced by him that they had been robbed.

Never missing an opportunity to stuff his financial coffers at the expense of others, Trump turned the country's sacred post-election period into a money grubbing opportunity. He abandoned the pretense of governing. His attention focused on golf and the scam of soliciting contributions from followers. He suddenly went silent on the pandemic as it ravaged the country with deaths running around 3,600 per day, heading to over 4,000 and a total of more than half a million dead citizens. And he ignored a Russian attack on our government systems.

Trump even disappeared from the public eye for ten days in December while he solicited money and railed against Republicans. His talon-like grip on them loosened. Some—not all—acknowledged the Biden win. There was no respite for White House workers either. They were subjected to non-mask-wearing masses at over ten White House parties by mid-December, with more planned.

Preparing for a coup, Trump purged senior leadership in the Pentagon by firing four of its main officers. He unloaded Attorney General William Barr, fired cyber security official, Christopher Krebs, and pardoned a slew of criminals in what some called a pardon-palooza that put his criminal cohorts above the law.

Numerous mental health professionals have stated Trump's behavior was at the highest level of the narcissistic spectrum. His abhorrent conduct is so frequent and blatantly in line with this conclusion that his condition is obvious all day every day, which implies it rises to the level of *malignant narcissism.*

One might suggest I've overshot the runway on this topic by accusing Trump of aspiring to be a fascist leader and suffering from mental acrobatics as bizarre as *I see dead people*. I stand by my conclusions. You be the judge.

− **June 22, 2020** − Trump expressed his opposition to mail-in voting. He tweeted: "RIGGED 2020 ELECTION. MILLIONS OF MAIL-IN BALLOTS WILL BE PRINTED BY FOREIGN COUNTRIES, AND OTHERS. IT WILL BE THE SCANDAL OF OUR TIMES!" There has been no evidence of significant fraud from mail-in ballots.

− **July 19, 2020** − Trump said he might not accept the results of the 2020 presidential election if he loses. He made similar statements before. His intention to stay in power indefinitely was expressed over and over.

− **July 22, 2020** − Trump's campaign published a Facebook picture showing Trump standing with police and another picture of protesters attacking a police officer. It read, "personal safety vs. chaos & violence." The photographer admitted taking the chaos photo in the Ukraine in 2014.

− **July 23, 2020** − Reaching out to suburban housewives in America, whom polls showed were pulling away from Trump, he made a comment with racist insinuations. He said he would repeal an Obama fair-housing rule, which he thought would appeal to them. He tweeted, "Biden will destroy your neighborhood and your American Dream. I will preserve it, and make it even better!"

− **July 30, 2020** − Trump criticized mail-in voting again. He used it to justify delaying the November election, which would keep him in power. He tweeted, "With Universal Mail-In Voting (not Absentee Voting, which is good), 2020 will be the most INACCURATE & FRAUDULENT

Election in history. Delay the Election until people can properly, securely and safely vote???"

– **August 6, 2020** – Trump, who never showed the slightest interest in spiritual matters except for photo ops, said Biden (a Catholic who attended Mass regularly) was "following the radical left agenda...no, no anything, hurt the Bible, hurt God. He's against God." All evidence to the contrary, Biden is a Christian. Trump professes to be one, but he uses and abuses people. He referred to *Second Corinthians* as *Two Corinthians,* exposing his ignorance of the Bible. He rarely attends church. On Sundays, he plays golf. Many so-called Christians, for some reason, are okay with all that.

– **August 11, 2020** – In an interview, Trump said, "China will own the United States if this election is lost by Donald Trump. If I don't win the election....you're going to have to learn to speak Chinese, you want to know the truth."

– **August 12, 2020** – Trump repeatedly called Kamala Harris, Biden's running mate, *nasty.* "She was nasty to a level that was just a horrible thing." He also said she "was the meanest, most horrible, most disrespectful of anybody in the U. S. Senate."

– **August 12, 2020** – Trump tweeted about Marjorie Taylor Greene, a Georgia Republican House candidate who supported the far-right conspiracy group QAnon, "Marjorie is strong on everything and never gives up—a real WINNER!" In 2019, the FBI identified QAnon as a domestic terror threat. On January 6, 2021, this was proven to be true as QAnon followers played a major role in the insurrection at the Capitol. Greene called for House Speaker Nancy Pelosi to be killed. The fact that Trump supports QAnon should frighten every American.

– **August 13, 2020** – Mail-in ballots were popular because of the pandemic. Congress proposed $25 billion in emergency aid for the U. S. Postal Service to process the ballots. Trump opposed the proposal, claiming funding would help process fraudulent mail-in ballots.

– **August 13, 2020** – After Kamala Harris was selected as Biden's vice president, Trump used his *flooding the zone with shit* tactic and claimed she could not be vice president because her parents were immigrants. He said, "I heard it today that she doesn't meet the requirements." (Trump's authoritative source of information is often: "I heard it," or "people are saying," or some other vague reference.) Harris was born in California and is thus eligible to be vice president and even president.

– **August 17, 2020** – Postmaster General Louis DeJoy— who, in spite of conflicts of interest, was appointed by Trump—was accused shortly after his appointment of deliberately slowing mail to help the president in the November election. The House Judiciary Committee asked the FBI to conduct a criminal probe, after which postal service delivery performance returned to near normal.

– **August 19, 2020** – Obama criticized Trump at the Democratic Convention. Trump responded by tweeting: "HE SPIED ON MY CAMPAIGN, AND GOT CAUGHT! When I listen to that and then I see the horror that he's left us, the stupidity of the transactions that he's made—look what we're doing, we have our great border wall, we have security."

– **August 19, 2020** – Convinced mail-in ballots would favor Democrats, Trump's campaign sued New Jersey over their plan to mail ballot forms to voters because of the pandemic.

– **August 19, 2020** – Regarding the November election, Trump said he would "see what happens. The only way we're going to lose this election is if the election is rigged." This is an interesting remark given Republicans made significant efforts across the country to restrict Democrats from voting.

– **August 21, 2020** – Trump said that if November's election results were not known by the end of 2020, "Crazy Nancy Pelosi would become president, you know that. No. No. I don't know if it's a theory or a fact, but I said, 'That's not good. That's not good.' The more success that we've achieved, the more unhinged the radical left has become. Anarchists and violent mobs have rioted in our Democrat-run cities, attacking police and tearing down statues. I'm the only thing standing between the American dream and total anarchy, madness, and chaos, and that's what it is."

– **August 23, 2020** – Twitter warned that a Trump tweet violated the company's rules about "civic and election integrity." Trump said in the post: "So now the Democrats are using Mail Drop Boxes, which are a voter security disaster. Among other things, they make it possible for a person to vote multiple times. Also, who controls them, are they placed in Republican or Democrat areas? They are not COVID sanitized. A big fraud!" The real story: Voting boxes were removed from Democratic populated areas.

– **September 2020** – After feuding with Puerto Rico's governor for three years, Trump sent $13 billion in hurricane relief after which she endorsed him for president. Trump, thereby, influenced voters from Puerto Rico living in America, and he did so with taxpayer money—lots of it. The good news is, Puerto Rico finally got the support it deserved.

– **September 3, 2020** – Trump belittled Joe Biden, for wearing a mask during the pandemic. He told Pennsylvania rally attendees, "If I were a psychiatrist, right, you know I'd say: 'This guy's got some big issues.'"

– **September 3, 2020** – Without any evidence of voter fraud, Trump's campaign and the Republican National Committee sued Montana Democratic Governor, Steve Bullock, to halt expansion of mail-in voting in his state.

– **September 23, 2020** – Trump claimed mail-in voting was fraudulent. He warned if he lost the election, he would not participate in a peaceful transfer of power. He said, "Well, we're going to have to see what happens."

– **September 29, 2020** – In the first presidential debate, Trump interrupted Biden almost every time he spoke. Moderator Chris Wallace pleaded with him to be quiet, to no avail. Trump was asked if he would condemn the Proud Boys, a group of white supremacists who promoted violence. The president called on them to "Stand back and stand by."

– **August 21, 2020** – Again, Trump said, "I'm the only thing standing between the American dream and total anarchy, madness, and chaos, and that's what it is."

– **October 8, 2020** – After being infected with COVID-19, Trump refused to take part in a scheduled debate with Biden unless it was in person. He said, "I'm not going to waste my time on a virtual debate. It's ridiculous, and then they cut you off whenever they want." The debate was cancelled.

– **October 8, 2020** – In a Fox interview, Trump said William Barr's legacy would be tainted if he didn't indict Joe Biden and Barack Obama. For what? He didn't say, but he called vice presidential candidate Kamala Harris "a monster and a communist."

– October 13, 2020 – Trump tweeted an altered photo of Joe Biden in a wheelchair surrounded by elderly people in what looked like a nursing home. The words "Biden for president" were changed to "Biden for resident."

– October 13, 2020 – At a political event, Trump again mentioned *herd immunity* for the virus, which proposes boosting immunity through widespread infection. Medical experts warned this would kill millions of Americans.

– October 14, 2020 – Trump's campaign took Dr. Anthony Fauci's comments out of context and made it appear as though Fauci was praising the president. He wasn't.

– October 15, 2020 – At a town hall, Trump, who had politicized the issue of mask wearing, refused to endorse wearing masks. "I believe we're rounding the corner," he said, praising his administration's response to the pandemic. Daily infections, however, were surging.

– October 17, 2020 – At a Michigan rally, Trump demanded Governor Whitmer reopen the state in spite of the raging pandemic. "Lock her up!" chanted the crowd.

– October 2020 – The FBI charged thirteen men of a plot to attack the Michigan Capitol and kidnap and potentially kill Governor Whitmer.

– October 18, 2020 – In Carson City, Nevada, Trump ridiculed Joe Biden for relying on scientists for pandemic information and advice. "He'll listen to the scientists. He will surrender your future to the virus," he said.

– **October 2020** – Trump called the nation's top infectious disease expert, Anthony Fauci, "a disaster." He told his staff, "People are tired of hearing Fauci and all these idiots." He claimed hundreds of thousands more would have died had they relied on Fauci's advice.

– **October 19, 2020** – At an Arizona rally, Trump accused the media of focusing too much on the pandemic. "You turn on CNN. That's all they cover. Covid, covid, pandemic. Covid, covid, covid. . . .CNN, you dumb bastards." At that time, the pandemic had killed more than 219,000 Americans and left many more with lingering health conditions.

– **October 24, 2020** – Five aides or advisers to Pence tested positive for the coronavirus. He had been in close contact with many of them but did not quarantine. Instead, he went on the campaign trail. Most people at the events he attended didn't wear masks.

– **October 24, 2020** – Speaking at a North Carolina rally, Trump said, "We're doing great, we're rounding the turn, our numbers are incredible." The previous day, more than 85,000 new coronavirus cases were reported in the U. S.—the highest number on any day since the pandemic began.

– **October 24, 2020** – At a Wisconsin rally, Trump introduced this conspiracy theory: "doctors get more money and hospitals get more money" if they classify any deaths as coronavirus deaths. Exactly how they made more money if someone died was not explained. Medical experts were appalled by the insult and maintained that Covid-19 deaths had been under-reported, not over-reported.

– **October 25, 2020** – "We're not going to control the pandemic," Trump's chief of staff Mark Meadows told

CNN, suggesting Trump's administration had given up on stopping the spread. The general public was not buying their messaging, Trump's ratings fell, so the daily updates ended.

– **October 26, 2020** – Trump held a campaign rally in Pennsylvania in October. Over the previous two weeks, the average of new daily coronavirus cases in the country had grown by 32 percent, and COVID had killed more than 225,000 Americans. There were no signs of the trend reversing. However, Trump announced, "We're rounding the turn. You know, all they want to talk about is Covid. By the way, on November 4, you won't be hearing so much about it. 'Covid Covid Covid Covid.'"

– **October 29, 2020** – People who attended a Trump rally in North Carolina on October 21 later tested positive for the coronavirus. Thousands attended and stood shoulder to shoulder cheering robustly, most without masks. The day before the rally, North Carolina broke its record for new coronavirus cases with 2,885 in one day.

– **October 29, 2020** – In a Fox News interview, Donald Trump Jr. said the number of Americans dying from the coronavirus is "almost nothing." More than 1,400 Americans died the day Trump, Jr. said that, bringing the total dead to almost 230,000 with no end in sight. This is over four times more than the number of soldiers lost in the Vietnam war, where 58,000 were lost.

– **October 31, 2020** – A Stanford University's study revealed that at 18 Trump rallies, at least 30,000 people had contracted the coronavirus. 700 of them died.

– **October 31, 2020** – Once again, Trump falsely claimed doctors inflated the number of deaths from the coronavirus in order to be paid more money. Exactly how they got paid more was a mystery. At a Michigan rally, he said, "Our doctors get more money if someone dies from COVID. You know that, right? I mean our doctors are very smart people. So what they do is they say, 'I'm sorry, but everybody dies of COVID.'" The medical community, immersed in the care of virus patients, many of whom died, was horrified.

– **November 1, 2020** – Trump celebrated supporters in Texas who blockaded a Biden campaign bus on a highway. According to Biden's camp, trucks flying Trump flags circled the bus as it traveled down a highway. There was fear they would run it off the road. Trump tweeted, "In my opinion, these patriots did nothing wrong."

– **November 2, 2020** – On the last day of his campaign, Trump held no less than five rallies, drawing in thousands of supporters, most not wearing masks or social-distancing. Trump made fun of Biden for having smaller events where many attendees stayed in cars to remain safe.

– **November 4, 2020** – Trump declared he had won the election, though many votes remained uncounted. The President has no authority to call an election. Trump didn't care that millions of ballots had yet to be counted in races too close to call. Without any authority to do so, he even asked that the counting stop while he was ahead.

– **November 4, 2020** – Trump proclaimed victories in key states. A president has no legal right to claim vote results. He said, "We have claimed, for Electoral Vote purposes, the Commonwealth of Pennsylvania (which won't allow legal observers), the State of Georgia, and the State of North Carolina, each one of which has a BIG Trump lead. Additionally, we hereby claim the State of Michigan if, in fact, ... there was a large number of secretly dumped ballots as has been widely reported!"

– **November 5, 2020** – After the election, which Trump lost both in popular and electoral votes and by wide margins, his campaign began soliciting donations from followers, supposedly to fight election fraud. Refusing to concede the elections allowed him over two months to keep donations flowing in. Much of the money eventually made its way into Trump's personal or business coffers.

– **November 5, 2020** – There was no evidence of voter fraud in any state. Nevertheless, Trump claimed the election had been rigged. He demanded the count be stopped in Georgia where he was ahead. In Arizona and Nevada where he was behind he demanded counting continue. Presidents have no authority to interfere with elections.

– **November 5, 2020** – *The Washington Post's* fact checker had tallied 29,508 Trump lies and false claims by November 2, including 4,000 in October alone. He was in a frenzy after his election defeat, and by the end of his term in office, 30,575 lies were reported by *The Post*. He was eventually kicked off of Twitter for lying and inciting an insurrection at the Capitol

– **November 7, 2020** – The *Associated Press* and all major TV networks, including Fox News, called the election for Joe Biden. Voting turnout was record breaking. More than 81 million people voted for Biden—the most votes any presidential candidate has ever received, and it was 7 million more than the Trump votes.

– **November 8, 2020** – A day after the election was called, Trump insisted he won and Democrats had committed fraud. He provided no evidence of this. "The big city machines are corrupt. This was a stolen election."

– **November 9, 2020** – In spite of the fact that Justice Department policies prevent prosecutors from getting involved in state election outcomes, Attorney General William Barr told federal prosecutors to investigate allegations of voting irregularities. On December 2, Barr admitted investigations found no significant voter fraud.

– **November 9, 2020** – Trump's campaign sued Pennsylvania secretary of state and seven counties, trying to block certification of election results. Similar lawsuits were rejected in Georgia, Michigan, and Nevada.

– **November 9, 2020** – Attendees didn't wear masks to a White House election night event. At least two people tested positive for the coronavirus. Historically, sitting presidents didn't consider it appropriate to host campaign activities at the White House.

– **November 9, 2020** – Two months before his term ended, Trump still refused to concede the election. He fired Defense Secretary Mark Esper as well as four high-level military appointees under him. This firing created instability at the top of the military command at an uncertain time. Without the voice of reason from these military leaders, the president's plan to withdraw troops from Afghanistan and Iraq was cleared, creating considerable angst among military and political leaders here and abroad. This introduced conjecture about what other radical, lame duck actions Trump might introduce. As it turned out, plenty, including a planned insurrection at the Capitol. Trump invited extremist to gather and "fight like hell." He said in the invitation, "It will be wild."

– **November 25, 2020** – Trump pardoned Michael Flynn, his ex-National Security Advisor—one of the most notorious of his posse of law breakers.

– **December 10, 2020** – The Electoral College elected Joe Biden President of the United States.

– **December 16, 2020** – CNN reported over fifty legal challenges submitted by Trump's team on election rigging were lost, two of them turned down by the Supreme Court. Trump's legal team continued fighting while he solicited followers for donations. Fine print in solicitation forms disclosed that funds would not be limited to this legal fight, meaning Trump could use them however he pleased.

– **December 2020** – Legal experts pointed out Trump's legal teams used election fraud stories publicly, but did not include them in formal legal filings because they were false, and attorneys could be disbarred for false claims.

– **December 16, 2020** – Forty-two days after Biden won the election, Mitch McConnell finally acknowledged Biden's win.

– **December 16, 2020** – Ex-Republican, Steve Schmidt, founder of *The Lincoln Project*, called Trump's fight to stay in office "a failed coup." He said Trump had poisoned America's democracy, and it is still on the critical list.

– **December 18, 2020** – Michael Flynn, whom Trump pardoned for convicted crimes, advised him to declare martial law and deploy the military to re-do elections in key states.

– **December 2020** – Gregory Treverto, former chairman of the National Intelligence Council, said Trump behaves like a Russian paid agent. Trump disappeared for ten days and made no response to Russia hacking numerous government systems, except to blame it on China.

– **December 24, 2020** – *The Washington Post* said Trump saved the worst for last. Laser focused on soliciting donations, spewing conspiracy theories, contemplating martial law to overthrow elections, and partying at the White House, Trump ignored Russian hacking attacks, the pandemic, and the people's business.

– **December 24, 2020** – Trump left the White House for Mar-a-Lago without signing a pandemic relief package.

– **January 6, 2021** – Trump followers invaded the Capitol.

– **January 20, 2021** – Joe Biden was inaugurated as the 46th President of the United States.

Historians will no doubt call Trump the most incompetent, least dignified, and worst president in U. S. history. His plan to disenfranchise 81 million voters nearly brought the country to its knees. And his claim that he is "the only thing standing between the American dream and total anarchy, madness, and chaos" is a confounding remark coming from a champion of anarchy and an election stealer.

He spent the last two months of his term challenging the election with over sixty lawsuits all of which failed, even two that went to the Supreme Court. In an unprecedented manner, he dishonored his position by protesting the election results, intimidating election officials, refusing to concede, obstructing the transition of power, and declining the long-standing tradition of attending his successor's inauguration.

In addition, he stopped governing—ignoring the pandemic raging across the country, Russian interference with government systems, and the people's business. Instead, he played golf and held numerous parties in the White house. He also incited extremist supporters to overthrow the government, which culminated in a violent attack on the U. S. Capitol that plundered this symbol of American democracy. For this, he was impeached for the second time. Then he betrayed those he inspired to riot. Still, many were so compromised they continued to support him.

Most Senate Republicans refused to convict him in the impeachment trial. The radical right-wing religious legislators in the party vote as a block no matter the facts. They do not vote issue by issue. Ex-NYC mayor Ed Koch said, "If you agree with me on 9 out of 12 issues, vote for me. If you agree with me on 12 out of 12 issues, see a psychiatrist." When a legislator votes with his party every time rather than issue by issue, he is not doing his duty.

Fortunately the country's systems held, a tribute to pivotal local government organizations administering the election and especially those Republicans who put country above politics. Also, the military and the courts stepped up and showed fidelity to the rule of law and the constitution. And the unwavering free press held its ground. For now, we are not looking down the barrel of the demise of democracy. However, Trump's twisted presidency shined a light on our vulnerabilities, and we must be vigilant in the future.

Post election, Republicans tried to install over 300 methods of preventing voting in Democratic strong holds and among minorities throughout the country. Georgia alone took 81 actions after losing two senate seats. The threat to democracy continues. Complacency is complicity. Because of Trump's pathologies and the effort of Republicans to restrict voting rights, we must remain tenacious and diligent.

No doubt, Trump will continue efforts to be the fascist leader of some place. Perhaps Florida.

SECTION V

RESILIENCE

Audacious

The measure of success when writing with finesse about a tough subject is: Are people still talking to you? Even more important is: Are you still talking to them? I'm not.

I never claimed to be a woman of infinite compassion, and I never believed wine, European cheese, or essential oils could heal anything or that Karma was a thing. I am even more hardened now. If someone were to ask how old I was when I learned to hate, I would answer seventy-three. Still, resilience prevails and I carry on, a brash and brassy old broad talking smack while on the cusp of redemption of some sort in an environment so gonzo I frequently ask, "Did that really happen?"

Chapter 12

THE COST OF COMPLICITY

A new normal in the face of depravity and the veracity of evil is in the arms of resilience, the power of resistance, and the courage of convictions.

Hate is fear with nowhere to go. I can't recall ever hating anyone until the Trump fiasco. His politics fostered a new intense and real emotion in me. I am afraid, and I hate —hard. I'm learning not to hate some of the cult-like followers who enabled him because they have been victims groomed over the years. Many know not what they do. I cannot forgive the complicity of right-wing Republican leaders, though. Abuse in the form of an attack on social programs, human rights, the lower and middle classes, and the weakest among us is unacceptable. And political cult leaders who use mind control to take advantage of people should have been buried with the German experience.

This book, an autopsy of the past five years, required considerable research, which revealed the vile nature of humanity. I set out to write in the interest of healing myself. Instead I came face to face with an abhorrent reality the magnitude of which was beyond unsettling. The residue of that shock and trauma exacerbated my unfortunate disposition. I am changed forever. Trust in human nature—the kindness, common sense, and astuteness of Americans, particularly professed religious people—has been destroyed. Their betrayal of country and tolerance of violent extremist ideologies has left me and many others disillusioned, making it difficult to respect religion. Some I still do. Most I don't.

Although forgiveness is a challenge, I do intend to lean into it. I hope others can pardon me as well for my lack of understanding of their predicaments and legitimate intentions to improve their lives. Appreciating the vulnerability of the human mind helps me see the human dynamics behind the mental shifts many have made.

Documenting the extent of Trump's aberrant behavior has validated my perceptions. I, like most Americans, spent four years watching him—a power-mongering, greedy, carnival barker—desecrate and plunder our democracy with actions so outrageous it was hard to accept they were real— that they could ever happen here. Chronicling them confirmed my interpretations of Trump and his cadre. Compelling messages cried out to be shared.

Building bridges with those who supported Trump's abusive and cruel policies without regret would suggest I'm willing to overlook the attack on the dignity and well-being of vulnerable citizens who are less powerful and less privileged. I don't know how to do that; therefore, forgiveness flounders. I tell myself, "Nik, you are better than that." But I am not. Neither do I expect those with whom I took a hard line to forgive me. I don't seek that or any prospect of reconnection. I've settled into a pocket of uncomfortable, reluctant acceptance of the reality of flaws in human nature.

Still, there is impetus for more unity after the 2020 election now that our country has regained its footing by soundly defeating Trump and neutralizing his threats—at least somewhat. There's still plenty of bluster from militant and angry Trump loyalists. The ludicrous nature of the Trump dogma, the degree of corruption, and the extent to which so many victims embraced it is troubling. Whether any of them come around to abandoning his hateful messaging will define our future. I must, and will, stand against him and his enablers while I try to understand what happened to once kindly folks seduced into not being kind.

In 2018, a year or so into the Trump term, I stopped watching shows that routinely made fun of him. Although his behavior was ludicrous and rich with clownish comedic fodder, which I appreciated initially, his meanness and obnoxiousness were off-the-charts, and the situation had become so grave that humor was no longer funny. Nothing about his pompous-ass nature and the enabling of Nazis and racists, Russian comrades, mean-spirited bullies, plunderers, fake Christians, and millions of people detached cult-like from reality was humorous. Looming threats were too real as the magnitude of Trump's influence and aspirations for authoritarian power became more clear and frightening.

I'm finding my rhythm in the aftermath as I warm up to his followers who got taken in and didn't realize it. At the same time, I accept the reality that there are those who continue to endorse violence, abuse, and cruelty, or who are complicit in the face of such behavior. These toxic people are taking a wrecking ball to democracy, and they need to stay away from me. They are either like Trump or so deep in cult-like behavior that they are not redeemable. They have bought The Big Lie and any other distorted messaging he deals out. Facts and truth count for nothing.

Buffeted by political chaos, my capacity to tolerate their support for someone who speaks nonsense, exploits citizens and country, and devastates people with impunity has been exceeded. They may have been conned, but they were not innocent. Trump and his loyal supporters burned the country to the waterline and shattered my trust in the good in people. That is no little thing to overcome.

In the past, at the end of every year, I looked forward to television shows featuring events of the past year. I couldn't watch the horror portrayed in the 2020 reviews, though. I tried, but the content was too awful. A multitude of desperate situations had me wondering when the swarm of locusts was coming.

Malignant narcissists never concede or admit defeat, and they believe their own lies. We've not seen the end of Trump and his spawn and goons. However, I and a multitude of others will stand against them with resolute determination, no matter what they dish out in the future.

As we navigate the mercy train of the future, I hope antidotes can be implemented for the imperfect political system and the mayhem it propagates. Awareness of cult behavior and the introduction of legislative changes, such as introducing term limits, lobbying controls, and better ways of funding elections, including eliminating Citizens United, would make a huge difference. Reinstitution of The Fairness Doctrine that requires truth in journalism, which was removed by Regan, would help. Unfortunately, the only ones who can make these changes are those who legislate, and they have the most to lose under any reform scenario. The root of the problem is that greedy people never get rich enough, as demonstrated by corporate America.

Mickey Edwards' book, *The Parties Versus the People— How to Turn Republicans and Democrats into Americans,* speaks to this issue. His analysis of how our country got into such a state is eyeopening and his recommended solutions doable—if politicians were stewards of democracy rather than focused primarily on personal power and wealth. At this point, we are stuck with a government with such an appetite for greed and power that the prospect of the current Congress solving divisiveness problems and reforming our broken systems is similar to a naked man offering you his shirt.

America is blessed with masses of rational, intelligent, determined and compassionate people, as demonstrated by the 2020 election. As we set about healing this nation and reaffirming the foundations of democracy and decency, there is hope. We are what our country is about: liberty and justice for all and the premise that all people are created equal.

Still, I'm haunted by a lingering fear the debacle will happen again. The poison is deep. Thirty-five percent of Trump's Twitter followers also follow at least one extremist hate group. Some people put up Trump Christmas trees. I thought Christmas was about Jesus. Christianity has been hijacked. Fake Christians, racists, Nazis, and extremists abound. Our country will never be the same. Neither will I.

Make no mistake, this is not the end of Trump. He is just beginning. He said so himself. As the darling of Russia, of greedy wealthy people, of religious charlatans, and of extremists of all sorts, he won't go away.

The Family, composed of powerful Washington legislators is still alive and well. Broadcasters are allowed to propagate lies with abandon. And, after the Capitol insurrection, 151 Republicans in Congress stood by the Trump lie that the election was stolen. Their loyalty to a cult is stronger than that to their state, country, constituents, and the Constitution. We must step up, be bold, and remain vigilant in the face of this depravity.

I've pondered whether it is arrogant of me to share such brazen opinions. What makes it okay for a circumspect, impertinent old woman to write such audacious things? And then I consider, what if I do not?

The last five years have assaulted my tranquility. Tolerance for depravity is exhausted and faith in humanity destroyed. As a result, I am no longer a nice person. Nor do I aspire to be so. This does not mean I have lost hope. I will not become numb, nor will I cocoon in my privilege, for I know the medicine is mine. It is also yours.

Chapter 13

THE MEDICINE IS MINE

Our lives begin to end when we become silent about things that matter.—Martin Luther King

When I feel I'm going to go all Joan Crawford on someone, I give them fair warning with "You ain't seen crazy yet." Such inclinations are often fostered by technology, social media, aging, or the brutalities and vulgarities of politics. I'm not a religious person, nor am I particularly spiritual. But I'm not an atheist, either. I haven't found a label that fits. I like to think I'm simply elegant in my weirdness, but I'm actually frazzled, adrift and, frankly, fed up.

From a political perspective, I prefer not to be divisive, but rather to have a reasonable social contract with everyone, no matter our differences. Fear has made this impossible. However, I'm hopeful this divide can be narrowed—with rational people at least.

To heal this country, truth must prevail over lies. Hateful and violent fringe groups emboldened by Trump must be disempowered. Legislators and other political leaders in Washington and throughout the country who are more loyal to cults than to country must be redeemed or replaced. The destructive shadow ministry, *The Family*, that has a vice-grip on many of our government leaders must be exposed. A covert, underground religious/political group, its members view Trump as an imperfect vessel, but also as a powerful Wolf King "chosen" by a divine source to lead his followers, to herd them like sheep. This group is a stalemate to progress that holds us back from all we could be. Few people in America know this cult exists in the upper ranks of our government. I heal by exposing it—at considerable risk —and by objecting to its influence.

How did we get to the point where we would experience an insurrection? The answer lies in cults, radical sources of news, corrupt leaders, and a mass of people who used to be loving Christians who are not so loving anymore, or at least they are complicit. Evil forces hijacked religion and invaded local and national politics.

The medicine for personal healing from what ails our country is brilliantly expressed by Valarie Kaur in her book, *See No Stranger*. She said, "I do not owe my opponents my affection, warmth, or regard. But I do owe *myself* a chance to live in this world without the burden of hate." My plan is to lean into that prospect while determinedly confronting the evil in our ranks.

DANCING ON THE EDGE

Looking for a soft place to land.

Political issues may come and go, but aging is a steady, continuous march to the inevitable. A person's response to that reality requires fresh perspectives and a massive dose of acceptance. Physical degradation from aging ranges from being laid up by hiccups to major life-or-death conditions, which are immensely scary and intrusive.

I was at a Eureka Springs, Arkansas, writing retreat at two in the morning putting the final touches on a manuscript due at the next day's workshop. My feet felt hot —a side-effect of diabetes—so I took off my socks to rub a cooling lotion on them. Shockingly, my toes had taken on a black tone and pale pink toenail polish had turned purple. *Oh, my god. It has happened. My diabetes is affecting my feet. Doctors will want to cut off my toes.* I panicked.

There was a small hospital in the community, but I considered hopping in my car and heading back home to a Tulsa hospital emergency room. You don't want just anyone cutting off your toes. Since my feet were hot, I decided to go ahead and rub on the lotion while considering my options. When I did so, the black color started smearing and rubbing off. It was dye from new black socks.

Most medical crises don't end so easily. Nature is fickle and rich with mystery but, in the end, she is predictable in the broad spectrum of things. We are all mortals. Dying is not an option. In the interim, unless I am unusually fortunate, I will be bombarded with health issues, the momentum of which will escalate as I grow older. Concerns in this regard have me feeling as though someone is doing a river dance in my head. But I've learned the soft place to land is in the arms of gratefulness.

AVOIDING A VICTIM MENTALITY

Reinvent like a caterpillar, evolve like a butterfly.

I'm actually not much into such lyrical caterpillar and butterfly crap. Fanciful rationalizations about reality may make a person feel better, but they will not solve aging problems. I prefer more realistic interpretations. Endurance, acceptance, gratefulness, and pragmatic interpretations of events are keys to sanity for me. Outcomes of struggles are unpredictable, which means irrational hope can promote an unachievable fantasy goal—an *irrational rational*—to which many older people subscribe. I don't.

Aging consequences can be severe. Sometimes I wonder, *Am I going to be able to land this plane?* Then I put it on the tarmac or at least roll it off into the grass. I haven't crashed and burned yet, leaving debris all around. I roll with the flow, do what I can, accept outcomes, and invoke personal forgiveness when I mess up. I know when things are really bad, they'll get better. Self talk says, *You cannot fall off the floor. Hold on. Tomorrow is a new day—a gift from the universe.*

I'm writing a story about old ladies jailed in Kansas for transporting marijuana in from Colorado. I got the idea for the story as two old gals and I drove home from Colorado and spotted a patrolman. The ladies in the story told their children to leave them in jail. The food, prepared by local women, was better than Meals on Wheels, and life was such that it no longer mattered where they were. Banter with jailers provided a distraction from loneliness, and the fellows supplied books and jigsaw puzzles from the library. The ladies' response to the arrest generated press attention throughout the state and, eventually, the nation, which created a dilemma for the judge when they asked not to be released. I don't recommend this approach to aging, but creative responses are possible if fresh interpretations are sought:

- Realizing no one cares what you look like but you is comforting.

- Contemplating do-overs may be interesting, but doing so doesn't heal. An emphasis on remembering things you did right heals.

- Novel goals, such as *to get drunk and swear*, are soothing and easily achieved.

- Replacing consumerism—the gospel of acquisition—with the introduction of empty space, simplifies life and lightens burdens.

- Exploring innate abilities reveals what a person was born to do. Find it, do that, and a sense of joy and purpose will prevail.

- Contentment blossoms from generosity and supporting others. Aging is not all about you.

There is medicine in not being stingy. Living like money is golden and you have forever to spend it is unfortunate. I wonder why so many people wait until they die to pass along inheritances. Once a baseline of personal support is achieved, why not give the rest away while you can observe those you love enjoy it? People often inherit from their parents when in their sixties or seventies. The money could have been more helpful when recipients struggled to raise families, fund college, and overcome financial or health crises—rather than when they are old folks in orthopedic shoes at Disneyland.

Another coping strategy is to do things you shouldn't —irreverent, inappropriate, batshit crazy things. Like a third-base coach waving a runner home, encourage others to do the same. When your children hear of your escapades and say, "Don't make me come over there," you're good. When you and your friends are barred from a coffee shop for being noisy or thrown out of a sushi bar for a food fight, your children might ask, "And how old are you people?" That's okay, if you leave a monster tip. When your children repeat a threat you made to them when they were teenagers, "Don't call me if you get thrown in jail," well, good for you.

Be brave, give the gift of a good goodbye, and leave things better for others. Oh, and be audacious.

BIBLIOGRAPHY

Albright, Madeline, *Fascism,* Harper Collins, New York, 2020

Benkler, Yochai; Faris, Robert; Roberts, Hal, Network *Propaganda: Manipulation, Disinformation, and Radicalization of American Politics*, Oxford University Press, New York, 2018

Bernays, Edward, *Propaganda,* Ig Publishing, New York, 2005

Brock, David, *Blinded by the Light*, Crown Publishers, New York, 2002

Buser, Steven, M.D., *DSM-5 Insanely Simplified*, Chiron Publications, New York, 2014

Cohen, Michael, *Disloyal*, Skyhorse Publishing, New York, 2020

Dáte, S.V., *The Useful Idiot*, 2020

Durvasula, Ramani S., Ph.D., *"Don't You Know Who I Am?"* Post Hill Press, New York, 2019

Edwards, Marvin Henry (Mickey), *The Parties Vs the People: How to Turn Republicans and Democrats into Americans*, Yale University Press, New Haven, 2012

Eisner, Juliette, *The Family*, Jigsaw Productions, Netflix 2020

Evans, Patricia, *Controlling People*, Adams Media Corp. Avon, Mass., 2001

Evans, Patricia, *The Verbally Abusive Relationship*, Adams Media, Avon, Massachusetts, 1996

Evans, Patricia, *Verbal Abuse Survivors Speak Out*, Adams Media Corporation, Avon, Massachusetts, 1993

Fox, Emily Jane, *Born Trump*, Harper Collins, New York, 2018

Hassan, Steven, *The Cult of Trump*, Free Press, New York, 2019

Hassan, Steven, *Combatting Cult Mind Control,* Park Street Press, Rochester, Vermont, 2015

Jamieson, Kathleen Hall, *Cyberwar*, Oxford Univ. Press, New York, 2018

Jonson, David Cay, *The Making of Donald Trump*, Scorpio Digital Press, New York, 2019

Kaur, Valarie, *See No Stranger*, One World, New York, 2020

Levitsky, Steven; Ziblatt, Daniel, *How Democracies Die*, Broadway Publishing, New York, 2018

Lifton, Robert J., M.D., *Thought Reform and the Psychology of Totalism*, Martino Publishing, Mansfield, Connecticut, 2014

Bibliography

Lifton, Robert J., M.D., *Losing Reality*, The New Press, New York, 2019

Luntz, Frank, *Words that Work*, Hyperion, New York, 2007

Mayer, Jane, *Dark Money*, Anchor Books, New York, 2017

McSweeney's: Parker, Ben; Steinbrecher, Stephanie; Ronan, Kelsey; McMurtrie, John; Durose, Sophia; Villa Rachel; Sumerton, Amy, *Lest We Forget the Horrors: Trump's Worst Cruelties, Collusions, Corruptions, and Crimes*; mcsweeney.net, 2020

Nance, Malcolm, *The Plot to Destroy America*, Hachette Books, New York, 2018

Oldham, John M.; Morris, Lois B., *New Personality Self-Portrait*, Bantam Book, 1995

QAnon: The Search for Q, iTunes, Peacock, and *youtube.com*

Ross, Rick A., *Cults Inside Out*, Independent publishing, Amazon, 2014

Perry, Samuel, M.D.; Frances, Allen, M.D.; Clarkin, John, Ph.D., *A DSM-III-R Casebook of Treatment Solutions*, Brunner/Mazel, Inc., New York, 1990

Reid, William H., M.D., M.P.H.; Wise, Michael G., M.D., *DSM-III-R Training Guide*, Brunner/Mazel, Inc., New York, 1989

Res, Barbara A., *Tower of Lies*, Graymalin Media, LLC, Los Angeles, 2020

Sargant, William, *Battle for the Mind*, Major Books, Los Altos, California, 2015

Schwartz, Tony, *The Truth About Trump*, YouTube, Oxford Union, 2016

Sharlet, Jeff, *The Family*, Harper, New York, 2008 and Netflix

Senko, Jen, *The Brainwashing of My Dad*, Amazon Prime, 2016.

Singer, Margaret Thaler, Ph.D., *Cults In Our Midst*, Jossey-Bass, San Francisco, 2003

Sperry, Len, M.D., Ph.D., *Handbook of Diagnosis and Treatment of the DSM-IV Personality Disorders*, Brunner/Mazel, Levittown, Pennsylvania, 1995

Taylor, Kathleen, *Brainwashing: The Science of Thought Control*, Oxford University Press, Oxford, UK, 2017

Timm, Jane C., *Trump vs. the Truth: The most outrageous falsehoods of his presidency*, NBC News, New York, 2020

Trump, Donald; Tony Schwartz, *The Art of the Deal*, Ballantine Books, New York, 2015

Trump, Mary L. Ph.D., *Too Much and Never Enough*, Simon & Schuster, New York, 2020

Wolkoff, Stephanie Winston, *Melania and Me*, Simon & Schuster, Gallery Books, New York, 2020

Zelizer, Julian E., *Burning Down the House*, Penguin Press, New York, 2020

WORKSHOPS AND PRESENTATIONS
BY NIKKI HANNA

LISTEN UP, WRITER
A Series on How *Not* to Write Like an Amateur

Find Joy and Purpose in Writing—Encourages writers to take a fresh look at why they write and to develop a definition of success that taps into innate talents and that is achievable.

Tap into Craft—The Road to Authorship—Reveals common craft mistakes writers make—the ones that shout *amateur.*

Get the Most Out of Revision, Editing, and Proofing—Ensures a writer produces work that is impressive enough to compete in the writing marketplace.

Nail the Structure—Beginnings, Endings, and In-Between—Covers how to write compelling beginnings and endings and how to keep the middle from slumping.

Write with Voice, Style, and Humor—Shows writers how to find personal voice and style so the writing stands out from that of other writers, delights readers, and impresses publishers.

Capture Life through Memoir—Writing the Hard Stuff—Shows how to write a captivating life story, how to write about difficult times and flawed characters, how to decide what to put in and what to leave out, and how to print and publish.

Create Compelling Nonfiction—Covers writing principles that apply to categories of nonfiction (biography/memoir, self-help, instructional, essay, inspirational, illustrative). Writing tips that apply to other genres and publishing options are included.

Apply Winning Strategies to Writing Contests—Demonstrates how to be more competitive in contests and how to strategically select them. Key tips increase the odds of winning.

Evaluate Printing, Publishing, and Marketing Options—Discloses nuances of the industry and describes the pros and cons of various publishing strategies so writers can make sound, informed decisions.

neqhanna@sbcglobal.net - www.nikkihanna.com

BOOKS BY NIKKI HANNA

Available on Amazon, Kindle, and at www.nikkihanna.com

OUT OF IOWA INTO OKLAHOMA
You Can Take the Girl Out of Iowa, but
You Can't Take the Iowa Out of the Girl

CAPTURE LIFE—WRITE A MEMOIR
Create a Life Story—Leave a Legacy

WRITE WHATEVER THE HELL YOU WANT
Finding Joy and Purpose in Writing

RED HEELS & SMOKIN'
How I Got My Moxie Back

NEAR SEX EXPERIENCES
A Woman in Crescendo, Aging with Bravado

HEY, KIDS, WATCH THIS
Go BEYOND Aging Well

LEADERSHIP SAVVY
How to Stand Out as a Leader, Promote Employee
Loyalty, and Build an Energized Workforce

LISTEN UP, WRITER
How *Not* to Write Like an Amateur—The Path
to Authorship

AUDACIOUS
Sometimes I Just Talk Crazy

www.nikkihanna.com

ABOUT THE AUTHOR

When asked to describe herself in one sentence, Nikki Hanna said, "I'm a metropolitan gal who never quite reached the level of refinement and sophistication that label implies." The contradictions reflected in this description are the basis for much of her humorous prose. She describes her writing as irreverent and quirky with strong messages.

As an author, writing coach, and writing contest judge, Hanna is dedicated to inspiring others. She speaks on writing and offers writing workshops on the craft of writing, memoir writing, contest strategy, writing with voice/style/humor, finding joy and purpose in writing, and other writing topics. She also speaks on aging, leadership, and women's issues.

In addition to numerous awards for poetry, essays, books, and short stories, Hanna received the Oklahoma Writers' Federation, Inc.'s *Crème de la Crème* Award and Rose State College's Outstanding Writer Award. As a self-published writer, her book awards include the National Indie Excellence Award, the USA Best Book Finalist Award, two International Book Excellence Awards, and four Independent Book Awards. Her books are available on Amazon and through her website.

Hanna has a BS degree in business education and journalism and an MBA from the University of Tulsa. A retired CPA and Toastmaster, her years of experience in management and as an executive for one of the country's largest companies fostered a firm grip on leadership. She also served as a consultant on national industry task forces, as a board member for corporations, and as an advisor on curriculum development and strategic planning for educational institutions and charity organizations.

Hanna lives in Tulsa, Oklahoma. She has three children. Four grandchildren consider her the toy fairy, and those in California believe she lives at the airport.

Made in the USA
Coppell, TX
30 April 2021

54836186R00162